GERMANY, PACIFISM, AND PEACE ENFORCEMENT

Manchester University Press

SERIES EDITORS: THOMAS CHRISTIANSEN AND EMIL KIRCHNER

The formation of Croatian national identity   ALEX J. BELLAMY

Committee governance in the European Union
THOMAS CHRISTIANSEN AND EMIL KIRCHNER (EDS)

Theory and reform in the European Union, 2nd edition
DIMITRIS N. CHRYSSOCHOOU, MICHAEL J. TSINISIZELIS,
STELIOS STAVRIDIS AND KOSTAS IFANTIS

German policy-making and eastern enlargement of the EU during the Kohl era
STEPHEN D. COLLINS

The European Union and the Cyprus conflict   THOMAS DIEZ

The changing European Commission   DIONYSSIS DIMITRAKOPOULOS (ED.)

Reshaping Economic and Monetary Union   SHAWN DONNELLY

The time of European governance   MAGNUS EKENGREN

An introduction to post-Communist Bulgaria   EMIL GIATZIDIS

Mothering the Union   ROBERTA GUERRINA

The new Germany and migration in Europe   BARBARA MARSHALL

Turkey: facing a new millennium   AMIKAM NACHMANI

The changing faces of federalism
SERGIO ORTINO, MITJA ŽAGAR AND VOJTECH MASTNY (EDS)

The road to the European Union
Volume 1   The Czech and Slovak Republics   JACQUES RUPNIK AND JAN ZIELONKA (EDS)
Volume 2   Estonia, Latvia and Lithuania   VELLO PETTAI AND JAN ZIELONKA (EDS)

Democratising capitalism?
The political economy of post-Communist transformations in Romania, 1989–2001
LILIANA POP

Europe and civil society
Movement coalitions and European governance
CARLO RUZZA

Constructing the path to eastern enlargement
ULRICH SEDELMEIER

Two tiers or two speeds?
The European security order and the enlargement
of the European Union and NATO
JAMES SPERLING (ED.)

Recasting the European order   JAMES SPERLING AND EMIL KIRCHNER

Political symbolism and European integration   TOBIAS THEILER

Rethinking European Union foreign policy
BEN TONRA AND THOMAS CHRISTIANSEN (EDS)

The European Union in the wake of eastern enlargement
AMY VERDUN AND OSVALDO CROCI (EDS)

Democratic citizenship and the European Union   ALBERT WEALE

The emerging Euro-Mediterranean system
DIMITRIS K. XENAKIS AND DIMITRIS N. CHRYSSOCHOOU

ANJA DALGAARD-NIELSEN
EDITOR

GERMANY, PACIFISM AND PEACE ENFORCEMENT

MANCHESTER UNIVERSITY PRESS
Manchester and New York

distributed exclusively in the USA by Palgrave

Copyright © Anja Dalgaard-Nielsen 2006

The right of Anja Dalgaard-Nielsen to be identified as the author of this work has been asserted by her in accordance with the Copyright, Designs and Patents Act 1988.

Published by Manchester University Press
Oxford Road, Manchester M13 9NR, UK
and Room 400, 175 Fifth Avenue, New York, NY 10010, USA
www.manchesteruniversitypress.co.uk

Distributed exclusively in the USA by
Palgrave, 175 Fifth Avenue, New York,
NY 10010, USA

Distributed exclusively in Canada by
UBC Press, University of British Columbia, 2029 West Mall,
Vancouver, BC, Canada V6T 1Z2

British Library Cataloguing-in-Publication Data
A catalogue record for this book is available from the British Library

Library of Congress Cataloging-in-Publication Data applied for

ISBN 0 7190 7268 9 *hardback*
EAN 978 0 7190 7268 0

First published 2006

15 14 13 12 11 10 09 08 07 06   10 9 8 7 6 5 4 3 2 1

Typeset in Minion
by Servis Filmsetting Limited, Manchester
Printed in Great Britain
by CPI, Bath

Contents

List of tables	*page* vi
Preface	vii
Acknowledgements	viii
List of abbreviations	ix

	Introduction From Iraq to Iraq: full circle?	1
	PART I **Research design and historical background**	5
1	Studying German strategic culture	9
2	A post-war history of German security culture	24
	PART II **A military role for Germany in international crisis management?**	45
3	From the Gulf War to Somalia: cracks in the old consensus	49
4	From Srebrenica to *Operation Allied Force*: reinterpreting the lessons of the past	70
5	Back to the Gulf: limits and possibilities of the new consensus	81
	PART III **The Bundeswehr: willing and able?**	99
6	The Bundeswehr: a force for good?	101
7	The Bundeswehr's projection capability	119
	Conclusion Germany, pacifism, and pre-emptive strikes	142
	Appendices	157
	Bibliography	163
	Index	183

List of Tables

6.1	Percentage willingness within different Bundeswehr ranks to accept internationl deployment in UN-mandated missions	*page* 102
6.2	Number of soldiers from different ranks within the Bundeswehr involved in right-wing extremist incidents, 1994–2000	111
7.1	German force structures, 2000	121
7.2	Projected force structure by 2010	124
7.3	The German defence budget, 1990–2000	128
7.4	Defence expenditure as a percentage of GDP, 1990–2003	128
7.5	Percentage distribution between expenditure categories: investment, maintenance & operations (M&O), and personnel in the Germany defence budget, 1990–2005	129
7.6	Percentage of total defence budget dedicated to investment, 1990–2003 (only EC Treaty area) in %	131
7.7	Investment relative to the number of active soldiers, 2003	131
8.1	Location, size, mandate, and national composition of the crises management missions to which Germany contributed, 1990–2003	149

Preface

The book describes and explains the transformation in Germany's stance on the use of military force in international crisis management that occurred during the 1990s – a conversion from strict military abstinence to participation in line with other major European countries. Relying on culturalism as a theoretical framework the book identifies competing domestic views on Germany's role in the world and on the legitimacy of the use of force. It shows how these domestic views moulded Germany's change and defined the limits and possibilities of the new policy that emerged at the end of the 1990s. Analysing the political premises of this new policy, as well as the approach and style of German peacekeepers, the book argues that a re-unified Germany developed a policy that from conception to implementation had a distinctly 'civilized' cast. Germany became willing to deliver a military contribution, but only in participation with other Western democracies, and taking a broad and non-forceful approach, including social, economic, and humanitarian measures. The book illustrates how a culturalist perspective affords a better understanding of both the process and outcome of Germany's change compared to an external structural theory such as realism. By capturing the peculiar and composite nature of post-war Germany's domestic security culture, it is possible to explain why Germany did not exploit its new favourable geostrategic position and European economic and demographic supremacy to realise its full independent military–political power potential. It also becomes clear where the limits and opportunities of Germany's new willingness to use force lie, and why the US lost Germany's support in the military part of the international efforts to combat terrorism somewhere between Afghanistan and Iraq.

Acknowledgements

The author would like to thank David Calleo, Michael Stürmer, and Stephen Szabo as well as her colleagues at the Danish Institute for International Studies, in particular Line Selmer Friborg. Special thanks are due to Patrick McCarthy for invaluable encouragement and support.

List of Abbreviations

ABC	atomic, biological, and chemical (weapons)
ACE	Allied Command Europa
AMF	ACE Mobile Force
c3	command, control, and communication
CDU	Christian Democratic Union of Germany
CFSP	Common Foreign and Security Policy
CRF	Crisis Reaction Force
CSU	Christian-Social Union of Bavaria
EC	European Community
ECSC	European Coal and Steel Community
EDC	European Defence Community
EDSP	European Security and Defence Policy
EMNID	German polling and media research institute
ESDP	European Security and Defence Policy
EU	European Union
FDP	Free Democratic Party
FRG	Federal Republic of Germany
GDP	gross domestic product
GDR	German Democratic Republic
IISS	Institute for International Strategic Studies
INF	intermediate-range nuclear force
ISAF	International Security and Assistance Force
KLA	Kossovo Liberation Army
KSK	*Kommando Spezialkräfte*
M&O	maintenance and operations
MAD	mutually assured destruction
MdB	Member of the Bundestag
MDF	Main Defence Force
NATO	North Atlantic Treaty Organisation
NCO	non-commissioned officer
NGO	non-governmental organisation
NPG	Nuclear Planning Group (NATO)
OOA	out-of-area deployment
OSCE	Organisation for Security and Co-operation in Europe
PDS	Party of Democratic Socialism
PPP	private–public partnership
PRT	Provincial Reconstruction Teams

R&D	research and development
RRC	Rapid Reaction Corps (NATO)
SACEUR	Supreme Allied Commander in Europe (NATO)
SAS	Special Air Service
SDP	Social Democratic Party
SOWI	Institute of Social Science (Bundeswehr)
UN	United Nations
UNHCR	United Nations High Commissioner for Refugees
WEU	Western European Union
WMD	weapons of mass destruction

Introduction

From Iraq to Iraq: full circle?

At the time of German re-unification in October 1990, Germany followed a policy of strict military abstinence in conflicts outside of Europe. The notion that the Bundeswehr (the German armed forces) could be used for other purposes than defence of Germany was inconceivable across the political spectrum. Thus, not a single German soldier participated in the 1991 Gulf War. Twelve years later, when another US-led coalition launched *Operation Iraqi Freedom* to oust the regime of Saddam Hussein, the Germans remained absent. Germany became the first Western power to issue a categorical 'no' to any participation in potential military action against Iraq. With this 'no' the German Chancellor fired the opening shot in a row that was to pitch Americans against Europeans and different European countries against each other.

Yet, in the meantime, much had changed. Between the first and the second Gulf War, Germany's position on the use of military force had taken a turn. Between 6,000 and 10,000 German soldiers were now permanently engaged in crises areas around the globe, German armed forces had been dispatched to as distant areas as East Timor, Indonesia, engaged in the first combat missions since the Second World War (*Operation Allied Force* in Kosovo) and contributed special operations forces to high-intensity operations such as *Operation Enduring Freedom* against the Taleban regime in Afghanistan.

During the 1990s a significant post-Second World War taboo was breached – the abstention from using military force for purposes other than self-defence. The projection of German military might beyond the NATO area in so-called 'out-of-area missions' had become acceptable to the Germans and German armed forces were undergoing a comprehensive restructuring to permit them to engage in these new international tasks.

The development in Germany's security policy and military posture throws up a number of questions:

- Why did Germany change, and what has it become?
- What are the limits and possibilities of Germany's new willingness to use military force?
- Do Germany's neighbours have any reason to be concerned over the German transformation?
- What does the German change entail for the organisation of Western security, and where will Germany look for partners in a world of terrorist violence and pre-emptive military strikes?

Drawing on theories of strategic culture this book analyses the process and outcome of Germany's transformation. It shows how the new German security posture is based on a working consensus between two very different domestic schools of thought about international security and Germany's role in the world. These two competing schools emerged after Germany's 1945 defeat and crystallised during the post-war period. One emphasised the importance of *international cooperation*, of Germany's image as a reliable partner, and its standing and leverage within international organisations. The other emphasised Germany's *historical and moral obligation* to work for peace, international law, and human rights.

The book shows how the German change was moulded by these two schools of thought and how the new willingness to use force in multinational out-of-area missions rested on a composite working consensus between them. This composite consensus between groups that had partially diverging notions about when it was legitimate to dispatch the Bundeswehr – the German armed forces – determined the possibilities and limits of Germany's new military role. It made possible the dispatch of German troops to still more far-flung regions of the world and their participation in ever-more intensive operations. The limits, however, were breached during the summer of 2002 in the run-up to the war in Iraq – a preventive military strike on a country, which in the view of many Germans did not pose a serious threat to the Western world.

The book examines the lengthy and at times acrimonious domestic German out-of-area debate as it unfolded in the German Bundestag – the debate's major public forum – in the period between the first Gulf War in 1991 and the war against Iraq in 2003. It analyses how external events and pressures influenced the debate and how Germany's actual policy towards the international crises of the post-Cold War era responded. It aims to understand why German policy makers abandoned the policy of strict military abstention in out-of-area conflicts and to discern the premises of the new policy that has taken its place. In other words, it seeks to answer the questions what kind of security actor Germany has become and what this means to Germany's partners and neighbours.

The importance of what's inside

With unification Germany re-emerged as Europe's biggest, most populous, and potentially most powerful state. The ratification of the two-plus-four Treaty of 12 September 1990 restored Germany as a united country enjoying full sovereignty over internal and external matters. Simultaneously, the Soviet collapse improved the country's security position dramatically, reducing the threat of a conventional attack and the danger of nuclear annihilation. The German dependence on alliances and on the American nuclear guarantee for territorial protection became more abstract and seemingly less urgent.

An observer informed by the notions of the realist theory of international relations might suggest that there was nothing surprising in the overall direction of Germany's change. As a number of external and structural constraints on Germany's power potential and security policy disappeared, it could be argued, Germany gradually started behaving like other major European states, drawing on the full foreign and security policy vocabulary in the pursuit of German national interests – military security, stability, and economic prosperity.

Though the culturalist analysis of this book looks inside Germany, it does not deny the realist's argument about the importance of the international context in which Germany's transformation took place. Without the undoubtedly momentous geostrategic changes that came with the end of the Cold War, Germany's transformation would never have got under way. Had Germany still faced an overwhelming threat at its Eastern border it is highly unlikely that it would have accepted an extended role in international security, or stood up to the American ally the way the German government did in the spring of 2003. It was a rapidly changing geostrategic context, unexpected events – among them a vicious war in the Balkans, and unanticipated international pressures that placed a question mark over the old beliefs and solutions. Thus systemic and international developments made a change both possible and necessary.

However, culturalism differs from realism in insisting that in order to understand fully the course and consequences of the German transformation it is necessary to examine the *domestic political dynamics* of the country. The realist can account for the general direction of change in Germany's policy on the out-of-area question. However, as this book illustrates, a culturalist approach offers a better account of the process, timing, and outcome of Germany's transformation and makes it possible to understand aspects of the new out-of-area policy that appear puzzling from a realist's perspective. The German change, though sparked by external pressures, was moulded by a domestic security culture which determined how German policy makers interpreted and reacted to the changes in the international system.

Organisation of the book

The book proceeds in three parts. Part I (Chapters 1 and 2) outlines the books theoretical approach and provides a historical background for understanding Germany's security culture and its rival schools of thought.

Part II (Chapters 3, 4, and 5) analyses the out-of-area battle as it unfolded in the Bundestag as well as the actual cases of German participation or abstention in international crisis management between the Gulf War of 1991 and the war against Iraq in 2003. It shows how the different schools of thought competed to define German policy, how external events and international pressure affected their relative strength, and how German policy – the actual military contribution to international crisis management – responded. It points to the possibilities and limits of the new German consensus – limits and possibilities illustrated as German policy makers dug in their heels and refused to even contemplate a German contribution to the 2003 war against Iraq, while less than six months later approving by an overwhelming majority the dispatch of German soldiers to help pacify a violence-wrecked area of Congo.

Part III (Chapters 6 and 7) proceeds to look at the instrument for carrying out the new policy – the Bundeswehr. It analyses the attitude and approach of German soldiers towards their new international tasks as well as the Bundeswehr's actual material ability to carry them out. It traces the development in German force structures and equipment profile during the 1990s and compares the German projection capability to French and British capabilities.

The Conclusion attempts to answer the threefold question why Germany changed, what it has become, and what that means to Germany's partners. It discusses the respective roles of systemic pressure, domestic culture, and individual political entrepreneurs in the German transformation process. It discerns an emerging pattern as to where, with whom, and for what German policy makers became willing to dispatch the Bundeswehr and discusses whether Germany's partners have any reason to be concerned over the new German assertiveness. Finally, the consequences of Germany's transformation for the organisation of Western security and for the way the Western world goes about managing the security threats of the post-Cold War world are discussed.

PART I
Research design and historical background

The German out-of-area debate did not, as an external observer might have expected, evolve around the question of re-unified Germany's national security interests in the post-Cold War era. Instead, it represented a battle over the lessons of the past and the expectations of Germany's partners. The debate looked backward much more than forward, and evolved around negative notions of what dangers Germany needed to avoid rather than positive notions of what could be achieved through engaging the Bundeswehr in international crisis management. There were few attempts to address the question of where, with whom, and for what German soldiers would be deployed internationally. Terms such as 'national security' and 'national interest' were hardly ever used. Instead, the debate centred on abstract notions such as 'Germany's historical responsibility', 'moral responsibility', 'international solidarity', and 'requirements of partnership'.

Military matters were either avoided or overemphasised for polemical purposes. The proponents of an extended German role stressed the humanitarian aspects of the new 'peace missions' and lauded the Bundeswehr as an 'army for integration' with Western partners and allies. Opponents denounced all out-of-area interventions as 'immoral' and issued ominous warnings against a 're-militarisation' of German policy.

Thus, the German debate provided few direct clues as to whether the Germans envisioned themselves as regional or global players and whether they preferred a global, Western, or European framework for their contribution to out-of-area crisis management. There was no direct indication of whether the Germans intended to throw their new military weight behind the UN, NATO, or the fledgling European Security and Defence Policy (ESDP).

German policy makers first had to confront the moral issues before they could discuss the nitty-gritty of out-of-area deployments. They first had to grapple with the past before they could deal with the present. Although the out-of-area debate took place in the 1990s, its conceptual coordinates cannot be understood without looking back to the 1945 defeat and the German post-war experience.

The out-of-area debate was set off by factors outside Germany – the end of the Cold War, the emergence of new types of conflicts, and pressure from Germany's partners for a German contribution to manage these conflicts. Yet, as this book will make clear, neither the course nor the outcome of the debate can be understood without looking inside Germany at competing domestic schools of thought about security. To structure the analysis of these domestic schools, the book draws on theories of political and strategic culture.

Part I of this book explains the theoretical framework for studying German security culture and provides a historical background for understanding it.

Chapter 1 opens with a discussion of the concept of 'strategic culture' and outlines the central tenets of culture theory. It explains how this theory provides a tool for analysing the domestic factors that influence security policy and introduces examples of culturalist analyses of post-unification German security policy. It argues that these accounts display a static bias due to their structural concept of culture, and explains how this book instead conceptualises culture as a dynamic and plural entity. Culture, it argues, limits the choices of German politicians, but simultaneously represents a resource for agents of change. The chapter also operationalises the concept of security culture and discusses how and where to study it, and argues that the sequence of Bundestag debates over the out-of-area question between 1990 and 2001 offers a window into the competing logics of German security culture. The chapter ends with an outline of the study's sources, and their reliability.

Chapter 2 traces the origin and post-war development of the competing logics of thinking within Germany's security culture. It shows the importance of the German past in the struggle for moral and intellectual leadership in security policy debates and illuminates the key issues, arguments, and taboos of the out-of-area debate by placing them in historical context.[1]

The chapter begins by showing how the German defeat of 1945 left a strong imprint on the security thinking of German elites and outlines how different political and social groups learned different lessons from the debacle, respectively 'never again war' and 'never again alone'. The first dictum represented a pacifist reaction to the two world wars, the second the conviction that to guard against a relapse, Germany needed to embed herself morally, economically, and strategically into common Western structures. Though adherents of the competing lessons of the past clashed on several occasions over the post-war period, the chapter shows how the political mainstream nevertheless started converging on a set of mutually acceptable security policy principles after the late 1950s.

The chapter also shows how the ostensibly puzzling focus and language of the 1990s out-of-area debate make sense when seen against the background of Germany's post-war experience. As the changing geopolitical environment of the post-Cold war era began to undermine the existing working consensus on security policy, the interpretation of the past, of Germany's historical responsibility, and of the requirements of partnership provided the conceptual coordinates for the renewed debate between rival German schools of security thinking.

Notes

1 The chapter concentrates on the foreign policy of the Federal Republic of Germany (FRG) rather than that of the German Democratic Republic (GDR). German re-unification has been described as a 'take-over' of the GDR by the FRG. This certainly was the case in the field of foreign and security policy. The backdrop against which the current security policy thinking of the German elite must be understood is the tradition of the FRG, not that of the GDR.

1
Studying German strategic culture

Culture theory and security policy

The first to explicitly apply the concept of culture to a study of security policy was Jack L. Snyder in his 1977 study, *The Soviet Strategic Culture*. Snyder, soon followed by other scholars, set out to explain why American and Soviet nuclear strategy apparently reflected different logics of thinking even though the two countries were facing the same geostrategic environment. Snyder's approach emphasised how differences in domestic factors such as historical experience, political culture, and national identity made for different kinds of international behaviour. The strategic culture approach stood in opposition to ahistorical and systemic frameworks for analysing the security policy of states.[1]

More recent studies have expanded the concept of strategic culture by drawing on insights from theories of political culture. Whereas strategic culture focused narrowly on explaining the war plans and operational doctrines of states, the newer approaches aspire to explain national security policy more broadly.[2]

The common and fundamental assumption of both the older and the newer culturalist approaches, however, is that domestic macro-level variables such as historical experience, national ideals, and collective beliefs about international affairs matter and must be taken into account when attempting to understand the behaviour of states in the international arena.[3]

Domestic ideational factors matter, it is argued, because of the infinite complexity of the material world. Systemic pressures are not irrelevant, but they underdetermine security policy because they tend to be ambiguous and sometimes contradictory. A variety of possible solutions and responses will normally appear viable; a reduction of the complexity of this material reality is a precondition for establishing a meaningful social reality, which decision makers can understand, evaluate, and act upon.

Culture helps to make sense out of a confusing reality by suggesting certain causal connections, interpretations, and solutions and downplaying others. It consists of systems of interacting symbols and interconnected ideas. It organises ideals, values, beliefs, and concepts into a coherent system or world-view that shapes a group or a society's orientation towards the external world. It functions as a mind-set that limits attention to less than the full spectrum of logically possible behaviours, affects the appearance and interpretation of these possible behaviours, and influences the formulation and evaluation of different policy options.[4]

Political and strategic culture is typically seen as rooted in the early and formative experience of a national community or in dramatic, existential events such as revolutions or major wars. It is regarded as a structural entity of significant inertia. Changes in culture and the policies it structures will be incremental and gradual if they happen at all.[5]

Culture and German security policy

Four scholars have applied culturalist approaches in attempting to account for Germany's post-Second World War security policy: Thomas U. Berger, John S. Duffield, Kerry Longhurst, and Hanns W. Maull – the last mixing elements of role-theory into the culturalist approach.[6] All four identify a pervasive culture of anti-militarism in German society. This culture, they argue, explains why the re-unified Germany in spite of strong external pressure remained reluctant to take on a greater share of the military burden in managing international security in the post-Cold War world.

The German anti-militarist culture, all four scholars contend, grew out of a reaction against the disastrous consequences of the aggressive policies of the Nazi-regime. The experience of total defeat prompted the development of a new German self-identification as a 'civilian power' – a power relying on political, cultural, and economic instead of military means of international influence.[7]

In line with the culturalist approaches mentioned in the previous section, Berger, Duffield, and Maull conceive of culture as a structural entity characterised by strong inertia. Longhurst, as will be discussed below, places more emphasis on the dynamic nature of culture.

Culture, according to Berger, Duffield, and Maull, will cause changes in policy to lag behind changes in 'objective' external circumstances and frequently prevent much change in policy at all. The end of the Cold War created pressure on Germany to give up its military exceptionalism. The domestic anti-militarist culture, however, functioned as a constraint on how fast and how far German security policy could move. Germany, they agree, largely maintained the behaviour of a civilian power.[8]

By emphasising Germany's national security culture Berger, Duffield, and Maull are able to explain why German behaviour after 1990 apparently confounded international and systemic pressures for a higher German security and defence profile. The extent of change fell short of what some neo-realist analysts had expected, as well as what some of Germany's NATO partners had wished.[9] However, these three scholars' strong focus on the structural and unitary quality of culture introduces a bias towards seeing regularity and repetition. They have difficulty accommodating pro-active political entrepreneurship. The changes that actually occurred in German security policy over the 1990s are thus conceived as the result of reluctant and reactive adaptation to appease the new international expectations directed at Germany.[10]

Multiple cultural logics and political entrepreneurship

It is true, as noted by Duffield, that national security culture is likely to have a great structuring impact in times of uncertainty and ambiguity. When well-known problems change and old solutions are challenged – as they were in Germany during a good part of the 1990s – decision makers are likely to fall back on existing beliefs and ideals to offer some guidance.[11]

But it is also true that in these very same times of rapid change, fluid environmental conditions, and unanticipated events, established beliefs and convictions are most likely to be challenged as the guidance they offer may appear less and less adequate.[12] Longhurst emphasises the possibility of change in security culture as a consequence of broader changes in the political culture of a nation. Security culture is dynamic in the sense that it is part of a broader political culture that changes over time as society reconsiders aspects and consequences of the nation's history.[13] This study, in line with Longhurst, approaches culture as a dynamic entity rather than a structural constant. However, it looks for the sources of change *within security culture itself*, first by emphasising the plural rather than monolithic nature of security culture, and second by pinpointing the possibility for political entrepreneurship and the possibilities for individual actors to alter culture.

The idea of a plural instead of a uniform culture is not in opposition to the basic assumptions of culture theory. According to the culturalists, national security culture is shaped by dramatic and existential events – in Germany's case the defeat in the Second World War. It could be argued, however, that the further the founding event recedes into history, the more likely that idiosyncratic experiences, beliefs, and ideals that are not shared by the whole national community assert themselves. Different groups would then come to carry different versions of the common culture. One could also imagine a situation in which different groups interpreted a culture-founding event in different ways. This would again result in competing notions instead of a coherent and uniform culture.

By abandoning the assumption of uniformity this study abandons part of the static bias of existing culturalist accounts of German security policy. The possibility of change is inherent in the existence of competing logics of thinking within a security culture, as the relative strength of these logics may change over time.

The study furthermore seeks to capture not only how culture structures perception and behaviour, but also how events and actors re-structure culture. It draws on the insights of Anthony Giddens' 'theory of structuration'. The structuration theory was formulated in the mid-1980s as an attempt to synthesise the insights of two opposing camps in the field of sociology – structuralism and voluntarism. Whereas the first granted ontological and causal priority to social structures, the latter emphasised the primacy of actors.

Giddens' theory does not deny the importance of structures in shaping the outcome of social processes, but it gives equal priority to actors. Structures and actors, it claims, are neither independent of, nor reducible to, each other. Both play a role in shaping the outcome of social processes by virtue of the dual nature of structure. Structure is both 'the medium and outcome of the conduct it recursively organises; the structural properties of social systems do not exist outside of action but are chronically implicated in its production and reproduction'.[14]

Structure – in this study the German security culture – should be conceived of as both *enabling* and *constraining*. It represents a barrier to change, but also a potential resource for agents of change. Political entrepreneurs might draw on one element of culture in order to attack another, or lend their argument for change legitimacy by linking it to a well-known and broadly accepted fundamental cultural belief.

Structuration theory points to the possibility of dynamic developments originating at the domestic micro-level – at the level of the individual policy maker. It points out that decision makers are not just puppets of culture, but also creators of culture. It emphasises the ability of political entrepreneurs to rise above the culture they are socialised into and actively attempt to manipulate it.

In sum, culture theory provides an analytical tool for grasping the influence of domestic factors on security policy. This study builds on the notion that systemic developments and international pressures do not work directly on the security policy of a country, but are mediated by a historically rooted culture that shapes the perceptions and reactions of policy makers. Attempting to remedy the static bias of most existing culturalist approaches, the study operates with a multiple and dynamic concept of culture and sees culture as both a constraint and resource for German policy makers.

Operationalising security policy culture

Jack L. Snyder originally defined strategic culture as 'the sum total of ideals, conditional emotional responses, and patterns of habitual behaviour that members of the national strategic community have acquired through instruction or imitation and share with each other with regard to nuclear strategy'.[15]

This definition drew criticism for being too amorphous and for conflating the dependent and independent variable by including behavioural elements in the definition of culture.[16] More recent approaches have excluded behavioural elements from their definition, though they are no less broad. John S. Duffield's, for example, includes basic empirical beliefs about the nature of the international system, affective elements of identification, norms regarding both the goals and the means of national security policy, and causal beliefs about the efficiency and legitimacy of different means, in his definition of national security culture.[17] The definition of Ronald L. Jepperson, Alexander Wendt, and Peter J. Katzenstein has much in common with Duffield's definition. The authors refer to culture as 'a set of evaluative standards, such as norms or values, and cognitive standards, such as rules or models defining what entities and actors exist in a system and how they operate and interrelate'.[18]

This study leans on the definition of Jepperson, Wendt, and Katzenstein, but draws more explicitly on the insights of cognitive and belief-system theories. This affords the advantage of being able not just to list ideas and values but also to rank them in relative importance and see how they form an internally coherent system.

Most cognitive theories make the fundamental assumption that belief systems consist of different layers of ideas. Though terminologies differ they all draw a distinction between central, operational, and peripheral beliefs.

Central beliefs are abstract beliefs and basic assumptions about the international system, about right and wrong, and about self and other. They silently inform and structure operational and peripheral beliefs, are rarely questioned, and tend to be very stable. *Operational* beliefs are beliefs about cause–effect relationships, and about the efficacy of different policy instruments and strategies. *Peripheral* beliefs concern concrete issues and objects. They tend to be influenced by many factors in the concrete situation and frequently have a transient character.[19]

The different layers possess different degrees of rigidity. As argued by Robert Jervis, it will typically be more stressful and costly for an individual to alter central beliefs than to adjust peripheral beliefs. Thus, individuals will tend towards minimal attitude changes, Jervis argues, and if possible limit changes to the peripheral layers of their belief system. It appears reasonable to assume that the same logic applies on the collective level.[20]

In mapping out the logics of German security culture, this study will attempt to look behind the peripheral day-to-day positions of German decision makers to discern their central and operational values and beliefs. It will look for their self-perception (Germany's role, interests, and obligations in international security), their beliefs about the generalised other (aversions and threat perceptions), and their operational beliefs about the efficacy and legitimacy of different ways of protecting German interests and dealing with the threat environment (the efficacy of diplomatic versus more forceful means).

The above definition of security culture is very broad. However, as a result of different national experiences, the key concepts, symbols, and arguments of security culture are likely to vary from state to state. They cannot be defined *a priori* on the basis of abstract theoretical reflection.

Measuring security policy culture: elite discourse and public opinion
In attempting to map Germany's national security policy culture, Berger and Maull rely on two sources: public opinion polls and elite discourse. Duffield and Longhurst concentrate on the latter, attempting to read elite culture through speeches, books, and articles by elite members.[21] This study will follow Duffield's and Longhurst's example and focus on the elite.

Public opinion polls are likely to provide sparse insights when it comes to understanding the competing logics of German security culture. Culture consists of an extensive system of interlocking beliefs, ideals, and assumptions and it is doubtful whether the average citizen is actually a bearer of security culture in this comprehensive form. Even if this is assumed, the measurement instruments of the polling institutes and the tabulation techniques used to process large sets of data pose a problem. They are unlikely to permit much insight into the meaning of key concepts and symbols, or into the complex connection between different beliefs and ideals. In order to capture this, it is necessary to apply a qualitative method of research such as text analysis or comprehensive elite interviews.

It could also be argued that while public opinion might reflect and sometimes influence the relative strength of rival logics of thinking within a security culture, ultimately elite opinion determines which way security policy goes. Historically, even when public opinion has been highly mobilised, governing elites have been willing and able to push through unpopular and contentious security policy decisions. German rearmament in the 1950s and the intermediate-range nuclear forces (INF) deployment in the 1980s were elite designs adopted in spite of public protests, as will be discussed in Chapter 2. The commitment of German troops to Afghanistan in 2001 was likewise pushed through in the face of popular opposition, as were other German international military engagements in the early 1990s. The German resistance to the 2003 war in Iraq provides the exception. In this instance the incumbent Chancellor Gerhard Schröder – in the middle of a domestic election campaign – decided to seize on widespread popular unease with the bellicose line of the American administration instead of going against it.

It is possible that the impact of public opinion on elite decisions will increase in the future. A blurring line between external and internal security might lead to greater public interest in elite decisions, by making the consequences of these decisions appear more palpable and relevant in the everyday life of normal people. The fact that a number of the 11 September 2001 hijackers had lived in Hamburg, and the subsequent arrests and terrorist alerts in Germany, arguably increased the public interest in security policy. The killing of fourteen German tourists in an Al-Qaeda-linked terrorist attack on the Mosque of Djerba, Tunisia in April 2002 might have had the same effect and increased popular German interest in how the international 'war on terrorism' was being conducted.

Simultaneously, it is conceivable that today's German elite feels more free to indulge public opinion on security matters than its Cold War predecessor, as the immediate stakes for Germany in matters of international security have declined. Security policy is no longer, at least not in the short term, an existential question.

Generally, the post-war cohorts of German voters are becoming progressively less inclined to accept responsibility for past German crimes, and increasingly supportive of an active German role in UN-mandated out-of-area operations. While strongly supportive of closer European integration they also support the notion that Germany should pursue its national interest in international fora, just like other 'normal' countries.[22]

Public opinion on actual out-of-area interventions has varied over time, from resistance to the first Gulf War to favouring UN-mandated operations in the former Yugoslavia after 1993, to resisting *Operation Enduring Freedom* in Afghanistan at the time of the Bundestag vote on the German contribution in November 2001. West Germans have generally been more inclined to favour a German international military engagement than East Germans, the latter being more sceptical towards Western security institutions. Though, on average, the German public developed a more permissive attitude over the period covered in this book there is no direct correlation between public opinion and the actions of the elite.[23]

Thus, while public opinion constitutes a constraint on and, at times, a temptation to the elite, it is not an absolute or immutable constraint, as demonstrated in the commitment of German troops to Afghanistan.

Moreover, elites are well positioned to shape popular opinion, due to their expert knowledge and privileged access to information and means of communication. Even if they do not manage to change popular beliefs about specific issues they are arguably still likely to have their way in the long run, as the general public interest in security policy, even if rising, tends to focus on specific issues and is ad hoc rather than permanent. Finally, though the public might have an opinion on a number of specific issues, new currents of thought normally originate at the elite level and will under all circumstances have to be filered through the elite to become translated into a comprehensive world-view or a security culture. In sum, the battle over German security and defence issues normally has to be won at the elite level.[24]

Therefore public opinion data will occasionally be used in this book to indicate limits or openings for the political elite. But in order to gain substantive insights into the logics of German security culture and in order to discern long-term trends the book focuses mainly on the elite.

The parliamentary elite and the Bundestag as a forum for elite debate

Traditionally, the making of German security and defence policy has been dominated by the executive and by a narrow circle of top politicians and security experts. This study, while retaining an elite focus, takes a broader view. It aims to understand the logic behind Germany's out-of-area policy by analysing the Bundestag debates and decisions between 1990 and 2003 on international deployments of the Bundeswehr.

Security and defence policy was not an area the average parliamentarian used to take much interest in. From the late 1950s to the early 1980s, the tone that dominated the infrequent security policy debates of the Bundestag was relatively congenial. The fault line in the most acrimonious disputes ran between an established parliamentarian mainstream and the extra-parliamentarian peace movement.

But with the Social Democratic drift to the left during the late 1970s and with the 1983 entry of the Green party into the Bundestag, strong anti-militarism and universal pacifism found expression in the parliament. Left-wing crusades against established security policies were transferred into the Bundestag. From the early 1980s, security policy debates thus became more frequent and more contentious, and the Bundestag became a forum that provided a window into competing schools of thought within Germany's security culture.

In the 1990s these two schools clashed over the question whether Germany should contribute to multinational military crisis management outside of the NATO area – a question that initially split the Bundestag down the middle and provoked a sequence of heated debates.

In June 1993 the German Constitutional Court ruled that the Bundestag should be fully involved in the decision making process about out-of-area deployments. All decisions should be properly prepared in the responsible parliamentary committees and debated 'substantially' in the Bundestag. One year later, in July 1994, the Court established that the Bundestag needed to approve each individual out-of-area deployment with a simple majority. These rulings confirmed the Bundestag as the major public forum for the out-of-area battle.[25]

The governments of Germany's post-Cold War decade – the CDU/CSU/ FDP coalition of Helmut Kohl and the SPD/Green coalition of Gerhard Schröder both disposed of parliamentary majorities.[26] Nevertheless, they tended to take the Bundestag debates and votes seriously, especially after the 1994 ruling of the Constitutional Court. In line with a German tradition for seeking cross-partisan consensus on important foreign and security policies, both attempted to garner broad parliamentary support for each individual international deployment.[27] Faced with deep public scepticism against such deployments, both governments were naturally reluctant to assume the sole responsibility for decisions that might cost German soldiers their lives. Cross-partisan support was particularly urgent for the SPD/Green government that came into office in 1998, since it had to live with the constant prospect of defection from its own left wing in out-of-area votes.

Though the Bundestag was not the forum in which decisions about out-of-area deployments of the Bundeswehr were made, it was the forum in which they had to be explained, defended, and approved. In the Bundestag's oppositional setting, the contenders in the out-of-area battle were repeatedly challenged to present and defend their assumptions and ideals regarding Germany's role in international security. The sequence of Bundestag debates and votes between 1990 and 2003 thus offers the opportunity to map out the central assumptions of competing groups and competing German schools of security thinking, assess how they responded to international pressures and events, and establish how their stance on the out-of-area question developed over time.

Other elites and the making of German security policy

The German strategic community is very small. The security experts of the parliamentary groups are typically recruited into government positions and incumbent government ministers and top decision makers almost without exception remain members of parliament. By focusing on the Bundestag one captures most of the influential individuals in security and defence policy, while surveying the beliefs of both present and future governmental elites.[28]

The study nevertheless occasionally includes the opinion of specific top bureaucrats, military leaders, academics, and editorialists.[29] However, it does not systematically study the communication of these groups in general. In Germany, the flow of people and ideas back and forth between politics, think tanks, and academia is limited. Occasionally the biggest foreign affairs think tank, *Stiftung Wissenschaft und Politik*, produces short studies or briefs for parliamentarians, and the yearly '*Friedensgutachten*' – peace assessment – published by a Hamburg-based peace research institute normally receive some political attention. But for the most part, academic communication tends to address itself instead of the outside world.[30]

The German military as an organisation exerts very limited influence on the German policy making process.[31] Occasionally, a few top bureaucrats from the Ministry of Defence play a role in shaping thinking and policy. But the post-war German political culture does not tolerate any overt attempt by military personnel to influence political decisions and the 'primacy of politics' is generally respected within the armed forces.[32] The post-war institutional civil–military relationship was constructed in a deliberate attempt to limit the potential of the military to influence politics. Military leaders report to the Minister of Defence, but have no institutionalised access to other top politicians, including the Chancellor and the members of the Bundestag's Defence Committee. Military leaders thus depend on the politicians themselves to request their advice or opinion. Such requests are scarce. The Defence Committee has called on military personnel to testify in connection with investigations into alleged right-wing extremism in the armed forces, but rarely to hear their opinion on issues of defence and security policy.

Yet, top military leaders at times exert influence by proxy via the Minister of Defence or via their counterparts in allied countries. At times German military leaders were able to plant ideas with these counterparts who would in turn feed them to their political superiors who would then promote them with the

German Government.[33] Accordingly, the study will take these instances into account and include the views of a few top military people among its sources.

In sum, to discern the competing schools of thought within German security culture the book focuses primarily on the German parliamentary elite. Beyond this group, it occasionally includes the ideas and beliefs of a handful of public academics, top bureaucrats, and military leaders that exerted direct or indirect influence on German out-of-area policy.

Sources

The sequence of Bundestag debates on out-of-area deployments between 1990 and 2001 constitute the study's major source. They are transcribed in *Plenarprotokoll Deutscher Bundestag,* accessible though the library of the Bundestag or through *Bundes Presse- und Informationsamt* in Berlin.[34] The study analyses the debates concerning all major and/or controversial cases of German out-of-area engagements between 1990 and 2001, including the Gulf War (1990–91), *Operation Sharp Guard* in the Adriatic Sea (1992–96), *Operation Deny Fly* over Bosnia-Herzegovina (1993–95), UNOSOM II in Somalia (1993–94), IFOR in Bosnia-Herzegovina (1995–96), SFOR in Bosnia-Herzegovina (since 1996), *Operation Allied Force* and KFOR in Kosovo (since 1998), INTERFET in East Timor (1999–2000), *Operation Essential Harvest* and *Operation Amber Fox* in Macedonia (since 2001), and *Operation Enduring Freedom* in Afghanistan (since 2001), as well as the debate over *Operation Iraqi Freedom* in the years 2002 and 2003 – an operation in which Germany did not participate. Finally, the 2003 debate over Germany's contribution to *Operation Artemis* in Bunia, Congo, is analysed. These deployments all proved domestically controversial and/or represented a fundamentally new step in the expansion of Germany's willingness to participate in international crisis management, provoking lively and contentious debate in the Bundestag.

The analysis omits four cases: the contribution of 140 German medical personnel in support of the UN transitional administration in Cambodia between 1991 and 1992 (UNAMIC), logistical support for an airlift to relieve the beleaguered city of Sarajevo between 1993 and 1995, the contribution of around ten German medical officers and observers as part of a UN-peace-keeping force in Georgia, since 1994 (UNOMIG), and the contribution of two German soldiers to a UN mission in Ethiopia/Eritrea since the year 2000 (UNMEE). Due to the mandate, scope, purpose, and/or deployment area of these missions, none of them was particularly controversial. Furthermore, they did not represent fundamentally new steps in the process leading Germany from total abstention to full participation. The debates relating to these three missions are therefore not analysed in detail.

Most of the Bundestag votes on out-of-area deployments were roll calls. This meant that the voting behaviour of each individual member of the

Bundestag (MdB) was recorded. The *Plenarprotokoll* thus offers insight into both the ideas and the actual voting behaviour of Germany's political elite.[35]

The Bundestag debates are supplemented with further written sources in the form of speeches and articles by top politicians, public academics, mass media leaders, top government officials, and military leaders regarding the out-of-area question. The sources will include *Aus Politik und Zeitgeschichte, Frankfurter Allgemeine Zeitung, Der Spiegel, Süddeutsche Zeitung, Die Welt, Die Zeit*, official publications and press releases from the Ministry of Defence and the Ministry of Foreign Affairs available in *Stichworte zur Sicherheitspolitik* and/or *Bulletin*, both published by *Bundes Presse- und Informationsamt*, journals such as *Europäische Sicherheit* and *Truppenpraxis*, publications from the German Defence Academy in Hamburg and the Centre for Civic Education and Leadership in Strausberg, annual reports of the Bundestag's ombudsman for military affairs, as well as *White Books* and *Planning Guidelines* from the Ministry of Defence. The written sources are supplemented with personal confidential interviews with government and party officials, former and previous political advisors to top politicians or parties, military leaders, mass media leaders, and academics.[36]

Methodological considerations

The study relies primarily on public sources of elite communication. The question remains to what extent such public communication is a reliable sources for gaining insights into competing schools of thought about security policy and for understanding why the German policy of military abstinence in out-of-area conflicts was abandoned.

Scholars working with culture, belief systems, and cognitive maps all face the same problem: as long as the social scientist remains unable to look into the minds of the objects of study, there is no foolproof way of distinguishing between sincere and tactical language. Most scholars, including the author of this book, rely on pragmatic solutions, such as surveying a variety of material, checking for congruence, and corroborating public sources with information obtained through confidential interviews.[37]

Moreover, the kind of insights sought in this analysis reduces the reliability problem. The analysis aims to discern long-term trends and broad logics. German parliamentarians may hide their true motivation for opposing or supporting a specific out-of-area deployment. But a systematic longitudinal study of more than twelve years of Bundestag debates pertaining to the out-of-area question is likely to provide insights into the general logic of security thinking of different groups. It is likely to reveal the ordinary patterns of thinking about security policy, the issues and arguments considered most important, notions about Germany's international role, and the prevalent threat perceptions or aversions.

Parliamentary debates are likely to contain plenty of instrumental language and tactical dodges. Yet, politicians acting in an oppositional setting like the Bundestag, debating a controversial issue such as the out-of-area question, are likely to probe and question each other's arguments and motives. If a politician is attempting to deceive, his opponent will attempt to uncover and display his 'true' motives. Even after Germany's major political parties started converging on a new working consensus on the out-of-area question towards the late 1990s individual *Mitglied des deutschen Bundestages* (Member of the German Bundestag, MdB) and the ex-Communist PDS maintained an unyielding resistance to international deployments of the Bundeswehr. The latter half of the 1990s saw these politicians take on a self-styled role as 'voice of conscience' or 'truth teller'. The Bundestag debates in effect consistently provide multiple versions of the truth. While this is no guarantee that deceptive language can be distinguished from sincere, it reduces the risk that the analysis overlooks and fails to consider important alternative explanations to the ones given by the responsible politicians themselves.

In sum, there can be no absolute certainty as to whether an elite culture is being measured and described accurately. However, by corroborating a longitudinal study of a sequence of contentious Bundestag debates with further public sources of elite communication, and confidential elite interviews, the research design should be able to claim a reasonable degree of reliability.

Summary

This book relies on the insights of culture theory to structure the analysis of Germany's changing out-of-area policy. Differing from most existing culturalist accounts of post-war German security policy, the study operates with a dynamic and multiple concept of culture, emphasising the opportunity of individual actors to promote cultural change. It concentrates on a sequence of Bundestag debates on out-of-area deployments of the Bundeswehr, which offers a window into the competing German schools of security thinking, their interaction, and their development over time. The reliability problem is sought to be reduced by corroborating the insights emerging through analysing these debates with other sources of elite-communication and with confidential elite intervie

Notes

1 Jack L. Snyder, *The Soviet Strategic Culture: Implications for Nuclear Options* (Santa Monica: Rand Cooperation, 1977); Colin Gray, 'National Styles in Strategy: The American Example', *International Security*, 6:2 (Fall 1981); Alastair Iain Johnston, 'Thinking about Strategic Culture', *International Security*, 19:4 (Spring 1995).

2 See for example Thomas U. Berger, *Cultures of Antimilitarism: National Security in Germany and Japan* (Baltimore: Johns Hopkins University Press, 1998); G. R. Boynton,

'The Expertise of the Senate Foreign Relations Committee', in Valerie M. Hudson (ed.), *Artificial Intelligence and International Politics* (Boulder: Westview Press, 1991); John S. Duffield, *World Power Forsaken: Political Culture, International Institutions, and German Security Policy after Unification* (Stanford, CA: Stanford University Press, 1998); Valerie M. Hudson (ed.), *Culture and Foreign Policy* (Boulder, Westview Press, 1997); Ronald L. Jepperson, Alexander Wendt, and Peter J. Katzenstein, 'Norms, Identity, and Culture in National Security Policy', in Peter J. Katzenstein (ed.), *The Culture of National Security: Norms and Identity in World Politics* (New York: Columbia University Press, 1996).

3 On the question of a culture's ontological status, the early culturalist approaches tend to lean towards an objectivist stand – culture is taken as a given. The newer approaches frequently incorporate reflectivist insights and treat culture as a social construct. This study takes the view that history, culture, and identity are social constructs, but that they nevertheless possess significant inertia and therefore have real and objective effects.

4 Gabriel Almond and Sydney Verba, *The Civic Culture* (Boston: Little, Brown, 1965), pp. 11–14; Duffield, *World Power Forsaken*, p. 27; Clifford Geertz, 'Ideology as a Cultural System', in David E. Apter (ed.), *Ideology and Discontent* (London: Macmillan, 1964), p. 56; Judith Goldstein and Robert O. Keohane, *Ideas and Foreign Policy* (Ithaca: Cornell University Press, 1993), pp. 8–10.

5 Berger, *Cultures of Antimilitarism*, p. 18; David R. Jones, 'Soviet Strategic Culture', in Carl G. Jacobsen (ed.), *Strategic Power: USA/USSR* (London: St Martin's Press, 1990), p. 35. See also K. J. Holsti, 'National Role Conceptions in the Study of Foreign Policy', in Stephen G. Walker (ed.), *Role Theory and Foreign Policy Analysis* (Durham: Duke University Press, 1987), p. 12; Robert Jervis, *Perception and Misperception in International Politics* (Princeton: Princeton University Press, 1976), p. 261; M. Sampson, 'Cultural Influences on Foreign Policy', in C. F. Hermann, C. W. Kegley, and J. N. Rosenau (eds), *New Directions in the Study of Foreign Policy*, (Boston: Allen & Unwin, 1987).

6 Role-theory argues that the foreign policy elite of a given country shares a set of ingrained beliefs about the role, function, mission, and obligations of their country in international affairs. The national role conception of the elite is seen as an important causal factor behind foreign policy. For an overview of different versions and uses of role theory see Stephen G. Walker (ed.), *Role Theory and Foreign Policy Analysis* (Durham: Duke University Press, 1987).

7 Kerry Longhurst, *Germany and the Use of Force: The Evolution of German Security Policy 1990–2003* (Manchester and New York: Manchester University Press, 2004), p. 25; Hanns W. Maull 'Germany and Japan: The New Civilian Powers', *Foreign Affairs*, 69:5 (1990), pp. 91–106.

8 Thomas U. Berger, 'Norms, Identity, and National Security in Germany and Japan', in Peter J. Katzenstein (ed.), *The Culture of National Security: Norms and Identity in World Politics* (New York: Columbia University Press), pp. 326 and 328; Duffield, *World Power Forsaken*, p. 27; Hanns W. Maull, 'Germany and the Use of Force: Still a "Civilian Power?"', *Survival*, 42:2 (2000), pp. 56–80.

9 For the original and most influential formulation of neo-realism, see Kenneth N. Waltz, *Theory of International Politics* (Reading, MA: Addison-Wesley, 1979). See also Christopher Layne, 'The Unipolar Illusion: Why New Great Powers Will Rise', *International Security*, 17:4 (1993); John J. Mearsheimer, 'Back to the Future: Instability in Europe after the Cold War', *International Security*, 15:1 (1990).

10 Berger, 'Norms, Identity, and National Security in Germany and Japan', p. 328; Duffield, *World Power Forsaken*; Hanns W. Maull, 'Germany's Foreign Policy, post-Kosovo: Still a "Civilian Power"?', in Sebastian Harnisch and Hanns W. Maull (eds), *Germany as a Civilian Power? The Foreign Policy of the Berlin Republic* (Manchester: Manchester University Press, 2001), pp. 119–120.

11 Duffield, *World Power Forsaken*, p. 27.

12 Robert W. Cox, 'Social Forces, States, and World Orders: Beyond International Relations Theory', in Robert O. Keohane (ed.), *Neorealism and its Critics* (New York: Columbia University Press, 1986), p. 210; Bernhard Giesen, *Die Intellektuellen und die Nation* (Frankfurt am Main: Suhrkamp, 1993); Peter M. Haas, 'Epistemic Communities', *International Organization*, 46 (1992), p. 5; Christopher Hill and Pamela Beshoff (eds), *Two Worlds of International Relations* (London: Routledge, 1994); Tony Judt, *The Burden of Responsibility* (Chicago: University of Chicago Press, 1998), p. 5.

13 Piotr Buras and Kerry Longhurst, 'The Berlin Republic, Iraq, and the Use of Force', *European Security*, 13:3 (2004), p. 217.

14 Anthony Giddens, *The Constitution of Society* (Cambridge: Polity Press, 1984), p. 376.

15 Snyder, *The Soviet Strategic Culture*, p. 9.

16 Johnston, 'Thinking about Strategic Culture', p. 37.

17 Duffield, *World Power Forsaken*, pp. 24–25.

18 Jepperson, Wendt, and Katzenstein, 'Norms, Identity, and Culture in National Security Policy', p. 56.

19 Goldstein and Keohane, *Ideas and Foreign Policy*, pp. 8–10; Robert D. Putnam, *The Beliefs of Politicians: Ideology, Conflict, and Democracy in Britain and Italy* (New Haven: Yale University Press, 1973), p. 125; Milton Rokeach, *The Open and the Closed Mind* (New York: Basic Books, 1960), p. 40. For a more elaborate cognitive theory, see Jervis, *Perception and Misperception in International Politics*.

20 Jervis, *Perception and Misperception in International Politics*, pp. 296–298.

21 Berger, 'Norms, Identity, and National Security in Germany and Japan', p. 328; Duffield, *World Power Forsaken*, pp. 34–35; Longhurst, *Germany and the Use of Force*, p. 21; Maull, 'Germany's Foreign Policy, post-Kosovo?', pp. 114–115.

22 Stephen F. Szabo, *Parting Ways: The Crisis in German–American Relations* (Washington, DC: Brookings Institution Press, 2004), pp. 120–122.

23 See Chapters 3–5.

24 Josef Joffe, 'Peace and Populism: Why the European Anti-Nuclear Movement Failed', *International Security*, 11:4 (Spring 1987), p. 11.

25 Bundesverfassungsgericht, 2 BvQ 17/93, reprinted in *Stichworte zur Sicherheitspolitik*, 7/1993, p. 14; Bundesverfassungsgericht, 'Urteil des Bundesverfassungsgericht vom 12. Juli 1994 zu Auslandseinsätzen der Bundeswehr', reprinted in *Stichworte zur Sicherheitspolitik*, 7/1994, pp. 17–34.

26 Christian Democratic Union of Germany (CDU), Christian-Social Union of Bavaria (CSU), Free Democratic Party (FDP), and German Social Democratic Party (SDP).

27 Joachim Krause, 'The Role of the Bundestag in German Foreign Policy', in Wolf-Dieter Eberwein and Karl Kaiser (eds), *Germany's New Foreign Policy: Decision-Making in an Interdependent World* (New York: Palgrave, 1998), p. 163.

28 Thomas Saalfeld, 'The West German Bundestag after 40 Years: The Role of the Parliament in a Party Democracy', in Philip Norton (ed.), *Parliaments in Western Europe*, Special Issue, *West European Politics*, 13:3 (1990), p. 72; Stephen F. Szabo, *The Changing Politics of German Security* (New York: St Martin's Press, 1990), p. 74.

29 In identifying these personalities the study has relied on the assessment of about thirty German security policy experts, think tank employees, government officials, and military leaders interviewed by the author between May 1999 and April 2002 (see Appendix A, p. 157). The group includes people such as Jürgen Habermas, Wolfgang Ischinger, Josef Joffe, Karl Kaiser, General Harald Kujat, General Klaus Naumann, Lothar Rühl, Hans-Peter Schwarz, Theo Sommer, Michael Stürmer, Walter Stützle, and Werner Weidenfeld.

30 Gisela Gantzel-Kress and Klaus Jürgen Gantzel, 'The Development of IR Studies in West Germany', in Ekkehart Krippendorf and Volker Rittberger (eds), *The Foreign Policy of West Germany: Formation and Contents* (Beverly Hills, CA: Sage, 1988); Michael Zürn, 'We Can

Do Much Better! Aber muss es auf amerikanisch sein?', *Politische Vierteljahreschrift*, 21 (1990), pp. 91–114.
31 For a more elaborate discussion of why this is the case, see Chapters 2 and 6.
32 Martin Kutz, *Berufsbilder und politische Orientierung: Zur soziologischen Typologisierung und politischen Entwicklungen des Offizierskorps der Bundeswehr*, Führungsakademie der Bundeswehr, Hamburg, October 1998, p. 15.
33 Author's interview, 'Forum Bundeswehr und Gesellschaft', Berlin, October 2001, Chancellery, Berlin, March 2002.
34 See Appendices A and B (pp. 157 and 159).
35 In some less controversial cases the Bundestag voted by hand raising and the *Plenarprotokoll* merely records whether a proposal was passed or defeated and adds a vague commentary such as 'passed with a few abstentions'.
36 See Appendix C (p. 160).
37 Duffield, *World Power Forsaken*, pp. 36–38; Ole R. Holsti, 'Foreign Policy Formation Viewed Cognitively', in Robert Axelrod (ed.), *Structure of Decision: The Cognitive Maps of Political Elites* (Princeton: Princeton University Press, 1976), pp. 43–44.

2

A post-war history of German security culture

'Never again!': reactions to the defeat of 1945

Theories of political culture point out how culture originates in events of existential significance for the national community. In Germany's case, the defeat of 1945 represented hour zero. It shook Germany to the core morally and physically and forced the Germans into a new conception of themselves.

More than 6 million Germans, half of them civilians, perished in the Second World War. All military personnel were imprisoned and many were transported to the Soviet Union to serve as slave labour. Most major German cities were transformed into heaps of rubble by allied bombardment, and the immediate post-war years saw acute shortages of food, clothing, and other necessities. About 12 million Germans were expelled from the territories east of the Oder and Neisse Rivers and Germany lost large tracts of land as the Soviet Union shifted the borders in Eastern Europe westwards. What remained was soon to be divided between East and West.[1]

With the Potsdam Agreement of 2 August 1945, the four victor powers agreed upon a complete disarmament and de-militarisation of Germany. Until the Korean War changed the American geopolitical calculus, the project was vigorously approached by the Western occupation authorities as a psychological as well as a physical task. They orchestrated a large scale re-education effort through the written press, radio, lectures, unions, schools, and churches, disseminating a pro-Western and anti-militarist message. Political and military leaders of the wartime regime were indicted, and the occupation authorities ensured that the Nuremberg Trials received extensive media coverage. Through exposing the dimensions of the crimes of the Nazi regime the Western occupation authorities sought to impress on the German population that the defeat had not just been military but also moral.[2]

German intellectuals and politicians needed little external spur. The defeat gave rise to self-reflection and soul-searching and a strong desire to understand when and why Germany had taken a wrong turn.[3] Different social and political groups eventually drew different conclusions. On the left, a pacifist interpretation took hold. 'Never again war' became the rallying cry for a disparate coalition of intellectuals, educators, unionists, politicians, and protestant clergy. On the centre right, the conclusion was different. 'Never again alone' was the precept for Germany's democratisation, rehabilitation, and reconstruction – a precept that guided and informed the policy of the first post-war German government, headed by the Conservative Konrad Adenauer.

Adenauer was convinced that the roots of the German disaster were to be found in the spiritual and strategic oscillation between East and West which had characterised German policy since unification in 1871. Germany's political and military elite had cultivated the idea of a German '*Sonderweg*' – a special path – bridging eastern communitarianism and western liberal individualism – an idea Adenauer renounced. He believed that the pursuit of a special path had undermined the stability of German society, contributed to the collapse of the Weimar democracy, and helped prepare the soil for Nazism.[4]

Sceptical as to the strength of the democratic instincts of his compatriots, he believed that moral, political, and strategic integration with the West was crucial to bolster Germany's nascent democracy. But if the defeated Germany was to earn a second chance it was necessary to pursue a policy that contained no new sources of mistrust. This called for clarity and consistency. A firm commitment to the West had to replace the perennial wavering of the past. The notion of Germany as part of a greater Western community had to take the place of excessive nationalism. 'Never again alone' became the guiding imperative of Adenauer's Western policy.[5] Adenauer's policy found support from his own party, the CDU/CSU, from the liberal FDP, from segments of the SPD, the Catholic Church, a number of intellectuals, and eventually a majority of the population.

The competing reaction to the German disaster – the pacifist 'never again war' – was promoted by a coalition of groups that did not share one coherent ideology. It comprised intellectuals, scientists, and clergy terrified by the potential consequences of nuclear warfare, trade unionists using the movement as a lever against the Government, left-leaning politicians propelled by both pacifist and tactical motives, and, from 1968, a radicalised student generation aiming for a far-reaching democratisation of German society. In spite of differences in focus and agenda, most of these forces held self-seeking nationalism, excessive militarism, Prussian authoritarianism, or crass capitalist materialism responsible for the two world wars. They converged on a principled objection to the use of force in international affairs and argued that Germany, because of its history, carried a special responsibility to work for peace and peaceful conflict resolution.

At various points in post-war history, the SPD closed ranks with 'never again war'. In spite of strong anti-militarist sentiments among the rank and file, however, the party leadership never subscribed to the full agenda of universal pacifism. Until 1983 when the Green Party broke into the Bundestag, 'never again war' thus found expression in extra-parliamentarian protest movements. Starting with the massive anti-rearmament demonstrations of the early 1950s, these movements became a recurrent phenomenon of post-war German political life.

'Never again alone' and 'never again war' represented competing interpretations of German history and diverging prescriptions regarding security and defence policy. The recognition of German responsibility for the crimes of the past, however, provided a unifying theme. The shared desire to learn from past mistakes and the resolution 'never again!' made for a community of aversion encompassing the two competing schools of thought within Germany's post-war security culture.[6] Intellectual and moral control of the past thus became a powerful instrument in the domestic political battle. It became a conscious pursuit and central aspect of post-war German political competition.[7]

Though the adherents of 'never again alone' and 'never again war' clashed on several occasions during the post-war era, the political mainstream gradually converged on a set of assumptions and policies that honoured both precepts: a strong urge to seek partnership and cooperation, emphasis on creating trust between Germany and its partners and neighbours, a defence posture that eschewed offensive strategies, and general restraint in security and military matters. The struggle over the past and the gradually emerging consensus was especially evident at three junctures – the re-armament battle of the 1950s, the initiation of Willy Brandt's new *Ostpolitik* (Eastern policy) in the 1970s, and the battle over the Euro-missiles of the 1980s.

The re-armament battle

In August 1949, Konrad Adenauer was elected the first post-war German chancellor. Under his leadership Western integration became the cornerstone of Germany's foreign and security policy. Though strongly suspicious of the military, Adenauer made rearmament a central part of his policy programme as he saw a German defence contribution as the only way to secure strategic, political, and economic integration with the Western victor powers on an equal basis.[8]

The quest for NATO membership

The North Atlantic Treaty Organisation (NATO) came into being in April 1949, while the Soviet Union was still perceived as a primarily ideological threat. NATO's main purpose was to stabilise the Western European democracies internally and provide them with a guarantee against a resurgent Germany. Though the Americans felt that German membership would be desirable to shield it from neutralist temptations, the continental Europeans resisted and Germany remained an outsider.

It would not be long, however, before the international climate started to deteriorate. In August 1949 the Soviet Union successfully tested its first nuclear device; less than a month later, the victorious Mao Zedong established a communist republic in China; and in June the following year communist North Korea launched an attack on South Korea. As the West's threat perception changed, Adenauer seized the opportunity to reopen the question of German NATO membership.[9]

The German chancellor realised that, in light of recent history, German rearmament and admission into NATO presupposed that Germany would appease the fears of its neighbours. In order to create trust and reassurance, he left no doubt about his willingness to embed Germany's power potential in common Western structures. Accordingly, he embraced two French proposals aimed at European integration: Jean Monnet's plan for a European Coal and Steel Community (ECSC), and the Pleven Plan for a European Defence Community (EDC). ECSC entailed the full integration of French and German coal and steel industries under a supranational authority – a move that would make war between the two countries difficult if not impossible in practical terms. The EDC, which eventually came to nothing as a majority in the French Assembly declined to consider it, foresaw an integrated European defence force. German soldiers and officers would serve in this force, but remain barred from senior positions.[10]

Though the French kept opposing Germany's admittance to NATO, Adenauer's policy of reassuring and building trust enabled him to gradually restore some aspects of German sovereignty. With the Petersburg Agreement of September 1950, Germany was allowed to establish a foreign ministry and a diplomatic service. And upon the signing of the EDC Treaty in 1952, the Western Allies formally removed the occupation statute.

As the EDC foundered and the international climate hardened, the French eventually, though grudgingly, accepted German NATO membership. Crowning the early achievements of Adenauer's Western policy, Germany was invited to join NATO in October 1954.[11]

The domestic re-armament battle

In Germany, Adenauer's re-armament plans met with a mixture of passive rejection and active resistance. To the population at large defeat, suffering, and humiliation had underlined the failure of power politics and installed a deep-seated scepticism towards the use of military force in international relations. 'Ohne mich' – count me out – was the reaction of the man in the street to the prospect of a new German army.[12]

The Social Democrats denounced re-armament as indefensible on strategic and moral grounds and criticised Adenauer for sacrificing German unification on the altar of Western integration.[13] Between 1952 and 1959 the party became the centre of a broad coalition of intellectuals, scientists, protestant clergy, and trade unionists advancing an anti-militarist, and, at times, anti-Western agenda.[14]

In 1954, the Eisenhower administration, forced by Western manpower shortages and budgetary constraints, abandoned the strategy of conventional deterrence. With the 'New Look' strategy, conventional forces would function as a shield to temporarily defend the alliance until NATO activated its nuclear forces to counterattack. Massive retaliation and the new emphasis on nuclear weapons aimed at maximising the West's deterrent capability. They also provided the German anti-re-armament movement with an issue of immense emotive power. Upon the NATO exercise 'Carte blanche' in June 1955, which simulated a nuclear attack on alliance forces in Germany, the German magazine *Der Spiegel* published staggering estimates of civilian casualties, allegedly obtained from an official source: 1.7 million dead and 3.5 million wounded as an immediate effect.[15] With the 'New Look' pacifism became able to leverage the fear of nuclear annihilation and 'count me out' sentiments were channelled into an anti-nuclear crusade.[16] Under the banner 'fight atomic death', the anti-rearmament movement staged a series of mass demonstrations against the deployment of nuclear weapons on German soil. The SPD called for a nuclear-free zone in Central Europe, withdrawal of East and West Germany from their respective alliances, and withdrawal of all foreign troops to ease tensions and pave the way for re-unification.

In light of the Soviet conventional superiority in Europe, the Adenauer government's first inclination had been to seek German control over tactical nuclear weapons. As this became publicly known, however, it provoked massive domestic uproar. Groups that had not earlier rallied around 'never again war' stepped forward against Adenauer's plans. Twelve renowned nuclear scientists from the University of Göttingen contended that 'once is enough', referring to the European havoc wrecked by Nazi Germany. Fellow Conservatives quietly warned that a national nuclear force might activate dormant primitive and atavistic desires within certain segments of German society and pose a challenge to the stability of the new democratic order.[17] The domestic storm and negative signals from Germany's partners soon removed the plan for nationally controlled nuclear weapons from the agenda.[18]

The deployment of American nuclear weapons on German soil, on the other hand, was pushed through in spite of massive popular protests. Invoking the past with terms such as 'nuclear holocaust', the peace movement attempted to establish a link between the new NATO defence doctrine and the cruel effectiveness of the Nazi extermination camps.[19] Adenauer responded by pointing to the consequences of the Western appeasement of Hitler's territorial claims in Eastern Europe in the 1930s. One could negotiate only with a totalitarian state, he charged, from a position of strength. The preservation of peace, freedom, and democracy in Germany and Europe, he argued, thus required Western solidarity and a German defence contribution.[20]

In order to appease opponents and sceptics, however, the Government designed a policy that combined Western military solidarity with an attempt to promote détente and negotiations with the East. In a government resolution of

March 1958, the superpowers were urged to enter into general disarmament talks. With the Harmel Report of 1967, the dual pillars of defence and negotiation were adopted as official NATO strategy to the great satisfaction of the German mainstream.[21]

'Non-offensive' defence and military restraint

As the peace movement protested in the streets and the SPD in parliament, the government went about reconstructing an army and a defence policy that on a number of accounts reflected and respected anti-militarist sentiments.

Adenauer himself harboured a strong suspicion of the military as an institution and considered the aggressive and excessive militarism of the past a major factor behind the German disaster. The founding fathers of the Bundeswehr – a group of former Wehrmacht officers summoned by Adenauer to the Himmerod Abbey in the Eifel Mountains in early October 1950 – were charged with creating a democratic and defensive army that would not figure as a threat to either Germany's neighbours or German democracy.[22]

To reassure sceptics both at home and abroad, a number of external and internal safeguards were installed. The German military was to be completely integrated in NATO, defensive in nature, and placed under a regime of strict civilian control.

The Bundeswehr was constructed as the first national army that could not function outside an alliance framework. Besides relying on the alliance nuclear guarantee, Germany lacked crucial command, control, and planning assets. The Bundeswehr's military command structure was deliberately kept weak. The inspectors of the individual services – the highest-ranking officers of, respectively, the army, navy, and air force – reported directly to the Minister of Defence. The Bundeswehr's military chief – the Inspector General – had no command power but filled a strictly advisory position ranking below both the minister and the civilian Deputy Minister of Defence. All active German forces were placed under the direct command of the Supreme Allied NATO Commander in Europe (SACEUR). The new Bundeswehr also lacked an independent military 'brain' in the form of Joint Chiefs of Staff and joint-service planning headquarters. Germany thus depended on the military planning capabilities of NATO headquarters in Brussels. Moreover, the size of the German army was restricted to 500,000 soldiers and Germany renounced production and possession of atomic, biological, and chemical weapons (ABC weapons), as well as strategic bombers and large warships that could be perceived as offensive in nature.[23]

Within Germany, civilian control and oversight were reinforced. The defence committee of the Bundestag was endowed with investigatory powers, and the office of the 'Wehrbeauftragte' – a parliamentary ombudsman for military affairs – was created.[24]

Furthermore, the internal organisation of the armed forces was democratised and the military culture sought to be civilised. The military ethos of the Reichswehr and the Wehrmacht – the military organisations of imperial and

Nazi Germany, respectively – was discarded and the traditional ideals of courage, manliness, and discipline gave way to a new ideal of well-informed and well-educated citizen-soldiers. The programmes of 'inner leadership' and 'citizen in uniform' entailed civic and political education of all Bundeswehr personnel and prescribed that the values of the German political and legal system should form the basis for internal discipline in the armed forces. It aimed on creating politically informed soldiers, capable of distinguishing between legitimate and criminal orders, between democracy and repression.[25]

Traditionalist and conservative critics of these reforms claimed that 'inner leadership' and 'citizen in uniform' overlooked the real differences between civilian and military society. The purpose of the army, it was claimed, was to be an effective military instrument, not an institution for democratic education. The profession of soldiering was of unchanging nature and therefore not in need of reform.[26] The programme of the Himmerod group, however, found broad political support. While its implementation was hampered by time pressure and material shortcomings, the army that emerged was, in the view of most analysts, decisively different from the military organisations of the German past. The ethos had been civilised, the civic rights of the soldiers secured to an extent unmatched in German history, the social diversity of the officer corps increased, and the variety of political attitudes and allegiances within the armed forces broadened.[27]

The introduction of universal conscription in 1956 aimed at ensuring a diversity of views and a variety of cross-cutting allegiances within the army, providing an insurance against the development of a military state within the state.[28]

Germany's new peaceful military posture found codification in the Basic Law from 1949. The Law's preamble committed Germany to work for European unity, international peace, and the protection of human rights. Article 87a (2) stipulated that German armed forces could be used for 'defence only' – an article whose interpretation would become a key point of contention during the 1990s out-of-area battle.[29]

Emerging consensus: accepting Western integration

Integration normally entails a loss of sovereignty. But by the end of the Second World War Germany had nothing to lose. Defeated, divided, and occupied, it was in no position to decide its own fate. Integration in NATO and Western European structures became the road leading back to respectability and self-determination.[30]

By cultivating ties to all the major Western democracies and by demonstrating a willingness to embed each piece of regained sovereignty in common institutions and structures, Adenauer gradually earned the trust of the Western world and managed to turn Germany's victorious opponents into allies.

Integration and access to the international regimes and organisations of the West in turn permitted Germany an influence it could never have obtained on a national basis due to the fear and mistrust of its neighbours.

By the late 1950s economic recovery and the partial restoration of German sovereignty through NATO and Western integration had bolstered political and public support for Adenauer's political line. Under the sheltering wing of NATO, the ECSC laid the foundation for Germany's economic revival through export-led growth. ECSC and its 1957 successor, the European Community (EC), ensured German industrial goods access to a large market, permitted the achievement of economics of scale, and gave German companies a platform for penetrating international markets.[31] Economic integration combined with the economic boom caused by the Korean War brought jobs and higher wages. Furthermore, the 1956 crackdown on the Hungarian revolt and the 1958 Berlin blockade tarnished the image of the Soviet Union and made the policy of defence and Western integration seem more necessary. Though re-unification remained a cherished goal across the political spectrum, few wished to see their country re-unified by the Red Army.[32]

Thus, whereas many German elites through the 1950s would have welcomed a withdrawal of American troops from Germany, the 1960s saw a reversal of these sentiments. A solid majority came to regard Western integration and the American military presence in Germany as desirable, even indispensable.[33] A majority had also come to terms with the existence of the Bundeswehr as part of this policy of Western integration. For many, however, it remained an acceptance devoid of enthusiasm – and contingent on the civilised and defensive character of German defence.[34]

Following a sequence of election defeats between 1957 and 1959 in which the SPD had run on an anti-NATO ticket, the Atlanticists within the party succeeded in winning a majority for the principle of defensive territorial defence within NATO. At the 1959 party congress in Bad Godesberg, the SPD embraced Western integration and the German defence contribution as a way of influencing Western policies in the direction of disarmament and détente.[35]

The SPD's conversion signalled an emerging German working consensus on security policy based on Western integration and defensive defence. Between the anti-re-armament demonstrations of the 1950s and the large anti-nuclear protests provoked by NATO's 1979 double-track decision, discussed below, there were no attempts on behalf of the opposition to stir up anti-NATO feelings.[36]

Willy Brandt's Eastern policy

Willy Brandt and Egon Bahr's Eastern policy, though initially divisive, broadened the nascent German foreign and security policy consensus. It extended the principles of Adenauer's Western policy – confidence building, negotiation, and accommodation – to Germany's Eastern neighbours, and eventually won acceptance on the centre right. Simultaneously, it imported many of the notions of the peace movement into mainstream policy and thus proved popular on the left. In the era of détente, it seemed to offer a way of combining a firm commitment to the West with peaceful coexistence and cooperation with the East.[37]

When Willy Brandt became chancellor in 1969, German partition looked like an enduring fact of life. The Cold War had turned out to be more than an episode in history and high politics and conventional diplomatic means appeared to have exhausted themselves in overcoming the 'bloc confrontation' that divided Europe and Germany. But within an international context of decreasing superpower tensions, Brandt and his close assistant and foreign policy advisor, Bahr, saw an opportunity to attempt a new approach to the German question. He concluded that civil society, not diplomats, should bridge the gap between East and West. The divisive effect of borders should be toned down and political, economic, cultural, and human links between the two Germanies strengthened.[38]

Brandt's strategy presupposed a critical level of trust between the East and West German governments. The GDR regime had to be convinced of the need to shed its fear of allowing East German citizens contact with the West – a fear embodied in the Berlin Wall. To re-assure and create trust, Brandt concluded a number of treaties with the East – the Moscow Treaty and Warsaw Treaty of May 1972, and the Basic Treaty between the two Germanies of December 1972. With these treaties, Bonn accepted the territorial status quo in Eastern Europe as well as the existence of East Germany, though it stopped well short of a formal recognition.

The status quo had to be accepted, Brandt believed, before it could be overcome. With time, increased human, economic, and cultural contact would let in enough fresh air to make East German autocracy untenable. It would become clear to people in the East how miserable their regimes were performing politically and economically, and Europe's division would eventually be overcome by popular pressure from below. 'Wandel durch Annäherung' – transformation through accommodation – was the motto of the new Eastern policy.[39]

Eastern policy, the past, and the peace movement

Brandt tied his new foreign and security policy into a broader agenda of how to deal with Germany's past. Public reflection on the darker sides of German history became part of his trust building strategy towards the East. In a series of acts of atonement and reconciliation, German political memory was extended back to the Nazi invasion of Poland in 1939 and the Soviet Union in 1941. Adenauer's policy of refusing to recognise the regimes of Eastern Europe, Brandt argued, had represented an act of insensitive omission towards countries in which the Wehrmacht had perpetrated its greatest crimes. His bent knee at the memorial to Jews killed in the Warsaw ghetto was a powerful symbolic gesture and an essential component of his diplomatic strategy. It signalled that Germany was not a revisionist power looking to regain lost territory in the East.[40]

Under the motto 'daring more democracy', Brandt linked his policy towards the East and the past to a domestic agenda that tapped into the sentiments fuelling the student movement of 1968. He criticised the restorational elements of Adenauer's reconstruction and rearmament policy, which had relied on the cooperation of a number of tainted elites. The '1968ers' fought for a radical democratisation of German politics and society as well as de-militarisation of international relations. They criticised the authoritarian streak in German education, the lack of democracy in the universities, and alleged residual authoritarianism in German society. Against the backdrop of the American war in Vietnam, they had reinvigorated the peace movement of the 1950s as they rallied against capitalist power politics and the use of force in international relations.

Brandt's new security policy thinking and approach to the East rested on a belief in 'soft' power – in the potential of economic, political, and cultural instruments of foreign policy – as well as on a belief that even structural enmity was not immutable and insurmountable. Though governments were at odds, societies and people shared common interests.

Instead of Adenauer's realist language and focus on balance of power, Brandt and Bahr employed an idealist and internationalist vocabulary. In the nuclear age, they argued, war could no longer serve as an instrument of policy. Mutually assured destruction (MAD) would deprive both parties of a conflict of any gains. There was no alternative to cooperation and reconciliation. Confidence building and cooperation would pave the way for a genuine peace that was not precariously perched on a nuclear balance of terror.

Such notions were reflected and confirmed in German academic life of the 1970s, where all shades and forms of peace and integration research flourished. A number of peace research institutes sprang up across Germany, focusing on topics such as socialisation and aggression, the arms race, and enemy images. Research informed by realist theories with emphasis on nation-states, national interest, and power, in contrast, remained almost absent from the German political science faculties.[41]

Brandt and Bahr's policy thus incorporated many of the notions of the peace movement – the immorality of power politics, the aversion against self-seeking international behaviour, and the suspicion against separating foreign policy from morality – and appealed to the anti-militarism of the German intelligentsia. But with Brandt and Bahr these sentiments were for the first time translated into a coherent and comprehensive political programme that, within an overall international climate of détente, did not seem utopian to a majority of German voters.

Accepting Brandt's Eastern policy

The new Eastern policy soon gained the favour of the general public. It facilitated travel and communication between East and West, expanded German trade and investment in Eastern Europe, and eased transit between West

Germany and West Berlin. The emphasis on cooperation instead of confrontation made fear of war, confrontation, and nuclear annihilation fade[42]

Though the CDU voted against the Eastern Treaties in 1972, the political controversy over the practical aspects of Eastern policy never grew particularly acrimonious. After an overwhelming SPD success in the general elections of 1972, the Conservatives quietly started adopting many of Brandt's ideas about how to deal with the 'other Germany'. This adoption was facilitated by the fact that Brandt never questioned the basic paradigm of the Conservative party – Adenauer's 'never again alone'.[43] Brandt's Eastern policy upgraded the importance of cooperation with the East without placing in doubt Germany's commitment to the Western camp and to NATO.[44]

Nevertheless, Adenauer's Western strategy and Brandt's Eastern policy were based on contradictory notions about German identity, the nature of the Soviet Union, and threats to German security. Adenauer was firmly committed to Western values and wished to see Germany develop economically and politically along Western lines. Brandt, in contrast, was committed to a different kind of society representing a 'middle way' between the Eastern and Western model. Adenauer saw the Soviet Union as the major external threat to German democracy. Brandt, while recognising the Soviet Union as a threat and while remaining firmly committed to German NATO membership, nevertheless placed more emphasis on armaments and nuclear weapons as threats in themselves. Adenauer saw military balance as the best way to avoid a military confrontation in Europe. Brandt believed cooperation, negotiation, and disarmament were more likely to prevent the use of force.

But in spite of these differences, Western integration and Eastern policy had common denominators: Both relied on cooperation and integration as means to pursue security, prosperity, and, in the long run, unity. Both emphasised the importance of creating trust between Germany and its neighbours and cultivating bonds of friendship and partnership among nations – former or current enemies. Both were aware of Germany's geostrategic vulnerability and the need to avoid violent confrontation in Europe.[45]

With the Bad Godesberg convention in 1959 the SPD had accepted the Western Alliance. The CDU, in turn, quietly endorsed many aspects of Brandt's Eastern policy during the 1970s, recognising its practical achievements and electoral appeal. The CDU/CSU/FDP government that came into office in 1982 continued its own mini-détente and a scaled-down version of Eastern policy, even as the international climate hardened and superpower tensions rose.[46]

The intermediate nuclear force battle

Brandt's new policy approach coexisted peacefully with the commitment to the West throughout most of the 1970s. However, with the hardening international climate of the early 1980s, the conflict between an Eastern and Western orientation returned with a vengeance. Brandt's internationalist vocabulary had provided new conceptual ammunition to the peace movement. The deployment of NATO Pershing II missiles in Europe pitted a reinvigorated 'never again war' against the old Atlanticist 'never again alone'.

The double-track decision

Though the German resistance to NATO's INF deployment proved more fierce than in any other European country, the demand for the INF actually originated in Germany. In 1975 the Soviet Union initiated a build-up of highly accurate, medium-range SS-20 nuclear missiles in its Western military zone. Two years later, Germany's Social Democratic chancellor, Helmut Schmidt, first voiced his concern about the resulting disparity between Soviet and NATO medium-range nuclear capabilities in Europe. The already existing nuclear parity on the strategic level, Schmidt argued, might prevent the US from coming to Europe's help in the case of a limited Soviet attack. Moscow might be tempted to exploit the tactical nuclear and conventional superiority it was in the process of building to attack Europe, calculating that the US would not risk general war by unleashing its strategic nuclear arsenal. Deterrence would remain effective, Schmidt argued, only if the gap in tactical nuclear capabilities was filled. Moscow had to be convinced that any aggression would lead to retaliation against its own territory.[47]

With the 1979 'double-track' decision, the NATO Council announced that it would deploy a new generation of tactical nuclear weapons in Europe to counter the Soviet SS-20s. Simultaneously, however, the alliance offered to enter negotiations for arms control aimed on limiting the number of long-range theatre nuclear weapons on both sides in concordance with a principle of parity and equality.

The domestic INF battle

The double-track decision and the increasingly belligerent superpower rhetoric caused anti-nuclear feelings to flare up in Germany. The strategy of massive retaliation had ironically done something to soothe nuclear angst by making it possible to imagine the Western military potential as an instrument to avoid, but not to fight war. The increased focus on tactical nuclear weapons and warfighting strategies pierced this psychological shield.[48] When Schmidt argued that a balance of military forces was necessary to deter aggression he was up against instinctive aversions as well as the moral and intellectual current of the détente era. This eventually undermined his position as party leader and a majority within the SPD, denounced the double-track decision.[49]

Drawing on the vocabulary of Brandt and Bahr's Eastern policy, the Social Democratic INF opponents argued that security could not be attained against the adversary, but rather, only in cooperation with it. The very deployment of new weapons, it was argued, made war more likely.[50] If both halves of Europe could be released from the confrontational logic of bloc-thinking, it was argued, the consciousness of a common European civilisation would re-emerge – a civilisation based on peaceful coexistence and a socioeconomic model that represented a third way between the backward Soviet model and the crass materialism of the US.[51] The party's left wing thus called for more distance between NATO and Germany, an immediate transfer to a purely conventional deterrent, and a non-nuclear Europe.[52] The mainstream, however, did not question Germany's NATO membership or the need to rely on nuclear deterrence for the foreseeable future. Instead, they advocated a greater Western European say within NATO in order to give peace policies a chance.[53]

Still, this apparent SPD drift away from the Atlantic Alliance alarmed the SPD's alliance partner, the liberal FDP. It warned against non-compliance with the double-track decision and eventually, in September 1982, brought down the government. Following a constructive vote of no confidence, power passed to a Conservative/Liberal coalition headed by the Christian Democrat Helmut Kohl.

The INF battle and the past

The lessons of the past became one of the most contended issues of the INF dispute. The left claimed that the Second World War experience and Germany's responsibility for the mass annihilation of Jews in extermination camps such as Auschwitz obliged the Germans to fight against the deployment of new means of mass annihilation. The centre right, in turn, argued that the years preceding the Second World War had shown that unbalanced power did not prevent war, but led to war. The pacifism of the 1930s, it was suggested, had made Auschwitz possible in the first place.[54] The left claimed that Germany, because of its past, carried a special responsibility to stand up for peace and reject INF. The centre right argued that since the Germans had failed to defend democracy and freedom in 1933 it was their special responsibility to do so in 1983 and accept INF.[55]

Meanwhile, the peace movement staged a series of mass demonstrations against 'Europe's Holocaust' and 'nuclear Auschwitz' drawing hundreds of thousands of Germans to the streets. The protests culminated in connection with a June 1982 NATO summit in Bonn where around 400,000 people attended an anti-nuclear rally.[56]

Yet, in the face of these massive public protests, Helmut Kohl reaffirmed his commitment to carry through the INF deployment and though the public aversion against new missiles was strong, support for NATO proved to be stronger. The general elections in March 1983 returned a solid majority for the new Conservative/Liberal Government. In November the same year Kohl was able to push the missile deployment through the Bundestag.[57]

Competing schools of thought in Germany's post-war security culture

The battle of the Euro-missiles recalled the anti-nuclear crusade of the 1950s and provided a reminder that the two schools of thought within Germany's security culture remained distinct. They rested on different core beliefs about Germany's role in international security, they diverged in their fundamental aversions and threat perceptions, and in their operational beliefs about the efficiency of various instruments of security policy.

To the adherents of 'never again alone' Germany's military exceptionalism and its policy of foreign and security policy restraint were necessary choices considering Germany's recent history and its special geostrategic circumstances. It was made necessary by Germany's inability to defend itself, its strong interest in avoiding military confrontation in Europe, and its urge to create trust and gain access to Western organisations and institutions. Military exceptionalism was not a goal in itself, but a means to an end.

In contrast, to the adherents of 'never again war', military restraint was not just a means to an end, but an end in itself. Germany's history, it was believed, placed a special moral obligation on Germany to abstain from ever again using military force for purposes other than self-defence. Germany's role, it was believed, was to work as a civilising force in international relations, promoting human rights and counteracting violence. According to this way of thinking, military restraint was a core element of Germany's role in international security.

As illustrated by their divergent approaches to the East bloc, the two schools also differed in their assessment of the nature of the international system. 'Never again alone' perceived of conflict as a basic premise of international politics and tended to perceive the East–West conflicts in zero-sum terms. 'Never again war' had stronger faith in the potential for peaceful coexistence and mutually beneficial solutions to international problems.

Following from these diverging core beliefs, the two schools also differed in their operational beliefs about the relative efficiency of diplomatic versus more forceful strategies. If both camps agreed that the world was no harmonious congregation of states, they differed in their assessment of what strategies were more efficient in dealing with threats to peace and security. 'Never again alone', with its emphasis on negotiation from strength, recognised, in principle, the effect of more forceful strategies. 'Never again war', with its emphasis on civilisation through cooperation and integration, tended towards diplomacy.

Despite these differences, the overlapping principle of 'never again!' was a paramount and uniting theme in Germany's security culture. This theme gave German security thinking a peculiar cast, for it often focused on abstract aversions instead of on concrete and contemporary threats. The two schools both conceived of the Soviet Union as a menace, but frequently the enemy images that figured most prominently in the debate were the core aversions of respectively 'never again alone' – a German separate path, isolation, and singularisation – and of 'never again war' – the excessive reliance on force and military means of the past.

Restraint and cooperation: the post-war working consensus

'Never again alone' and 'never again war' represented competing lessons from the first half of Germany's twentieth century. But as illustrated above German politicians, despite their philosophical differences, gradually converged on a number of mutually acceptable policies. This working consensus comprised integration with the West, cooperation with the East, renunciation of national nuclear weapons, and a defensive military posture with the role of the Bundeswehr circumscribed to homeland defence.

By the 1980s, the Social Democrats no longer questioned the German tie to the West.[58] In turn, the central tenets of Brandt's Eastern policy – the value of 'low politics', negotiation, cooperation, and non-confrontation – had been recognised on the centre right.[59]

The Liberal Hans-Dietrich Genscher's continued service as Minister of Foreign Affairs provided for continuity between the foreign and security policy of the two camps. Genscher in many ways personified the working consensus between left and right. While strongly committed to the Atlantic Alliance he nevertheless shared many of the basic philosophical tenets of the idealist and internationalist Social Democratic security thinking developed during the détente era. Genscher's 'policy of responsibility' emphasised Germany's historical obligation to exercise a maximum of restraint in military matters as well as an obligation to tie German policy to values such as democracy, peace, and human rights.[60]

The legacy of this policy was impressive. From a war-devastated outcast deprived of even the most basic sovereign state rights, Germany rose to a position of prosperity, peace, and unity. By October 1990, at the outset of the out-of-area debate, a re-unified Germany found itself surrounded by friendly nations in a re-unified Europe where the Soviet threat was quickly receding. Arguably, international cooperation had proved beneficial to the extent that it obtained inherent value across the political spectrum. It proved instrumental in realising German goals to the extent that it became a goal in itself. Moreover, the search for non-military solutions to international problems became ingrained and the aversion against offensive and pro-active military strategies was shared across the political spectrum in a country for which even a limited East–West confrontation would most likely have entailed total destruction.[61]

A realist might charge that the focus on historical responsibility, past, and partners, and the lack of discussion about national interests and military matters that characterised the 1990s out-of-area battle were nothing but window-dressing aimed at reassuring nervous neighbours. This chapter, in contrast, has indicated that concern for these issues was sincere in the sense that it was deeply rooted in Germany's post-war experience. The focus on responsibility and partnership as well as the apparent aversion against all things military were not just window-dressing aimed at seducing foreigners, but were deeply rooted in Germany's history and in the security policy culture of Germany's political elite.

The out-of-area question prior to unification

The question of rearmament, national control with nuclear weapons, and nuclear deployments on German soil made the two rival schools of thought within German security culture – 'never again war' and 'never again alone' – clash violently at various times over the post-war era. But on the out-of-area question, German politicians quickly united: there would be no German military involvement in potential conflicts beyond Europe.

Beginning with a request for military support in the Vietnam War, the Americans occasionally called on Germany to extend its military role. German leaders consistently declined.[62] In 1964, they pointed to the fact that the Bundeswehr had not yet been fully built up, making a diversion of resources away from the central European front problematic. Later, they invoked the 'defence-only' clause in the German Basic Law. These arguments were generally accepted among Germany's NATO allies. The central European front remained the major potential battlefield and a concentration of German forces there seemed appropriate. Moreover, most of Germany's European neighbours were anything but eager to see Germany take on a higher military profile in world affairs.

When Germany became a member of the UN in 1973, the question of participation in UN peacekeeping missions was raised. Some argued that Germany's economic weight obliged it to carry part of the burden for upholding world security. But a political majority, pointing to the presumed constitutional prohibition, rejected any German military presence out-of-area, whether under NATO or United Nations (UN) auspices. German support for international crisis management would be financial, political, and humanitarian, but not military.[63]

This rejection was based on a mixture of motives. On the left, the conviction that Germany's history obliged the country to show maximum restraint in military matters prohibited the consideration of an out-of-area role. The left-wing aversion against playing a role outside of NATO area was reinforced during the Vietnam War. It was completely unacceptable to this group that Germany should lend its support to global US policies that were perceived as relying excessively on military force, as opposed to political and diplomatic instruments.

The centre right, in turn, worried about creating concern among Germany's neighbours by taking on a higher military profile. Policy makers on the centre right were also reluctant to endorse a global NATO strategy that would divert resources away from Central Europe and worried that German involvement in proxy confrontations in extra-European theatres might provoke the Soviet Union to extend the conflict to Central Europe and thus undermine Germany's policy of cooperation and negotiation with the East.[64]

It was only when superpower tensions turned into détente in the mid-1980s that individuals on the German centre right came around on the out-of-area question. They reasoned that if Germany wished to preserve its standing within

NATO at a time where Soviet reforms reduced the likelihood of conflict in Central Europe, German armed forces would have to take on a broader role

NATO's 1991 Strategic Concept and the 1992 Petersburg Declaration of the Western European Union (WEU) eventually confirmed this line of thinking. NATO's new Strategic Concept emphasised global risks and stressed the need for flexible and mobile forces to meet these new challenges. The Petersburg Declaration established that the armed forces of WEU member states would henceforth serve not just collective defence purposes, but could also be deployed beyond WEU area in humanitarian and rescue missions, peacekeeping, and peace-enforcing missions.[65]

With the *Defence Policy Guidelines* published by the German ministry of defence in 1992, the thoughts of the converted German strategists and security experts for the first time found their way into an official German government document. The *Defence Policy Guidelines* came directly from the hand of the then-Inspector General of the Bundeswehr, General Klaus Naumann. The *Guidelines* suggested that the Bundeswehr would henceforth 'serve world peace and international security in accordance with the UN Charter' and 'assist in humanitarian aid-missions'.[66]

The handful of German strategists that favoured extending Germany's international security role in the 1980s did so based on what could be characterised as 'realist' reasoning – a calculation of how best to secure and enhance Germany's international political influence in Western security organisations. Their thoughts and mode of reasoning, however, did not resonate within Germany's political culture. The great majority of German politicians in the 1980s rejected any suggestion that Germany should take on a greater global security role. They kept believing that the best way to heed Germany's historical responsibility and remain a good partner was through predictability, continuity, and general restraint in military matters. By the time of unification, all political parties thus subscribed to a policy of strict military abstinence in conflicts outside of NATO area.[67]

The strategists and security experts, however, came to play a crucial role during the early 1990s as they translated their own 'realist' reasoning into different arguments that resounded within Germany's political culture. Only then did Germany's policy start to hange, prodded by external pressure and a succession of crises that questioned the old thinking of both schools of thought within Germany's security culture.

Notes

1 David Gress, *Peace and Survival: West Germany, the Peace Movement, and European Security* (Stanford, CA: Hoover Institution Press, 1985), p. 8; 'Die Deutschen als Opfer', *Der Spiegel*, 25 March 2002, pp. 36–39.
2 Lucius D. Clay, *Decision in Germany* (New York: Doubleday & Co, 1950), pp. 282–284.
3 Kenneth Dyson, *The State Tradition of Western Europe* (New York: Oxford University

Press, 1980), p. 178; Rudolf von Thadden, *Nicht Vaterland, nicht Fremde: Essays. zu Geschichte und Gegenwart* (Munich: C. H. Beck Verlag, 1989), p. 121; Bernard Giesen, *Die Intellektuellen und die Nation* (Frankfurt am Main: Suhrkamp, 1993), p. 237; Michael Stürmer, *Die Grenzen der Macht: Begegnung der Deutschen mit der Geschichte* (Berlin: Siedler Verlag, 1990), p. 118.

4 Hans-Peter Schwarz, *Konrad Adenauer*, I (Providence: Berghahn Books, 1986), p. 612; Jeffrey Herf, *War by Other Means: Soviet Power, West German Resistance, and the Battle of the Euromissiles* (New York: Free Press, 1991), p. 14; Jeffrey Herf, *Divided Memory: The Nazi Past in the Two Germanies* (Cambridge, MA: Harvard University Press, 1997), p. 216.

5 Stürmer, *Die Grenzen der Macht*, p. 140.

6 Dyson, *The State Tradition of Western Europe*, p. 178; Giesen, *Die Intellektuellen und die Nation*, p. 237; Gress, *Peace and Survival*, pp. 4–5; Stürmer, *Die Grenzen der Macht*, p. 118; Thadden, *Nicht Vaterland, nicht Fremde*, p. 121.

7 Detlef Bald, *Militär und Gesellschaft 1945–1990* (Baden-Baden: Nomos Verlagsgesellschaft, 1994), p. 54; Thomas U. Berger, 'Norms, Identity, and National Security in Germany and Japan', in Peter J. Katzenstein (ed.), *The Culture of National Security: Norms and Identity in World Politics* (New York: Columbia University Press, 1996), p. 331; Herf, *Divided Memory*, p. 8; Hannah Vogt, *The Burden of Guilt: A Short History of Germany, 1914–1945* (New York: Oxford University Press, 1964), pp. 285–286.

8 Wolfram F. Hanrieder, 'West German Foreign Policy, 1949-1979: Necessities and Choices', in Wolfram F. Hanrieder (ed.), *West German Foreign Policy 1949–1979* (Boulder: Westview Press, 1980), p. 18.

9 Carl Cavanagh Hodge, 'Konrad Adenauer, Arms, and the Redemption of Germany', in Cathal J. Nolan (ed.), *Ethics and Statecraft: The Moral Dimension of International Affairs* (London: Praeger, 1995), p. 156; Catherine M. Kelleher, 'Fundamentals of German Security: The Creation of the Bundeswehr – Continuity and Change', in Stephen F. Szabo, *The Bundeswehr and Western Security* (New York: St Martin's Press, 1990), p. 19; W. R. Smyser, *From Yalta to Berlin: The Cold War Struggle over Germany* (New York: St Martin's Griffin, 1999), p. 105.

10 The EDC was conceived by the French premier René Pleven as a pre-emptive move aimed at averting the partial restoration of Germany, which would follow from its re-armament and admission to NATO. The scheme may not have appeared particularly attractive from a German viewpoint, but Adenauer embraced it and signed the EDC Treaty in May 1952. Smyser, *From Yalta to Berlin*, pp. 110–111.

11 In order to reconcile the French to the prospect of a re-armed Germany in NATO, Great Britain committed to permanently deploy at least four divisions in Germany. Smyser, *From Yalta to Berlin*, p. 128.

12 More than half the population resisted the creation of the Bundeswehr in 1950. Mark Cioc, *Pax Atomica: The Nuclear Defense Debate in West Germany During the Adenauer Era* (New York: Columbia University Press, 1988), pp. 12–13; Schwarz, *Konrad Adenauer*, p. 590.

13 Thomas U. Berger, *Cultures of Antimilitarism: National Security in Germany and Japan* (Baltimore: Johns Hopkins University Press, 1998), p. 43; Smyser, *From Yalta to Berlin*, pp. 111, 128.

14 Herf, *Divided Memory*, pp. 246, 268; Smyser, *From Yalta to Berlin*, p. 212.

15 Cioc, *Pax Atomica*, p. 30.

16 Bald, *Militär und Gesellschaft 1945–1990*, p. 90; Ludwig von Friedeburg, 'Rearmament and Social Change', in Jacques van Doorn (ed.), *Armed Forces and Society: Sociological Essays* (The Hague: Mouton, 1968), p. 172; Hans-Peter Schwarz, *Die Zentralmacht Europas: Deutschlands Rückkehr auf die Weltbühne* (Berlin: Siedler Verlag, 1994), p. 174.

17 Karl W. Deutsch, Lewis J. Edinger, Roy C. Macridis, and Richard L. Merritt, *France, Germany and the Western Alliance* (New York: Charles Scribner's Sons, 1967), p. 191.

18 Adenauer and his successor, Ludwig Erhard, both hesitated formally to renounce the option of co-ownership of nuclear weapons. This owed less to a desire to dispose of nuclear weapons than a wish to maintain a bargaining lever with the Soviet Union on the question of German unification. With the establishment of NATO's Nuclear Planning Group (NPG) in 1964, the issue was effectively closed. NPG gave the non-nuclear states a greater say in the formulation of alliance strategy without granting them direct physical access to nuclear weapons. Stephen F. Szabo, *The Changing Politics of German Security* (New York: St Martin's Press, 1990), p. 17.
19 Herf, *War by Other Means*, pp. 24–25.
20 Herf, *Divided Memory*, p. 298; Schwarz, *Konrad Adenauer*, p. 292.
21 Cioc, *Pax Atomica*, pp. 42, 49; Anne-Marie LeGloannec, 'West German Security: Less of a Consensus?', in Catherine McArdle Kelleher and Gale A. Mattox (eds), *Evolving European Defense Policies* (Lexington, MA: Lexington Books, 1987), p. 180; Szabo, *The Changing Politics of German Security*, p. 17.
22 Donald Abenheim, *Reforging the Iron Cross* (Princeton: Princeton University Press, 1988), p. 101; Donald Abenheim, 'The Citizen in Uniform: Reform and its Critics in the Bundeswehr', in Stephen F. Szabo (ed.), *The Bundeswehr and Western Security* (New York: St Martin's Press, 1990), pp. 35–36; Count Wolf von Baudissin, 'The New German Army', *Foreign Affairs*, 34:1 (October 1955), p. 3; Herf, *Divided Memory*, p. 219.
23 Abenheim, 'The Citizen in Uniform', p. 35; Smyser, *From Yalta to Berlin*, p. 128.
24 Abenheim, 'The Citizen in Uniform', p. 39.
25 Bald, *Militär und Gesellschaft 1945–1990*, p. 7; Sameera Dalvi, 'The Post-Cold War Role of the Bundeswehr: A Product of Normative Influences', *European Security*, 7:1 (1998), p. 103.
26 Abenheim, 'The Citizen in Uniform', p. 45; Martin Kitchen, *A Military History of Germany: From the Eighteenth Century to the Present Day* (London: Weidenfeld & Nicolson, 1975), p. 340.
27 Bald, *Militär und Gesellschaft 1945–1990*, p. 55; Rudolf Hamann, 'Abscheid vom Staatsbürger in Uniform', in Paul Klein and Dieter Walz (eds), *Die Bundeswehr an der Schwelle zum 21. Jahrhundert* (Baden-Baden: Nomos Verlagsgesellschaft, 2000), pp. 67–68.
28 Baudissin, 'The New German Army', p. 3.
29 Article 87a (2) of the German Basic Law restricts the use of Bundeswehr forces to 'defence' only. Article 24 (1) and (2) opens the possibility of transferring sovereign rights to collective security institutions. Article 26 prohibits acts intended to disturb international peace.
30 Schwarz, *Die Zentralmacht Europas*, p. 7.
31 David Calleo, 'Germany and the Balance of Power', in Wolfram F. Hanrieder (ed.), *West German Foreign Policy 1949–1979* (Boulder: Westview Press, 1980), p. 11; Rudolf Hrbek and Wolfgang Wessels (eds), *EG-Mitgliedschaft: Ein vitales Interesse der Bundesrepublik Deutschland?* (Bonn: Europa Union Verlag, 1984); Carl Lankowski, 'Modell Deutschland and the International Regionalization of the West German State in the 1970s', in Andrei Markowits (ed.), *The Political Economy of West Germany: Modell Deutschland* (New York: Praeger, 1982), pp. 90–115.
32 Cavanagh Hodge, 'Konrad Adenauer, Arms, and the Redemption of Germany', p. 162.
33 Deutsch, Edinger, Macridis, and Merritt, *France, Germany and the Western Alliance*, p. 152. See also Timothy Garton Ash, *In Europe's Name: Germany and the Divided Continent* (London: Jonathan Cape, 1993), p. 81; Hans Rattinger, 'The Federal Republic of Germany: Much Ado About (Almost) Nothing', in Gregory Flynn and Hans Rattinger (eds), *The Public and Atlantic Defense* (London: Rowman & Allanheld, 1985), p. 141; Hans Rattinger, 'The Bundeswehr and Public Opinion' in Stephen F. Szabo (ed.), *The Bundeswehr and Western Security* (New York: St Martin's Press, 1990), pp. 107–109.

34 Deutsch, Edinger, Macridis, and Merritt, *France, Germany and the Western Alliance*, p. 152.
35 LeGloannec, 'West German Security', p. 171.
36 Hanrieder, 'West German Foreign Policy, 1949–1979', p. 30.
37 Garton Ash, *In Europe's Name*, p. 53.
38 Lothar Gutjahr, *German Foreign and Defence Policy after Unification* (London: Pinter, 1994), p. 107.
39 Herf, *War by Other Means*, p. 33.
40 Berger, *Cultures of Antimilitarism*, p. 93; Herf, *Divided Memory*, p. 391.
41 Gerhard Brandt, 'Diverging Functions of Military Armament', in Jacques van Doorn (ed.), *Armed Forces and Society: Sociological Essays* (The Hague: Mouton, 1968), p. 199; Friedeburg, 'Rearmament and Social Change', p. 183; Giesela Gantzel-Kress and Klaus Jürgen Gantzel, 'The Development of International Relations Studies in West Germany', in Ekkehart Krippendorf and Volker Rittberger (eds), *The Foreign Policy of West Germany: Formation and Contents* (Beverly Hills, CA:x, 1988); Reinhard Meyers, 'Weltmarkt oder Weltpolitik?', *Neue Politische Literatur*, 31:2 (1986), pp. 190–193; Kitchen, *A Military History of Germany*, p. 353.
42 Szabo, *The Changing Politics of German Security*, p. 18.
43 Gutjahr, *German Foreign and Defence Policy after Unification*, p. 30.
44 As a reflection of this, the Americans were generally supportive of Bonn's efforts and working relations between Germany and its Western partners remained good. The virtuous alliance policy of Brandt's predecessors had won Germany enough trust to permit it a more independent stance towards the East. Smyser, *From Yalta to Berlin*, p. 260.
45 Dieter Dettke, 'Multilateralism and Re-Nationalization: European Security in Transition', in Paul Michael Lützeler, *Europe After Maastricht* (Providence: Berghahn Books, 1994), p. 178.
46 Christian Hacke, *Weltmach wider Willen* (Stuttgart: Ernst Klett Verlag, 1988), pp. 365–367.
47 Herf, *War by Other Means*, pp. 40, 55; Helmut Schmidt, *Perspectives on Politics* (Boulder: Westview Press, 1982), p. 26.
48 Hanrieder, 'West German Foreign Policy, 1949–1979', p. 30; Josef Joffe, 'Peace and Populism: Why the European Anti-Nuclear Movement Failed', *International Security*, 11:4 (Spring 1987), p. 17.
49 Joffe, 'Peace and Populism', p. 3.
50 Hans Günter Brauch, 'SDI – The Political Debate in the Federal Republic of Germany', in Hans Günter Brauch (ed.), *Star Wars and European Defense* (London: Macmillan, 1987), pp. 167–168.
51 Herf, *War by Other Means*, pp. 122–123.
52 LeGloannec, 'West German Security', p. 178.
53 Szabo, *The Changing Politics of German Security*, pp. 71–73.
54 Berger, *Cultures of Antimilitarism*, p. 128; Berger, 'Norms, Identity, and National Security in Germany and Japan', p. 349.
55 Herf, *War by Other Means*, p. 192; Stürmer, *Die Grenzen der Macht*, p. 249; Manfred Wörner, 'West Germany and New Dimensions of Security', in Wolfram F. Hanrieder (ed.), *West German Foreign Policy 1949–1979* (Boulder: Westview Press, 1980), p. 41.
56 Hans-Peter Schwarz, *Die gezähmten deutschen* (Stuttgart: Deutsche Verlagsanstalt, 1985); Smyser, *From Yalta to Berlin*, pp. 163, 296–299.
57 Rattinger, 'The Federal Republic of Germany', p. 134.
58 LeGloannec, 'West German Security', p. 180.
59 Elizabeth Pond, 'Federal Republic of Germany: Westpolitik, Ostpolitik, and Security', in Catherine McArdle Kelleher and Gale A. Mattox (eds), *Evolving European Defense Policies* (Lexington, MA: Lexington Books, 1987), p. 227.

60 Gutjahr, *German Foreign and Defence Policy after Unification*, p. 89.
61 J. J. Anderson and J. B. Goodman, 'Mars or Minerva? A United Germany in a Post-Cold War Europe', in Robert O. Keohane, Joseph S. Nye, and Stanley Hoffmann (eds), *After the Cold War: International Institutions and State Strategies in Europe, 1989–1991* (Cambridge, MA: Harvard University Press, 1993), p. 60.
62 With two early exceptions: in 1964 the Government of Ludwig Erhard voted in favour of deploying a German contingent as part of a NATO force on Cyprus, and in 1967 the Kurt-Georg Kiesinger government voted in favour of deploying German ships, again within a NATO framework, in response to a naval blockade against Israel announced by Egypt. Lothar Rühl, 'Security Policy: National Structures and Multilateral Integration', in Wolf-Dieter Eberwein and Karl Kaiser (eds), *Germany's New Foreign Policy: Decision-Making in an Interdependent World* (New York: Palgrave, 1998), p. 110.
63 Arthur Hoffmann and Kerry Longhurst, 'German Strategic Culture in Action', *Contemporary Security Policy*, 20:2 (1999), p. 37.
64 Karl Kaiser and Klaus Becher, 'Germany and the Iraq Conflict', in Nicole Gnesotto and John Roper (eds), *Western Europe and the Gulf* (Paris: Institute for Security Studies of the WEU, 1992), p. 41; Nina Philippi, 'Civilian Power and War: The German Debate about Out-of-Area Operations 1990–99', in Sebastian Harnisch and Hanns W. Maull (eds), *Germany as a Civilian Power: The Foreign Policy of the Berlin Republic* (Manchester: Manchester University Press, 2001), pp. 50–51; Pond, 'Federal Republic of Germany', p. 224.
65 *Strategic Concept 1991*, NATO's on-line library, www.nato.int/docu/basictxt/b911108a.htm; *Petersburg Declaration*, WEU Document, www.weu.int.
66 V*erteidigungspolitische Richtlinien für den Geschäftsbereich des Bundesministers der Verteidigung*, Bundesministerium der Verteidigung, Bonn, 26 November 1992, p. 29–30. See also Bald, *Militär und Gesellschaft 1945–1990*, pp. 161–162; General Klaus Naumann, *Die Bundeswehr in einer Welt im Umbruch* (Berlin, 1994), p. 135; Peter Schmitz, 'The Out-of-Area Issue: Is NATO an Island?', in Catherine McArdle Kelleher and Gale A. Mattox (eds), *Evolving European Defense Policies* (Lexington. MA: Lexington Books, 1987), p. 67; Wörner, 'West Germany and New Dimensions of Security', p. 39.
67 Gutjahr, *German Foreign and Defence Policy after Unification*, pp. 41–42.

PART II

A military role for Germany in international crisis management?

The process of redefining the role of military means in Germany's foreign and security policy can be divided into three phases. A first phase ran from German unification through 1994 when the German Constitutional Court ruled out-of-area deployments constitutional. The second phase began with the massacre on Muslim men and boys in the enclave of Srebrenica in Yugoslavia in the summer of 1995 and ended with the Kosovo War in 1999. A third phase lasted from 1999 to the outbreak of war in Iraq in the spring of 2003 and the first major EU-led intervention of the same year, *Operation Artemis* in Congo. Changing constellations of proponents and opponents and changing issues characterised the three phases that gradually moved Germany away from principled military abstention to a policy of conditional engagement in the full spectrum of out-of-area engagements.

Phase one: cracks in the old consensus

Between 1990 and 1994 the paramount issues in the domestic German battle were the requirements of partnership and the lessons of Germany's past. The fault line ran between the centre right and the left. The former argued that the expectations of Germany's partners towards the bigger and more secure Germany as well as the lessons of Germany's history called for an extended German engagement in international security, the latter claimed the opposite. The battle evolved around the attempt, launched by a handful of Conservative security experts, to win the political mainstream for an extended German role in international security. Two factors aided this effort. First, increased international pressure for a German contribution to multinational peace missions made it possible to harness the sentiments condensed in 'never again alone' to the project. Second, the Gulf War, the crisis in Somalia, and, most forcefully, the break-up of Yugoslavia indicated the limits of unarmed diplomacy in managing the crises of the new era and protecting innocent civilian lives. This threw into doubt the coherence of the consensus policy of 'responsibility' forged by Hans-Dietrich Genscher during his long reign in the foreign office – a policy which simultaneously committed Germany to Western integration, a maximum of restraint in military matters, and to values such as democracy, international law, and human rights.

The existing beliefs and old solutions of the German centre right came under pressure, eventually leading to a process of rethinking among Conservatives, Liberals, and some Social Democratic leaders. That rethinking found external expression as Germany gradually increased its engagement in international crisis management. In spite of strong international pressure for a German show of solidarity, the German government had declined military involvement in the Gulf War and in the early peacekeeping initiatives in Yugoslavia in 1991–92. But beginning in 1992 and 1993, respectively, German ships and aircraft helped monitor a sea embargo against Serbia-Montenegro and a no-fly zone over Bosnia-Herzegovina. The policy of strict abstention had been abandoned. In 1993 Germany went one step further and deployed logistical and medical Bundeswehr units as part of UNOSOM II, a UN mission in Somalia. With UNOSOM II, German ground troops were dispatched beyond NATO area for the first time since the Second World War.[1]

A majority on the left, however, remained opposed to any expansion of Germany's military role. Even after the Constitutional Court in 1994 ruled out-of-area deployments constitutional, German politics remained split on the issue and the out-of-area battle was to continue throughout the second half of the 1990s.

Phase two: reinterpreting the lessons of the past

In the battle's second phase, the focus and fault line moved. The lessons of the past became *the* paramount topics and the dividing line no longer ran between the centre right and the left but through the left. On the one side were those left wingers who argued that Germany had a historical responsibility to oppose and abstain from the use of military force. On the other side were those who argued that Germany's historical responsibility was not just a responsibility to resist war, but also a responsibility to stand up to aggression and massive human rights violations, if necessary by threatening or using force. Eventually, the latter position prevailed.

The mass killing of Bosnian Muslims in the UN 'Safe Area' of Srebrenica in the summer of 1995 constituted the turning point for numerous pacifists. It shook fundamental moral convictions and important operational beliefs in German left wingers' world-view. As a result, the common understanding of the precept 'never again war' was amended: Germany's historical responsibility was not only a responsibility to oppose war, it was also a responsibility to stand up to aggression. Among segments of the German left 'never again war' underwent a literal inversion. From having advocated total German military abstention in international crisis management, 'never again Auschwitz' became the new rallying cry for converted pacifists, advocating far-reaching German engagement against the violation of human rights in unstable crisis areas around the world.

As greater and greater segments of the left came around to an active understanding of Germany's historical responsibility Germany crossed several lines that had earlier defined the limits of its international military engagement. With IFOR in 1996 German troops were for the first time deployed on Yugoslav soil. IFOR's follow-up mission, SFOR, represented the first deployment of combat troops charged with security tasks. With the 1999 *Operation Allied Force* over Serbia and Kosovo, Germany crossed the line between peacekeeping and peace enforcement. For the first time in the history of the Bundeswehr German soldiers participated in a combat mission.

Different groups within Germany, however, had different reasons to revise their thinking – the centre right had moved for the sake of partnership, the left for the sake of human rights. The new working consensus thus rested on quite different logics of thinking.

Phase three: limits and possibilities of the new consensus

In phase three of Germany's conversion process – the years after the Kosovo War – it became clear how these different logics defined the limits and possibilities of the new German willingness to engage in international crisis management.

In 1999, at the behest of Green foreign minister Joschka Fischer – a former ardent opponent of out-of-area deployments – Germany dispatched Bundeswehr personnel as far from home as East Timor in a mission with a clear humanitarian purpose. In 2001, however, the commitment of German soldiers to a NATO-led mission in Macedonia proved domestically controversial because the deployment did not serve to prevent an impending humanitarian disaster or stop ongoing violence against civilians. The commitment of almost 4,000 troops, including elite units, to the American anti-terror campaign in Afghanistan was vigorously disputed on similar grounds, and eventually passed the Bundestag by only a very narrow margin.

The deployment to Afghanistan approached the limit of what Germany's new consensus could sustain – a limit that was eventually breached by the circumstances of the brewing crisis in Iraq in the Summer and Fall of 2002. Calculations of domestic politics and the bellicose rhetoric of the US administration made the German government dig in its heels and issue a firm 'no' to any German participation. Yet, Germany had not, as a superficial glance might suggest, come full circle. Less than six months later an overwhelming majority embraced a German military contribution to the EU's *Operations Artemis*, aimed at halting expulsions and persecution of civilians in Bunia, Congo.

The crises of the years following the Kosovo War thus revealed how the dispatch of German soldiers to distant trouble spots had become possible on the condition, however, that Germany's partners participated and that the mission served a clear and primarily humanitarian purpose.

Chapters 3–5 tell the stories of the different phases in Germany's transformation. Reasons for the transformation, the nature of the new Germany that emerged, and consequences for Germany's partners and neighbors are discussed along the way as well as in the book's conclusion.

Note

1 Apart from an uncontroversial deployment of an unarmed medical unit and a German field hospital that formed part of the UN peace mission UNTAC in Cambodia from May to November 1992. The German hospital did not fill a military function, but treated locals and civilians. Peter K. Fraps, 'Unter dem Blauen Barett', in General Peter Goebel (ed.), *Von Kambodscha bis Kosovo: Auslandseinsätze der Bundeswehr* (Frankfurt am Main: Report Verlag, 2000), p. 73.

3

From the Gulf War to Somalia: cracks in the old consensus

Prelude: Gulf War, 1991

The end of the Cold War delivered Germany from more than four decades at the world's geostrategic centre. But German policy makers were not allowed a lengthy respite from world affairs. The crisis sparked by Saddam Hussein's invasion of Kuwait in August 1990 placed the question of the new Germany's role in international security on the agenda even before the two-plus-four negotiations for German unity had been wrapped up. It caused the two rival schools of security thinking – 'never again alone' and 'never again war' – to clash head on. As all of Germany's major partners rallied behind the US in the Gulf, and the German CDU/FDP Government bent over backwards to support the effort without appearing to do so, hundreds of thousands of Germans took to the streets to protest against war.[1]

Eventually, the international coalition in the Gulf had to do without German soldiers. On the surface, German reactions to the conflict thus indicated a continuation of the post-Second World War line on the use of force. Underneath, however, cross-pressures on the government and internal contradictions in the consensus 'policy of responsibility', which incorporated some of the core notions of both 'never again alone' and 'never again war', prompted a beginning of a rethink on the centre right of German politics.

Cross-pressures on the government: Conservative and Liberal reactions
The situation in the Gulf placed the ruling CDU/FDP coalition in an unpleasant dilemma. On the one hand, international partners pressed for a German show of solidarity. On the other hand, the notion of a military solution ran counter to the Liberal grain of thinking and to the German 'policy of responsibility' forged by Hans-Dietrich Genscher.[2]

Trying to straddle opposing demands, the German government eventually extended material and financial help to the US-led coalition while declining any direct military involvement.[3] Besides covering a substantial part of the costs of *Operation Desert Storm* and aiding countries indirectly hurt by the conflict, Germany permitted American and British armed forces unrestricted use of their German bases and installations, supported the movement of US and British troops to the Gulf, and supplied several ammunition shipments to the international coalition.[4]

Yet, the absence of German troops in the international coalition made Germany the target of criticism and accusations of security free-riding and risk avoidance from both its European allies and the US.[5]

Against this backdrop, the Conservative proponents of out-of-area engagement were able to gain the ear of the party mainstream, arguing that Germany's standing and influence as a partner in Europe and NATO was threatened by the policy of strict military abstinence.[6] In other words, 'never again alone' was successfully invoked in the attempt to change the party's position on the out-of-area question. In the Fall of 1990, the CDU announced its plan to work for a clarification of the German Basic Law to enable the Bundeswehr 'to participate in actions agreed upon by the Security Council within the framework of the UN Charter'.[7]

The Gulf Conflict also modified the position of the Liberals. The crisis mounted an intellectual challenge to the Liberal party, which over the post-war era had inclined more and more towards a belief in international cooperation and pacific conflict resolution. The new bloc-free world and the peaceful process of German re-unification had initially seemed to confirm these notions and to promise even greater room for negotiation and mutual accommodation between states.[8] Thus, during the first months of the crisis Foreign Minister Genscher stressed the need to find a peaceful solution and, up to the last minute, many Liberals believed this would in fact be possible. When diplomatic efforts eventually failed they were caught unprepared. Though they harboured a strong aversion to using military measures to restore the independence of Kuwait, the Liberals were unable to offer an operational alternative.[9]

Prior to the Gulf War, the FDP had rejected German engagement in international security that went beyond UN 'blue helmet' missions. Peacekeeping missions were considered acceptable, but not peace-creating or peace-enforcing missions permitted under the UN Charter's Article VII. The Gulf War prompted a modification of this stance. Though the Liberals insisted on a prior amendment to the Basic Law, they aligned themselves with the Conservative view that Germany needed to be able to join all international crisis management efforts covered by the UN Charter.[10]

The domestic debate
The Gulf War permitted the proponents of an extended international military role for Germany to catalyse a process of rethinking on the centre right. However, the government in turn lost the domestic battle for the minds of the

German centre left. Nonetheless, the two suggestions that would later turn into powerful arguments for extending Germany's out-of-area role did appear in embryonic form during the debate over the Gulf War: the responsibility for the past and the country's partners required a German engagement.

History, the Government argued, ought to have 'sensitised' the Germans to the danger of appeasing a determined aggressor.[11] This suggestion was adopted by a few left-wingers. 'Saddam is Hitler!' wrote Hans-Magnus Enzenberger, a prominent left-leaning novelist, in *Der Spiegel*.[12] A majority on the centre left, however, remained unimpressed by the government's version of the lessons of the past. They called for diplomatic initiatives and denounced 'military solutions' as historical dead-ends.[13]

The opposition also brushed off the government's suggestion that Germany's 'credibility as a partner' was threatened.[14] On the contrary, it was charged, it was the credibility of Germany's partners that was challenged: on the eve of German re-unification part of the French and British press had indeed been busy warning against revived German militarism and a renewed drive for global power. Only a few months later, the Germans were scolded for abstaining from military action in the Gulf.[15] 'Our foreign friends must clarify what exactly they wish to criticise', suggested Hans-Jochen Vogel, the SPD chairman.[16]

While the government was feeling its way on new ground, opponents of the Gulf War could fall back on well-known and well-tested arguments honed over the past forty years. Under the 'never again war' banner, Social Democrats, Greens, ex-Communists, intellectuals, and church leaders mobilised significant segments of the public against the pending violence. When *Operation Desert Storm* was launched in January 1991, it was greeted with a wave of protest. More than 200,000 people attended the biggest anti-war demonstration in Berlin on 26 January 1991.[17]

Reactions on the left wing

The Social Democrats shared many tenets of Liberal security thinking. They placed emphasis on negotiation, cooperation, and integration, non-military instruments of security policy, and a 'morally responsible' policy wedded to principles such as respect for international law, democracy, and human rights. During the latter part of the 1980s the SPD had focused on devising a post-bloc cooperative security order for Europe while issues of global crisis management had received little or no attention. Like the FDP, the Social Democrats proved conceptually ill equipped to cope with the crisis.[18] On the one hand, they criticised the Iraqi violation of international law. On the other hand, they rejected a military intervention to restore the sovereignty of Kuwait, even after several months of fruitless diplomatic efforts.[19]

The geography of the crisis, however, helped the German left to deflect attention from the emerging internal tension in its own position. *Operation Desert Storm* was denounced as a battle for 'cheap oil' thinly veiled as a defence of international law.[20] The UN was cast as a fig leaf for the self-interested policy of its dominant power – the US. Germany, it was argued, should not enrol in America's 'neo-colonial' ventures.[21] 'Should we let ourselves be convinced that we are once again on our way down a German separate path because we do not go along with the jingoism of the English boulevard press?' asked the German weekly *Die Zeit* in the wake of the war.[22] On the far left, members of the PDS characterised the American President George Bush as a 'war-criminal' and rejected the legitimacy of any intervention by the 'imperialist' North in the affairs of the South.[23] On the German left wing the pacifist 'never again war' thus prevailed as a guide to German policy.

The war nevertheless forced the issue of Germany's role in post-bloc global security on to the SPD agenda. Urged on by a few security experts, the 1991 SPD party convention in Bremen with a narrow margin passed a resolution that cautiously endorsed German participation in UN blue helmet peacekeeping missions. It specified some highly restrictive requirements that had to be met before German participation would be acceptable: the peace keepers should be permitted to use force only in self-defence; the parties to the conflict had to agree to their deployment; and the Bundestag had to approve each individual out-of-area deployment. All other forms of out-of-area operations, including UN peace-creating and peace-enforcing missions, were rejected.[24]

The break-up of Yugoslavia

The Gulf War placed a question mark at the viability of Germany's old policy solutions in the new security environment. The violent break-up of Yugoslavia brought home a similar message, but this time in a starker form. A string of broken ceasefires highlighted the question as to how pacifists could counter determined aggressors, and there was no North–South dimension to deflect from this question. The shock of the conflict's atrocities and ethnic violence was heightened by its geographic proximity to Germany; and the arrival of about 300,000 refugees at German borders gave the conflict a reality that by far surpassed that of the Gulf War.

As the number of civilian victims mounted, a deep-felt frustration edged the Liberals towards endorsing an extended German role in UN peacekeeping. When the UN Secretary General himself appealed directly for German help, the prospect of domestic and international isolation also made the Social Democratic leaders reconsider their restrictive stance. The pacifist 'never again war', they reckoned, risked isolating Germany as the only Western democracy that in all situations would decline the use of military measures to end massive human rights violations.

The failure of diplomacy
Political relations between the republics of the Yugoslavian federation started to deteriorate during the Fall of 1990. The Yugoslavian economy's disintegration

during the winter of 1990–91 did not improve matters, and referenda held during that winter in Croatia and Slovenia resulted in majorities for secession. On 25 June 1991, both Croatia and Slovenia declared their independence. Two days later, fighting broke out between Slovenia and the mainly Serb Yugoslav People's Army. On 3 July hostilities also broke out between Croatia and the Yugoslav People's Army, later spreading to the ethnically mixed province of Bosnia.[25]

Propelled by moral outrage and fear of a refugee influx, the German government became a leading force behind several diplomatic initiatives during the first six months of the crisis.[26] Foreign Minister Genscher pressed for the dispatch of EC observers to Slovenia and Croatia and in September 1991 proposed an EC-sponsored peace conference. The efforts were fruitless. Yugoslav leaders proved immune to political and economic pressure and by the end of the year, fourteen separate EC-sponsored ceasefires had collapsed.[27] The German government then, in vain, pressed for the creation of a WEU or UN buffer force – an ironic policy given that German soldiers would not, due to the presumed constitutional prohibition, be able to participate.[28]

There followed the much-criticised German policy of recognising the republics of Croatia and Slovenia. Picking up on a press campaign spearheaded by the *Frankfurter Allgemeine Zeitung*, German decision makers had begun to believe that formal recognition of the two republics would deter the warmongers by internationalising the conflict. Urged on by Germany, European leaders in December 1991 agreed to recognise the republics on 15 January 1992 – provided they introduced adequate measures to protect the political and civic rights of minorities. In spite of this agreement, Genscher, acting under strong parliamentary pressure, went ahead on his own and recognised Croatia and Slovenia prior to the date agreed on by European leaders.[29]

Yet, fighting and ethnic violence continued and Germany subsequently became the target of fierce criticism from its European partners. By breaking ranks, it was argued, Germany had undermined the credibility of the EU diplomacy. Further, German policy was seen to have relied on rhetoric only, as Germany proved unwilling and unable to help implement the policy that flowed logically from Bonn's recognition: protection of the smaller ex-Yugoslav republics from Serb aggression, if necessary by military power. Finally, on a more extreme note, it was suggested that Bonn was pursuing hegemonic ambitions in the Balkan area and, by supporting the Croat and Slovenian independence ambitions, sought to circumvent the European order designed by the First World War victor powers.[30]

As it became clear that recognition in itself was not enough to end the conflict, German diplomacy became almost invisible. Initiative passed to those countries, mainly France and Great Britain, who, with the creation of the United Nations (UN) Protection Force (UNPROFOR) in February 1992, put their troops in the line of fire in an attempt to manage the evolving crisis. European diplomacy, however, could not end the war. Internal divisions in the Western camp left the Serb and Bosnian Serb leadership ample room to manipulate the international community – ignoring agreements, obstructing humanitarian aid efforts, exploiting UNPROFOR troops to consolidate territorial conquests, and taking international peace keepers hostage when threatened with air strikes.

The major fissure within the Western camp ran between the US on the one hand and the European countries with peacekeepers on the ground on the other. Washington's main priority was to avoid commitment of US ground troops in a conflict where no direct American interests were at stake. Both the Bush and the Clinton administrations favoured a policy of 'lift and strike': lift the UN-imposed arms embargo against ex-Yugoslavia to permit the Bosnian Muslims and others under fire to arm themselves. NATO air-power, this line of thinking went, should be deployed to back them up against the Serb forces.

The European states opposed this policy. Escalation of hostilities and aggressive use of NATO airpower, it was feared, would either place UNPROFOR peace keepers in intolerable danger or force their withdrawal. The Europeans were convinced that more could be done through UNPROFOR, which in their view had substantially contributed to dealing with the humanitarian nightmare in Bosnia, than by taking the uncertain and difficult course of lifting the arms embargo and withdrawing the peace keepers.[31]

Effective American leadership materialised only during 1995 as the Serb siege of Sarajevo and attacks on UN-declared 'safe areas' exposed the ineffectiveness of the hitherto attempts to manage the crisis. The atrocities came to an end only as US shuttle diplomacy backed up by a credible military threat succeeded in pushing through the Dayton Peace Agreement in December 1995.[32]

Rethinking among the liberals

The Gulf War had challenged core liberal beliefs about the power of political and economic instruments in settling disputes. The crisis in Yugoslavia shattered them. The outbreak of ethnic violence on Germany's very doorstep derided the liberal belief in progress towards a peaceful post-bloc world in which conflicts would be settled according to reason and international law. Ethnic cleansing of conquered areas brought back lurid memories of Europe's own past. The initial reaction was shock and disbelief; as Foreign Minister Klaus Kinkel said: 'We are talking about human beings, we are talking about children, women, old people, innocents. It shocks us, revolts us; in the end, however, we are powerless, impotent. And that is embittering.'[33]

The Liberals had staked high hopes on the civilising force of institutions such as the UN and the EC in the post-Cold War era. The inability of both to stop the violence in Yugoslavia added to the frustration. As the war dragged on, the number of victims increased, the stream of refugees swelled, and ceasefire after ceasefire broke down, foreign minister Klaus Kinkel openly acknowledged the limited effectiveness of a policy of restraint, which *a priori* excluded the use of military means; as Kinkel said: 'The horror inspiring developments in the former Yugoslavia have made it sadly clear – and it makes no sense to try to deny it – that the traditional instruments of our peace policy are insufficient.'[34]

In sum, the break-up of Yugoslavia placed in question important Liberal beliefs about the nature of the international system and the relative efficiency of different instruments of policy. A policy for peace, it was reckoned, that could not turn to military measures as a last resort, would remain impotent if faced with determined warmongers.

In August 1990, the CDU had already stated its support for extending Germany's role in international security, a position brought about by the Gulf War and international criticism of Germany's military abstention.[35] The Conservatives held that the German Basic Law already permitted engagement in all international military measures covered by the UN Charter. But at the time, the opposition and the FDP insisted that any engagement beyond UN blue-helmet peacekeeping would violate the Basic Law.[36] During the Gulf War, the CDU did not push the issue. Officially, the party said it considered a 'clarifying Constitutional amendment' desirable to ensure a cross-partisan consensus.[37] Such an amendment would require a two-thirds majority in the Bundestag. It therefore depended on the votes of the SPD, which in the 1991 party convention had posed a number of criteria for when the Bundeswehr could be deployed out-of-area. The Conservatives, however, considered these criteria unduly restrictive. The political process had therefore been stalled.[38]

Propelled by events in Yugoslavia, however, the Conservatives resumed the attempt to expand Germany's multilateral military options. And this time, the Liberals were willing to go along. As a result, the government initiated a step-by-step process decried by its opponents as 'salami-tactics', gradually expanding the type and number of Bundeswehr out-of-area operations[39]

The ruling coalition, however, maintained one reservation regarding this expansion. The deployment of German peace keepers directly on Yugoslav soil was not considered tenable. According to what was later termed 'the Kohl doctrine', German troops could not be deployed in areas that had suffered under the Wehrmacht's campaign in the Second World War. The presence of German soldiers in such areas, it was believed, would increase rather than defuse tensions.[40]

Operation Sharp Guard and *Operation Deny Fly*

The gradual expansion of out-of-area engagements started with the Government's decision to contribute Bundeswehr units to monitor a sea and air embargo against Serbia and Montenegro – *Operation Sharp Guard* – and to enforce a no-fly zone over Bosnia – *Operation Deny Fly*.

In May 1992 the UN Security Council adopted comprehensive economic sanctions against Serbia and Montenegro. In July, NATO and the WEU decided to deploy air and sea patrols in the Adriatic Sea to monitor the embargo. Twelve nations, including the US, Great Britain, Italy, Turkey, Greece, and the Netherlands contributed to *Operation Sharp Guard*. From July 1992 to June 1996, when the operation was suspended, Germany contributed with three sea-surveillance aircraft and two destroyers to patrol the shores of Montenegro and Albania.[41]

The opposition protested against the deployment, warning against a 're-militarisation' of German policy.[42] Social Democrats, Greens, and ex-Communists united in calling for political and economic measures to put pressure on the Belgrade regime, but still rejected the idea of a 'military solution'. 'In this specific case there are no military options', claimed the leader of SPD's parliamentary fraction, Hans-Ulrich Klose, 'especially not for Germany'.[43]

When the government nevertheless went ahead with the deployment, the SPD lodged a complaint with the Constitutional Court. The German contribution to *Operation Sharp Guard* did not qualify as a humanitarian mission, it was argued, and therefore it violated the Basic Law's Article 87. This case – the main case in which the Court was asked to determine whether the deployment of Bundeswehr units outside of NATO area violated the German Basic Law – was not decided until July 1994.

In October 1992, NATO AWACS aircraft, partially manned by German crews, began to monitor a UN-imposed no-fly zone over Bosnia, which prohibited all military flights in Bosnian airspace other than UN mission flights. In March the following year the Security Council voted to enforce the flight ban as Serbian aircraft and helicopters continued to violate the no-fly zone and attack villages in eastern Bosnia. Fighter jets from the US, France, Great Britain, Italy, the Netherlands, and Turkey joined the mission. *Operation Deny Fly* began on 13 April 1993 and lasted until December 1995. The German contribution to *Operation Deny Fly* was substantial, amounting to almost 500 AWACS airmen out of the total 4,500 soldiers involved in the mission.[44]

With the March 1993 vote to enforce the no-fly zone over Bosnia, the German AWACS contribution became controversial domestically and internally in the governing coalition. From that point on German soldiers were not only involved in an intelligence gathering exercise. German crews would become indirectly involved in a combat mission due to the crucial role of the AWACS aircrafts in relaying information to fighter jets.[45] The German government split on the question of whether this would violate the constitution – the FDP believing that it did, the CDU/CSU that it did not.[46]

During Genscher's long reign in the foreign office, the FDP had become closely associated with a restrictive interpretation of the Basic Law. A sharp reversal on the issue would have been politically awkward for a party that cast itself as the major defender of liberty and the rule of law. Nevertheless, the events in Yugoslavia had convinced most Liberals that the German military had to contribute to international crisis management. The coalition parties therefore engaged in an intricate political manoeuvre aimed at a quick settlement of the constitutional question – a settlement they hoped would permit the German crew to remain part of the AWACS team in Bosnia.

The FDP filed for a temporary injunction at the Constitutional Court, seeking a quick ruling in the AWACS case. The Court was asked to decide whether there was an 'overwhelming reason' to prevent the deployment of German troops in *Operation Deny Fly* while the Court's final ruling in the out-of-area question was still pending. The Government thus sued itself, hoping that the ruling would go against it.[47]

On 8 April 1993, the Court decided that the German crews could stay in the AWACS aircrafts. The judges argued that the negative political consequences of a withdrawal would outweigh the potential negative consequences of letting the airmen stay, even if it later turned out to be in conflict with the Basic Law. The loss of confidence of Germany's partners in case of a withdrawal would be irreparable, they held.[48] The Court thus applied a mainly political reasoning and seemed to nod to 'never again alone' in the ruling.

The domestic debate

The Government invoked two factors as it tried to rally domestic support for *Operation Sharp Guard* and *Operation Deny Fly*: Germany's past, and Germany's obligation to be a good partner. The arguments that had appeared in embryonic form in 1990 and 1991 were now given a more definite and compelling formulation. Against the backdrop of the atrocities and the ethnic violence in ex-Yugoslavia, they found stronger resonance among the adherents to 'never again war'.

Pointing to Germany's historical experience and invoking one of the most powerful symbols of German political memory – the Nazi extermination camps – the Government argued that military measures were sometimes necessary to stop an aggressor and end large-scale human rights violations; as Defence Minister Volker Rühe said: 'The concentration camps in Germany were shut down by soldiers and not by diplomatic declarations! Again, in the future it may be possible to stop the deepest immorality only by using soldiers. In such cases the deployment of military means is required on moral grounds.'[49]

Appealing to the ingrained urge to cooperate and integrate condensed in 'never again alone' the government also argued that Germany's international standing and credibility as a partner and as a responsible member of the international community was at stake.[50] When Germany joined the UN in 1973, it was argued, it had joined as a full member without claiming special treatment. As long as German armed forces had to hold the central Cold War front in Europe they were exempted from wider global responsibilities. But the bigger and safer re-unified Germany had an obligation to support international efforts to safeguard peace and stability in line with other civilised Western democracies.[51] The SPD's policy of principled military abstinence, it was charged, would send Germany down a new national and nationalist 'separate path' dividing it from the rest of the world's democracies.[52] 'The SPD', Kohl claimed, 'has ended up completely isolated internationally'.[53]

Germany's insistence on special treatment, the government further argued, damaged the credibility and effectiveness of the UN and other organisations of collective security, particularly in Yugoslavia.[54] Finally, the strong though ill-fated European engagement during the first four years of diplomatic and peacekeeping efforts in ex-Yugoslavia made it possible to exploit the positive connotations of 'Europe' and 'European integration' in the attempt to break the German out-of-area taboo. All Germany's major European partners – France, Great Britain, and Italy – were contributing to UNPROFOR, *Operation Sharp Guard*, and/or *Operation Deny Fly*. Against this backdrop, proponents of an extended German role in international security could present a German contribution to manage the Balkan crisis as a precondition for further European political integration. If Germany insisted on special treatment, it was argued, it would jeopardise the prospect of Europe developing into a real political union: 'How exactly do you imagine you can build Europe if the German ships as a matter of principle take a course that differs from the ships of all our allies?' Volker Rühe asked in the face of opposition to *Operation Sharp Guard*.[55]

Rethinking on the left wing

Between the Gulf War and the Yugoslavian crisis the government had introduced no new arguments. But the circumstances of the crisis in ex-Yugoslavia made the basic line of argument – that the past and the partners required a German contribution to out-of-area peacekeeping – seem more plausible, both intellectually and emotionally.

The occurrence of ethnic cleansing and religiously based violence made the invocation of Germany's own past a powerful device in the debate. Against the background of a string of broken ceasefires and failed diplomatic initiatives, the suggestion that Germany had a 'historical responsibility' to contribute to peacekeeping as a final resort to protect civilians, seemed increasingly compelling. Publicly, SPD leaders kept up their resistance to German participation in *Operation Sharp Guard* and *Operation Deny Fly*. But at the same time, the government's arguments tapped into mounting frustration with the performance of Germany and the international community in attempting to stop the violence: 'With hindsight we are forced to ask the self-critical question whether, in this situation, we ought not to have done more than send protest after protest to Belgrade', said Günther Verheugen (SPD).[56]

The circumstances of the Gulf War had permitted the proponents of abstention to maintain the moral high ground. The circumstances of the violent break-up of Yugoslavia were different. The peace keepers of UNPROFOR, struggling to protect humanitarian convoys and unarmed civilians, could not be depicted as instruments of a neocolonial venture driven by oil interests. The UN could not be cast in the role as a US fig leaf and, if anything, seemed to be doing too little rather than too much. The geography and the heavy European involvement in the crisis also permitted the government to emphasise the importance of displaying European – as opposed to simply international – solidarity and exploit the positive connotations carried by European integration across the German political spectrum. Whereas large segments of the German left were at the least indifferent to the prospect of appearing out of line with a coalition led and dominated by America, appearing anti-European was much less palatable.

Whether the centre right's invocation of 'Europe' signified a real will to promote a more Europe-centred security order for the continent or whether it was simply an effective rhetorical strategy will be discussed later. The argument certainly proved effective in moving the position of the Social Democrats.

The international criticism of Germany's posture in the Gulf had limited impact on the centre left. But in the case of Yugoslavia, it stung. The German policy of early recognition of Slovenia and Croatia had not brought the hostilities to an end. It was France and Britain that, together with a number of smaller European states, put their soldiers in the line of fire to stabilise the area and stop the atrocities, while Germany, in concordance with the prevailing interpretation of the Basic Law, declined to commit peace keepers.[57] In the wake of the recognition debacle, the demand for solidarity from Germany's allies became more and more insistent, and in January 1993 Secretary General of the UN, Boutros Boutros Ghali, appealed for full German participation in the entire range of UN peace missions. He placed special emphasis on the importance of a German contribution to aid the efforts in Yugoslavia.[58]

Against the background of this rising chorus of international calls for solidarity the government's argument about the requirements of partnership seemed increasingly plausible to more and more Social Democrats. The invocation of 'never again alone' thus proved more effective than it had been in connection with the Gulf War.[59]

The fact that both the CSU/CDU and FDP accused the SPD of causing Germany's international and European isolation also illustrated the domestic isolation that threatened. With the conversion of the FDP on the out-of-area question, a number of SPD leaders were getting uncomfortable with the inflexible stance of their party.[60] Headed by the party's chief whip, Hans-Ulrich Klose, SPD parliamentary leaders at the end of 1992 stepped up pressure for a revision of the restrictive Bremen decision from May 1991. The party, it was suggested, should back a constitutional amendment that would authorise German participation in the whole range of UN peace missions carried out under UN command, including peace enforcement.[61]

But the rank and file was not yet ready for such a step. At an extraordinary party congress in November 1992, and again at the Wiesbaden party congress in November 1993, a majority reconfirmed that Germany should participate only in UN blue helmet missions. It was acknowledged that UN soldiers might occasionally need to fire their weapons in self-defence, but reiterated that Germany should not contribute to operations that from the outset were intended to involve the threat or use of force – the SPD thus insisted on a clear distinction between peacekeeping and peace enforcement. Nevertheless, an important concession was made. Party members recognised that the spectrum of possible blue helmet missions had become broader than the traditional monitoring of ceasefires on the invitation of both parties to the conflict. In the new security environment, a majority of the party recognised, acceptable missions included the monitoring of UN embargoes, the safeguarding of humanitarian aid, and protection of UN safe zones.[62]

The Yugoslavian crisis made the Social Democrats take a cautious step down the road from military abstention towards accepting a spectrum of different UN blue helmet missions. Though the rank and file moved slowly, the decision in Wiesbaden indicated that a reinterpretation was on the way.

Further to the left, in contrast, a majority of Greens and ex-Communists stuck to their pacifist convictions. In the wake of the Gulf War, the Greens, at their party convention in April 1991, took a clear stand against any deployment of German soldiers abroad.[63] The bloodshed in Yugoslavia did cause a couple of Green MdBs to call for a UN military intervention to end the atrocities – an intervention, though, in which Germany because of its history could not possibly participate. Occasionally, it was reluctantly acknowledged, military intervention might represent the only way to protect civilian lives: 'As a very last resort, when all other means have failed, when there is no other way of protecting defenceless people, it might be the case that the dispatch of UN soldiers is necessary', said Gerd Poppe, Bündnis (90/Die Grünen).[64]

But such voices were quickly rebuked. The party leadership and a majority of the parliamentary faction reiterated the party's pacifist ideals.[65] The combination of arguments that had started to impress a number of Social Democrats was less effective in making the Greens question their existing position. Pacifism, after all, was a founding value of the party – and a value that enjoyed clear priority over the need to act like a reliable ally or to display international solidarity. Finally, the PDS, in line with the Greens, also denounced any suggestion that Germany should play a military role in international peace missions.

UNOSOM II in Somalia

In April 1993, while the Constitutional Court's final ruling on the out-of-area question was still pending, the German government pledged troops to a UN mission in Somalia – UNOSOM II. The purpose of the mission was to ensure the arrival of humanitarian aid in a famine-stricken country – which in 1991 had collapsed into a chaos of warring factions – and to disarm these factions.[66] The general environment for the mission was non-permissive. The United Task Force – the predecessor of UNOSOM II – had come under direct hostile fire on several occasions during 1992. UNOSOM II was therefore given a robust mandate, authorising the use of force for self-defence, or if necessary to secure the implementation of the missions goals.[67]

Twenty-eight nations contributed to the intervention, among them a number of Germany's NATO and European partners, including the US, Turkey, Norway, France, Greece, and Italy. As part of the force, 1,700 German soldiers, stationed in a pacified area of Somalia, were to provide logistical supply and back-up for the troops of other participating nations.[68] UNOSOM II involved the greatest number of Bundeswehr soldiers to date – and for the first time put them on foreign soil with a mandate to shoot in self-protection or mission defence.

In the domestic battle over this deployment the government adopted mainly a 'never again alone' argument, pointing to the involvement of a number of Germany's major Western and European partners. The government was not successful, however, in forging a resounding moral or humanitarian argument for why it was necessary to dispatch German soldiers instead of civilian aid workers to alleviate the situation in the pacified area of Belet Weyne where German troops were to be deployed. While SPD leaders and foreign policy experts were by 1993 approaching the stance of the FDP on the out-of-area question, UNOSOM II nevertheless caused the party to backtrack. A complaint over the deployment was lodged with the Constitutional Court.

The domestic debate
In its attempt to garner support for UNOSOM II the German Government repeated many of the points brought up in connection with *Operation Sharp Guard* and *Operation Deny Fly*. Re-unified Germany's 'greater responsibility', the 'expectations of Germany's partners', and the need to display 'international solidarity', were invoked.[69] However, the arguments that had found resonance on the left in connection with the crisis in Yugoslavia did not work in the case of Somalia.

The opposition, while declaring its support for the humanitarian goals of UNOSOM II, rejected the need to dispatch soldiers and questioned the government's motivation for doing so. It would be more appropriate to support the UN efforts by contributing civilian aid workers and police units, it was argued, since the German area of deployment was considered pacified. 'Soldiers', the opposition scoffed, 'are not development workers'.[70]

Instead of attempting to counter these suggestions and forge a convincing moral argument for Germany's military contribution, the government made itself vulnerable to left-wing criticism by bad political timing: three days after announcing its decision to contribute to UNOSOM II, an application for a permanent German seat in the UN Security Council was lodged. This proved to be a tactical mistake. The government appeared to be using the Bundeswehr for the purpose of increasing Germany's international influence.

The government's proclaimed concern about 'international responsibility' was now denounced by the opposition as a veiled grab for international power.[71] In reality, it was charged, the German contribution to UNOSOM II was not about humanitarian relief, it was about proving German 'normalcy' so that it might re-enter the league of major powers: 'We [the SPD] can also not exclude that situations may arise in which one has to risk the lives of German soldiers, but never in order to prove something ladies and gentlemen – never in order to prove something', said Peter Glotz (SPD).[72]

The 'instrumentalisation of German soldiers' in the service of a 'policy of global military interventionism' was likewise decried further on the left, among Greens and ex-Communists.[73]

The double appeal to Germany's historical responsibility and the requirements of European partnership that characterised the debate over Yugoslavia prompted the SPD to start redefining its stance on the out-of-area question. Blue helmet interventions as a last resort to protect civilians were gaining acceptability among the rank and file. UNOSOM II, however, hit the boundaries of the acceptable. The dispatch of the Bundeswehr did not appear to be the policy option of last resort and the government did not succeed in arguing why civilian helpers could not have carried out the humanitarian tasks in Belet Weyne.

On 14 June 1993, the SPD filed a complaint with the Constitutional Court. The plaintiffs requested a temporary injunction in which the Court decided whether there was an 'overwhelming reason' to stop the ongoing deployment in Somalia until the Court had handed down its decision in the main case discussed above.[74]

In June 1993 the Court endorsed UNOSOM II. The justices argued that Germany's foreign policy credibility would suffer if it reneged on its pledge to the UN and emphasised the negative consequences for UNOSOM II if the promised German contribution did not materialise. The mission would be delayed by several months and the credibility of the UN might suffer, the Court argued.[75] Once again, then, the justices appeared to lean towards the notions condensed in 'never again alone' in their ruling.

The Constitutional Court ruling on the out-of-area question

On 12 July 1994 the Constitutional Court handed down its final decision on the out-of-area question. The Court ruled that the deployment of German troops in military operations outside of NATO area was constitutional, provided they formed part of a multilateral operation designed to uphold international peace and security, carried out by an organisation of collective security such as NATO, WEU, or the UN. The German Bundestag, the justices further decided, needed to approve each individual deployment with a simple majority.[76]

The 1994 ruling marked a watershed. It approved a policy that broke with the practice of the previous fifty years. Yet, it did not give rise to a political debate of issues that, from an external observer's perspective, would appear crucial: there was no debate of how potential out-of-area interventions might serve Germany's interest, no debate over what multinational framework would best serve German interest, and finally, no discussion of the geographical and military limits, if any, to the missions in which Germany would participate.

The centre right simply greeted the result as a victory for the 'policy of international solidarity and responsibility'. Simultaneously it was stressed that Germany remained a 'civilian power' whose international engagement would remain mainly humanitarian, political, and economic. Very few of the world's most pressing challenges, it was emphasised, were soluble by means of tanks and soldiers. Germany would decide to support multilateral military measures only as a 'last resort'.[77]

Foreign Minister Klaus Kinkel stressed that Germany would never act alone. He also emphasised that Germany would consider military measures only in missions where they formed part of a broader approach aiming at a lasting political solution to the conflict. He emphasised that any military mission would need a UN or Organisation for Security and Cooperation in Europe (OSCE) mandate and had to serve the interest of 'Germany, Europe or the international community' – a condition that was not specified further. Finally, the Kohl doctrine was reiterated: German soldiers would not participate in crisis management in areas in which they for historical reasons could be expected to fuel rather than defuse tensions.[78]

The Social Democratic leaders echoed most of the foreign minister's points about displaying 'international responsibility', 'continued military restraint' and accepting military interventions, but only as 'a very last resort'.[79] The striking similarity in the rhetorical reaction to the ruling indicated that the moderate wing of the party had come around to a view that resembled the Liberal position: Germany needed to contribute to all out-of-area missions covered by the UN Charter. The Court's ruling, though in principle a defeat, was received with quiet relief by the SPD leaders as it would aid the ongoing attempt to edge the party's left wing towards a more flexible stance on the out-of-area question.[80]

The Constitutional Court ruling closed the first chapter of the out-of-area battle – the period over which the political mainstream and the leaders of the major parties had been persuaded to accept an extended engagement in out-of-area peace missions. However, numerous left-wingers maintained uncompromising resistance to German military engagements abroad. They kept defending 'never again war' as the most important and still valid lesson of Germany's past – and mounted a forceful insistence on the civilian aspects of German foreign and security policy. The belief in 'military solutions', they insisted, was an illusion and a historical blind alley.[81] The out-of-area battle was thus to continue throughout the second half of the 1990s.

Notes

1 Though there was resistance to the war in other European countries, the German anti-war movement was by far the largest and loudest. Ulf Hedetoft, *Signs of Nations: Studies in the Political Semiotics of Self and Other in Contemporary European Nationalism* (Aldershot: Dartmouth, 1995), p. 599.
2 Hans-Dietrich Genscher, interview with SAT 1, 5 January 1991, reprinted in *Stichworte zur Sicherheitspolitik*, 1/1991, p. 24.
3 Germany delivered an indirect military contribution in the form of eighteen German Alpha Jets, forming part of NATO's ACE Mobile Force, which was dispatched to Turkey

upon the request of the Turkish government. The German jets took no part in the hostilities and were dispatched to a NATO member country, thus remaining in the NATO area.

4 Germany's financial contribution amounted to more than $11 bn by February 1991. 'Kooperation in der Golfkrise', Informationserlass des Auswärtigen Amts, 19 February 1991, reprinted in *Außenpolitik der Bundesrepublik Deutschland: Dokumente von 1949 bis 1994* (Bonn: Auswärtiges Amt, 1995), p. 792; Helmut Kohl, 'Erklärung der Bundesregierung zur Lage in der Golfregion', 14 January 1991, reprinted in *Außenpolitik der Bundesrepublik Deutschland: Dokumente von 1949 bis 1994* (Bonn: Auswärtiges Amt, 1995), p. 782; Bundes Presse Amt, press release No. 92/91, 6 March 1991; Gerhard Stoltenberg, interview with ZDF, 6 January 1991, reprinted in *Stichworte zur Sicherheitspolitik*, 1/1991, p. 24.

5 Lothar Gutjahr, *German Foreign and Defence Policy after Unification* (London: Pinter, 1994), p. 89. For criticism of Germany in the US Senate, see *New York Times*, 12 September 1990 and *New York Times*, 26 January 1991, p. 8; Jeffrey Garten, *Cold Peace: America, Japan, Germany, and the Struggle for Supremacy* (New York: Times Books, 1992), pp. 162–167; Karl Kaiser and Klaus Becher, 'Germany and the Iraq Conflict', in Nicole Gnesotto and John Roper (eds), *Western Europe and the Gulf* (Paris: Institute for Security Studies of the WEU, 1992), p. 39; 'Make Arms, Not War?', *The Economist*, 16 February 1991.

6 Helmut Kohl, debate in the Bundestag, 6 June 1991, reprinted in *Bulletin*, No. 64, 7 June 1991, p. 514; Gerhard Stoltenberg, interview with SDR 1, 3 March 1991, reprinted in *Stichworte zur Sicherheitspolitik*, 3/1991, pp. 41–42.

7 *Bulletin* (Presse und Informationsamt der Bundesregierung), No. 102, 25 August 1990, p. 858. See also 'Beschluss des Bundeshauptausschusses der FDP', 25 May 1991, reprinted in Bundes Presse Amt, Referat III B 5, Dokumentation, *Freiheit und Verantwortung gehören zusammen*, June 1991. The UN Charter deals with international conflicts in Chapter VI and VII. Chapter VI concerns the pacific settlement of disputes; Chapter VII concerns possible UN actions, including the use of force, to counter threats or breaches of international peace as well as acts of aggression. Traditional blue helmet missions are referred to within the UN system as belonging to 'Chapter six and a half'. Blue helmets were normally deployed in a strategically static situation with the consent of the parties to the conflict to monitor a ceasefire or oversee the implementation of a peace agreement. However, UN soldiers can also be given more robust mandates under Chapter VII permitting the use of force for self-, mission, or third-party defence. www.un.org and www.un.int.

8 Hans-Dietrich Genscher, 'Die neue europäische Friedensordnung', *Europa-Archiv*, No. 15 (1990), pp. 473–478; Norbert Ropers, 'Security Policy in the Federal Republic of Germany', in Colin McInnes (ed.), *Security and Strategy in the new Europe* (London: Routledge, 1992), p. 230.

9 Hans-Dietrich Genscher, 'Bericht der Bundesregierung', 23 August 1990, reprinted in *Bulletin*, No. 102, 25 August 1990. See also 'Bemühungen der Bundesregierung zur friedlichen Lösung der Golf-Krise', *Bulletin*, No. 2, 11 January 1991; 'Bundesregierung bedauert Ergebnislosigkeit der Genfer Gespräche zur Lösung der Golfkrise', *Stichworte zur Sicherheitspolitik*, 1/1991, p. 25.

10 'Beschluss des Bundeshauptausschusses der FDP', reprinted in *Stichworte zur Sicherheitspolitik*, 6/1991, p. 39; Hans–Dietrich Genscher, quoted in *Frankfurter Allgemeine Zeitung*, 7 February 1991, p. 1 and *Berliner Zeitung*, 27 February 1991, p. 3.

11 Genscher, Bericht der Bundesregierung; Kohl, 'Erklärung der Bundesregierung zur Lage in der Golfregion', p. 782; Helmut Kohl, Erklärung der Bundesregierung zum Krieg am Golf', reprinted in *Bulletin*, No. 6, 19 January 1991; Gerhard Stoltenberg, interview with *Bonn Direkt ZDF*, 6 January 1991, reprinted in *Stichworte zur Sicherheitspolitik* 2/1991, p. 24; Richard von Weizsäcker, interview with *Die Zeit*, 8 February 1991.

12 Hans-Magnus Enzenberger, 'Hitlers Wiedergänger', *Der Spiegel*, 1 February 1991, pp. 26–28. See also Hans-Ulrich Klose (SPD), 'Die Deutschen und der Krieg am Golf – eine schwierige Debatte', *Frankfurter Allgemeine Zeitung*, 25 January 1991.
13 Hans-Jochen Vogel, debate in the Bundestag, 31 January 1991, reprinted in *Das Parlament*, No. 7–8, 15 February 1991; Olaf Feldmann, *Gemeinsame europäische Golf-Initiative nötig*, FDP Fachinfo, Irak, 11 January 1991.
14 Helmut Kohl, 'Regierungserklärung', 14 January 1991, reprinted in *Bulletin*, No. 4, 15 January 1991; Helmut Kohl, 'Regierungserklärung', 30 January 1991, reprinted in *Bulletin*, No. 11, 31 January 1991; Gerhard Stoltenberg, speech, CDU Congress, Bonn, 15 May 1991, reprinted in *Stichworte zur Sicherheitspolitik*, 6/1991, p. 38.
15 Dieter Dettke, 'Civil Foreign Policy: German Domestic Constraints and New Security Arrangements in Europe', in Beverly Crawford (ed.), *The Future of European Security* (Berkeley, University of California Center for German and European Studies, Research Series, No. 84, 1992), p. 257; Richard von Weizsäcker, interview with *Die Zeit*, 8 February 1991.
16 Hans-Jochen Vogel, intervention during debate in the Bundestag, 31 January 1991, reprinted in *Das Parlament*, No. 7–8, 15 February 1991.
17 Kaiser and Becher, 'Germany and the Iraq Conflict', p. 44. Opinion polls indicated that a clear majority among the German public rejected the participation of German troops in hostilities. However, the actions of the US-led coalition were tolerated, 57 per cent were 'supportive' or 'somewhat supportive' of the use of military means to push Iraq out of Kuwait, whereas 33 per cent 'rejected' or 'strongly rejected' a military solution. EMNID survey conducted between 29 January and 4 February 1991. Reprinted in MBMVc, press release, No. 28/7, 8 February 1991. For further data on German public opinion see Hedetoft, *Signs of Nations*, pp. 599, 604.
18 Gutjahr, *German Foreign and Defence Policy after Unification*, p. 132.
19 Oskar Lafontaine, 'Verzweifelte Aussichten', *Die Tageszeitung*, 9 February 1991; Hans-Jochen Vogel, intervention during debate in the Bundestag, 31 January 1991, reprinted in *Das Parlament*, No. 7–8, 15 February 1991.
20 Katrin Fuchs, 'Keine deutschen Soldaten an den Golf', *Vorwärts*, January 1991.
21 Theo Sommer, 'New World Order?', *The Guardian*, 13 April 1991; Uwe Stehr, 'Damit deutsche Soldaten in der Krieg ziehen können?', *Frankfurter Rundschau*, 30 November 1990.
22 *Die Zeit*, 8 February 1991.
23 *BRD im Golfkriege: Von der Wiedervereinigung an die Nah-Ostfront*, PDS-Pressedienst, Bonn, 30 January 1991.
24 *Außen-, Friedens-, und Sicherheitspolitik*, Beschlüsse des SPD Parteitages in Bremen, 28–31 May 1991.
25 Carl Cavanagh Hodge, 'Germany and the Limits of Soft Security', *European Security*, 7:3 (1998); Beverly Crawford, 'Explaining Defection from International Cooperation: Germany's Unilateral Recognition of Croatia', *World Politics*, No. 48 (July 1996), pp. 482–521.
26 See debate in the Bundestag, 15 November 1991 and 15 January 1993, *Plenarprotokoll Deutscher Bundestag*, 12/58 and 12/132; Hans Schauer, *Europäische Identität und demokratische Tradition: Zum Staatsverständnis in Deutschland, Frankreich und Großbritannien* (Munich: Günter Olzog Verlag, 1996).
27 John S. Duffield, *World Power Forsaken: Political Culture, International Institutions, and German Security Policy after Unification* (Stanford, CA: Stanford University Press, 1998), p. 191.
28 *Frankfurter Allgemeine Zeitung*, 8 October 1991, p. 2; Hanns W. Maull, 'Germany in the Yugoslav Crisis', *Survival*, 37:4 (Winter 1995–96), p. 101.
29 Maull, 'Germany in the Yugoslav Crisis', p. 102.

30 James Gow, *Triumph of the Lack of Will: International Diplomacy and the Yugoslav War* (New York: Colombia University Press, 1997), p. 172; Michael Libal, *Limits of Persuasion: Germany and the Yugoslav Crisis, 1991–1992* (Westport: Praeger, 1997), p. 162.
31 Gow, *Triumph of the Lack of Will*, p. 180.
32 Gow, *Triumph of the Lack of Will*, p. 277.
33 Klaus Kinkel, 'Regierungserklärung', 7 July 1992, reprinted in *Bulletin*, No. 83, 23 July 1992, p. 806.
34 Klaus Kinkel, 'Regierungserklärung', 7 July 1992, reprinted in *Bulletin*, No. 83, 23 July 1992, p. 806. See also Ulrich Irmer (FDP), *Plenarprotokoll Deutscher Bundestag*, 12/58, p. 4858; Klaus Kinkel, 'Regierungserklärung', 7 July 1992, reprinted in *Bulletin* No. 83, 23 July 1992, p. 805.
35 *Bulletin*, No. 102, 25 August 1990, p. 858. See also 'Beschluss des Bundeshauptausschusses der FDP', 25 May 1991, reprinted in Bundes Presse Amt, Referat III B 5, Dokumentation, *Freiheit und Verantwortung gehören zusammen*, June 1991; Helmut Kohl, debate in the Bundestag, 6 June 1991, reprinted in *Bulletin*, No. 64, 7 June 1991, p. 514.
36 The Basic Law permits the maintenance and use of armed forces for defence purposes only (Article 87 (1, 2)). However, it empowers the Federal Republic to participate in systems of collective security (Article 24 (2)). The Conservative leadership argued that Article 24 (2) permitted Germany to participate in UN or NATO-led peacekeeping activities taken in accordance with the UN Charter. The SPD and FDP, on the other hand, argued that Article 87 (1, 2) superseded Article 24 (2). Any expansion of the Bundeswehr's tasks beyond blue helmet peacekeeping would thus require, in their view, an amendment of the Basic Law. Harald Müller, 'Military Intervention for European Security: The German Debate', in Lawrence Freedman (ed.), *Military Intervention in European Conflicts* (Oxford: Blackwell, 1994), pp. 128–129.
37 *Die Zukunft gemeinsam gestalten: Die neuen Aufgaben deutscher Politik*. Resolution passed at the CDU party convention, 14–17 December 1991. CDU-Dokumentation 39/40, 1991.
38 Duffield, *World Power Forsaken*, p. 186.
39 Gregor Gysi, *Plenarprotokoll Deutscher Bundestag*, 13/76, p. 6647.
40 Helmut Kohl, interview with SAT 1, 2 April 1993, reprinted in *Stichworte zur Sicherheitspolitik*, 5/1993, p. 8. This Conservative doctrine was quickly adopted by the foreign policy and security experts of the SPD. Helmut Schmidt, 'Zum AWACS-Beschluss des Bundeskabinetts', *Stichworte zur Sicherheitspolitik*, 4/1993, p. 12.
41 Frank Ropers, 'Embargo-Überwachung in der Adria', in Peter Goebel (ed.), *Von Kambodscha bis Kosovo: Auslandseinsätze der Bundeswehr* (Frankfurt am Main: Report Verlag, 2000), p. 101.
42 Karsten D. Voigt, *Plenarprotokoll Deutscher Bundestag*, 12/132, p. 1993.
43 Hans-Ulrich Klose, *Plenarprotokoll Deutscher Bundestag*, 12/101, pp. 8613–8614.
44 Walter Jertz, 'Einsatz der Luftwaffe über Bosnien', in General Peter Goebel (ed.), *Von Kambodscha bis Kosovo: Auslandseinsätze der Bundeswehr* (Frankfurt am Main: Report Verlag, 2000), p. 136.
45 Günther M. Wiedemann, 'Das Frühwarnsystem AWACS', *Kölner Stadtanzeiger*, 26 March 1993.
46 'Regierungserklärung and Erklärung der FDP-Minister', 2 April 1993, press release, No. 116/93, Presse- und Informationsamt der Bundesregierung.
47 Regierungsbeschluss, 'Überwachung des Flugverbots über Bosnien-Herzegowina unter deutscher Beteiligung', *Bulletin*, No. 29, 7 April 1993.
48 'Beschluss-Begründung des Bundesverfassungsgerichts im AWACS-Streit', *Süddeutsche Zeitung*, 10 April 1993; Müller, 'Military Intervention for European Security', p. 130.
49 Volker Rühe, *Plenarprotokoll Deutscher Bundestag*, 12/132. See also Hans-Peter Schwarz, *Die Zentralmacht Europas: Deutschlands Rückkehr auf die Weltbühne* (Berlin: Siedler Verlag, 1994), p. 157. See also Klaus Kinkel, *Plenarprotokoll Deutscher Bundestag*, 12/132.

See also Klaus Kinkel, 'Die Außenpolitik der Bundesrepublik Deutschland nach der Wiedervereinigung', *Europäische Sicherheit*, 1/1993, p. 14.
50 Ulrich Irmer, *Plenarprotokoll Deutscher Bundestag*, 12/169, p. 14590; Volker Rühe, speech at 'Forum Bundeswehr und Gesellschaft', Berlin, 22 March 1994. See also Volker Rühe, *Plenarprotokoll Deutscher Bundestag*, 12/101, pp. 8639–8640.
51 Klaus Kinkel, 'Regierungserklärung', 21 April 1993, reprinted in *Bulletin*, No. 32, 23 April 1993.
52 Rupert Scholz, 'Auch Deutschland muss UNO-Friedensaktionen mittragen', *Truppenpraxis*, No. 2, 1993. See also statements by Klaus Kinkel and Volker Rühe in the Bundestag, 22 July 1992, transcribed in Foreign Broadcast Information Service, Daily Report: West Europe, pp.12–17.
53 Helmut Kohl, interview with SAT 1, 2 April 1993, reprinted in *Stichworte zur Sicherheitspolitik*, 5/1993, p. 10.
54 Wolfgang Schäuble (CDU), *Plenarprotokoll Deutscher Bundestag*, 12/101, p. 8624. See also 'CDU will Bundeswehreinsatz außerhalb Europas', *Stichworte zur Sicherheitspolitik*, 6/1991, p. 38; Helmut Kohl, debate in the Bundestag, 6 June 1991, reprinted in *Bulletin*, No. 64, 7 June 1991, p. 514; Heinrich Lummer, *Plenarprotokoll Deutscher Bundestag*, 12/58, p. 4855; Gerhard Stoltenberg, BMVg, press release XXVIII/1, 22 January 1991.
55 Volker Rühe, *Plenarprotokoll Deutscher Bundestag*, 12/101, p. 8639.
56 Günter Verheugen, *Plenarprotokoll Deutscher Bundestag*, 12/58, p. 4856. See also Dieter Dettke, 'Multilateralism and Re-Nationalization. European Security in Transition', in Paul Michael Lützeler, *Europe After Maastricht* (Providence: Berghahn Books, 1994), p. 186.
57 William Drozdiak, 'Germany Vows Balkan Recognition', *Washington Post*, 11 January 1992, p. 14A; Hodge, 'Germany and the Limits of Soft Security'; Jeffrey S. Lantis, 'Rising to the Challenge: German Security Policy in the Post-Cold War Era', *German Politics and Society*, 14:2, 1996, p. 26; Daniel Vernet, 'Le retour de la question allemande', *Le Monde*, 22–23 December 1991.
58 *Frankfurter Allgemeine Zeitung*, 12 January 1993, pp. 1–2.
59 Karsten D. Voigt, debate in the Bundestag, 15 January 1993, reprinted in *Stichworte zur Sicherheitspolitik*, 2/1993, pp. 7–9.
60 In addition, German public opinion had become more favourable towards a German military contribution to international crisis management. In February 1993, an *Allensbacher* survey indicated that 31 per cent opposed German participation in UN-mandated peace missions, whereas 54 per cent supported it. 56 per cent expressed support for a 'decisive' international intervention in ex-Yugoslavia to end the war. Allensbacher Monatsbericht, reprinted in *Frankfurter Allgemeine Zeitung*, 11 February 1993.
61 See statements by Günter Verheugen, Karsten D. Voigt, Rudolf Scharping, Hans-Ulrich Klose, Heidemarie Wieczorek-Zeul, and Peter Struck reprinted in *Stichworte zur Sicherheitspolitik*, 9/1993, pp. 13–26.
62 *SPD-Sofortprogramm*, Bonn, November 1992; SPD, *Perspektiven*, Wiesbaden, November 1993.
63 Ordentliche Bundesversammlung der Grünen, Resolution A3, 13, Neumünster, 26–28 April 1991.
64 Gerd Poppe, *Plenarprotokoll Deutscher Bundestag*, 12/166, p. 14338. See also Wolfgang Ullmann, *Plenarprotokoll Deutscher Bundestag*, 12/169, p. 14592.
65 Jürgen Trittin, *Der Spiegel*, 5/1993, pp. 76–83.
66 Holger Kammerhoff, 'Unter Blauhelm am Horn von Afrika', in General Peter Goebel (ed.), *Von Kambodscha bis Kosovo: Auslandseinsätze der Bundeswehr* (Frankfurt am Main: Report Verlag, 2000), p. 120.
67 UNOSOM II represented the first attempt to enforce peace inside a UN member state under Chapter VII of the UN Charter. Traditional blue helmet peacekeeping missions did

not foresee the use of force. UNOSOM II, however, did from the outset authorise forceful measures to ensure the arrival of humanitarian aid and disarm Somalia's warring factions, www.un.org and www.un.int.
68 'Beschluss der Bundesregierung zur Unterstützung von UNOSOM II in Somalia', *Bulletin*, No. 32, 23 April 1993; William J. Durch, 'Introduction to Anarchy: Humanitarian Intervention and "State-Building" in Somalia', in William J. Durch (ed.), *UN Peacekeeping, American Politics, and the Uncivil Wars of the 1990s* (New York: St Martin's Press, 1996), p. 345.
69 Paul Breuer, interview with Deutschlandfunk, 8 June 1993, reprinted in *Stichworte zur Sicherheitspolitik*, 7/1993, p. 18; Michael Glos, *Plenarprotokoll Deutscher Bundestag*, 12/166, p. 14580; Karl-Heinz Hornhues, *Plenarprotokoll Deutscher Bundestag*, 12/240, p. 21198; Klaus Kinkel, statement in front of the Constitutional Court, 19 April 1994, reprinted in *Bulletin*, 22 April 1994; Günther Friedrich Nolting, *Plenarprotokoll Deutscher Bundestag*, 12/240, p. 21204; Volker Rühe, press release, BMVg, 17 June 1993; Jürgen Rüttgers, interview with ZDF, 22 July 1993, reprinted in *Stichworte zur Sicherheitspolitik*, 8/1993, p. 38; Wolfgang Schäuble, *Plenarprotokoll Deutscher Bundestag*, 12/166, p. 14328.
70 Konrad Weiss, *Plenarprotokoll Deutscher Bundestag*, 12/169, p. 14607.
71 Nina Philippi, 'Civilian Power and War: The German Debate about Out-of-Area Operations 1990–99', in Sebastian Harnisch and Hanns W. Maull (eds), *Germany as a Civilian Power: The Foreign Policy of the Berlin Republic* (Manchester: Manchester University Press, 2001), p. 54.
72 Peter Glotz, *Plenarprotokoll Deutscher Bundestag*, 12/169, p. 14599; Hans-Ulrich Klose, *Plenarprotokoll Deutscher Bundestag*, 12/169, p. 14585.
73 Gerd Poppe, *Plenarprotokoll Deutscher Bundestag*, 12/166, pp. 14336–14337. See also Manfred Opel (SPD), *Plenarprotokoll Deutscher Bundestag*, 12/169, p. 14602; Konrad Weiss, *Plenarprotokoll Deutscher Bundestag*, 12/169, p. 14607.
74 The plaintiffs argued that the German UNOSOM II contingent would become indirectly involved in combat through its logistical back-up function, which entailed the transportation of fuel and ammunition to other UN troops. It therefore did not qualify as a humanitarian relief effort and violated the Basic Law's Article 87. Günter Verheugen, *Plenarprotokoll Deutscher Bundestag*, 12/166, p. 14332.
75 Bundesverfassungsgericht, 2 BvQ 17/93, reprinted in *Stichworte zur Sicherheitspolitik*, 7/1993, p. 17.
76 Urteil des Bundesverfassungsgericht vom 12. Juli 1994 zu Auslandseinsätzen der Bundeswehr, reprinted in *Stichworte zur Sicherheitspolitik* 7/1994, pp. 17–34.
77 Michael Glos, *Plenarprotokoll Deutscher Bundestag*, 12/240, p. 21174; Klaus Kinkel, *Plenarprotokoll Deutscher Bundestag*, 12/240, p. 21168; Günther Friedrich Nolting, *Plenarprotokoll Deutscher Bundestag*, 12/240, p. 21203; Volker Rühe, *Plenarprotokoll Deutscher Bundestag*, 12/240, p. 21186; Herman Otto Solms, *Plenarprotokoll Deutscher Bundestag*, 12/240, p. 21177; Rudolf Scharping, *Plenarprotokoll Deutscher Bundestag*, 12/240, pp. 21169–21174; Karsten Voigt, *Plenarprotokoll Deutscher Bundestag*, 12/240, pp. 21199–21203.
78 Klaus Kinkel, 'Germany's Role in Peacemissions', *NATO Brief*, 10/1994; Helmut Kohl, 'Aufbruch in die Zukunft: Deutschland gemeinsam erneuern', *Bulletin*, No. 108, 24 November 1994, p. 991; Volker Rühe, interview with *Welt am Sonntag*, 27 November 1994.
79 Hans-Ulrich Klose, *Plenarprotokoll Deutscher Bundestag*, 12/169, p. 14585; Hans-Ulrich Klose, interview with ZDF, 30 August 1993, reprinted in *Stichworte zur Sicherheitspolitik*, 9/1993, p. 17; Günter Verheugen, interview with ZDF, 7 June 1993, reprinted in *Stichworte zur Sicherheitspolitik*, 9/1993, p. 13.
80 Author's interview, Ministry of Defence and Ministry of Foreign Affairs, Berlin, 25 July 2000 and German Embassy, Washington, DC, 24 June 2002.
81 For these critical voices, see Anlage 1 and Anlage 2, *Plenarprotokoll Deutscher Bundestag*,

12/240, pp. 21216–21218. From the vote following the debate in which the government asked the Bundestag to endorse UNOSOM II as well as the German contribution in the Adriatic Sea embargo and the AWACS airspace surveillance over Bosnia, it is clear that this faction was rather small. Fourteen SPD members voted against and twelve abstained.

4

From Srebrenica to *Operation Allied Force*: reinterpreting the lessons of the past

From 'never again war' to 'never again Auschwitz'

'I recall only with agony' wrote *Die Zeit*'s columnist in June 1998, 'how German peace lovers during the years of the ethnic mayhem in the former Yugoslavia turned their heads away from the images of dismembered, lacerated, murdered women, children, men, and, coldheartedly pronounced their mantra: under no circumstances should one intervene with military force'.[1]

As these lines were written, left-leaning Social Democrats and Greens had already gone through a painful reappraisal of the lessons of Germany's past. The critical event that triggered this process was the massacre of Bosnian Muslims in Srebrenica in the summer of 1995. In November 1994, Serb forces had penetrated the designated UN 'Safe Area' of Bihac, and in February 1994 a Serb mortar attack on the market place of Sarajevo killed dozens of civilians.[2] But with Srebrenica the tragic absurdity of a UN unable to protect unarmed civilians reached a pitch. In early July 1995, Serb security forces overran the 'Safe Area' of Srebrenica in the Eastern part of Bosnia-Herzegovina. The Dutch peace keepers supposedly protecting the enclave were confined to their compound outside of the city while Serb forces went on a rampage lasting several days, systematically killing Bosnian Muslims that had sought refuge in the city. The outside world appeared to be doing nothing to stop the atrocities, which cost an estimated 8,000 Muslim men and boys their lives.[3]

Srebrenica left German pacifists speechless. Diplomatic means and economic sanctions had done nothing to prevent the biggest single mass-murder in post-war European history. The potential price of pacifism and the inner contradiction between humanism and principled military abstention had been exposed in the most gruesome manner.

In the domestic battle, the proponents of a German military contribution to the peace efforts in Yugoslavia now gained the offensive. They took on the core pacifist dictum 'never again war' by using the pacifists' own language – that of morality: 'From my point of view it has nothing to do with morality and especially not with higher morality, when people threatened by genocide are denied help', argued Friedbert Pflüger (CSU).[4] 'It can be highly immoral not to resist injustice by deploying soldiers', added Defence Minister Volker Rühe.[5]

The shock of Srebrenica caused soul-searching and re-thinking on the left. It prompted initial steps towards a more active definition of Germany's historical responsibility – an active definition that later found its strongest expression in the motto 'never again Auschwitz'. Action instead of abstention gradually became the order of the day, as reflected in the arguments and voting behaviour of the left between 1995 and 1999.[6]

IFOR

On 26 June 1995 the ruling CDU/FDP coalition decided to contribute German troops to IFOR – the NATO-led peacekeeping force established to implement the Dayton Peace Agreement.[7] IFOR's task, authorised by the UN Security Council, was to enforce a demilitarised zone between the parties to the Yugoslavian conflict and to create a secure environment for the return of refugees. The force was also mandated to support, when possible, the civilian reconstruction efforts in Bosnia. The force was given a robust mandate under the UN Charter's Chapter VII, authorising prompt and comprehensive military action to suppress any breaches of the ceasefire. All of Germany's NATO partners along with France contributed to the 60,000-strong force, together with twenty-two non-NATO members.[8]

The German contribution to IFOR amounted to 4,000 soldiers and included transportation aircraft and Tornado fighter jets. An army contingent of about 2,700 Bundeswehr soldiers stationed in Croatia provided logistical support and back-up for the IFOR peace keepers in Bosnia-Herzegovina.[9] Compared to the tasks of French, British, and American peace keepers, the German contingent's mission was modest. It was stationed in a pacified area, was not charged with security duties, and needed only light armour.

For Germany, however, IFOR marked a turning point. For the first time since the Second World War, German troops were deployed on Yugoslav soil equipped with a robust mandate permitting the use of force for self-protection or mission defence. IFOR clearly went beyond what a political majority had so far been willing to accept.[10] Nevertheless, when the CDU/FDP government asked the Bundestag to approve the contribution, numerous converted pacifists were willing to go along. On 6 December 1995, a broad parliamentary majority endorsed the IFOR contribution with 543 votes in favour, 107 against, and six abstentions.[11]

To rally support for IFOR, the CDU/FDP government stressed that Germany's international responsibility and the expectations of its partners required engagement.[12] The ideas behind 'never again alone' were easily mobilised behind a force to which all Germany's major Western and European partners contributed. But the argument that dominated the debate and eventually found resonance on the German left was that, given the events of Sarajevo, Bihac, and Srebrenica, it was no longer morally defensible to abstain.[13]

The debate over IFOR made it clear that the political dividing line in the out-of-area battle no longer ran between the centre right and the left; it ran through the left and through the SPD. Targeting pacifists and anti-militarists within their own ranks, Social Democratic leaders echoed and at times sharpened the government's arguments: 'Not only he who acts but also he who looks away incurs guilt', argued Karsten Voigt (SPD).[14] And 'The war in former Yugoslavia has made it brutally clear that unfortunately words, good intentions, and humanitarian aid alone were not sufficient to stop that genocide', added SPD Chairman Rudolf Scharping.[15]

A majority of Social Democrats eventually came out in favour of the German IFOR contribution. On 6 December, 187 Social Democrats voted in favour, 55 against, and one abstained.[16]

Further on the left, Srebrenica had thrust the Greens into an agonising questioning of deep-seated and cherished beliefs, which threatened to split the party. The internal woe was openly displayed in the parliamentary debates where numerous Greens admitted that they found themselves torn between different values. Pacifism was a pillar of Green political identity, but it appeared difficult to argue with Srebrenica.[17]

The 'fundis', led by Jürgen Trittin, still rejected any use of military means.[18] However, the 'realos' around party leader Joschka Fischer were edging towards accepting participation in humanitarian interventions. Fischer came out in favour of IFOR, while lamenting 'the cursed dilemma of being able to save peoples' lives only by dispatching the military'.[19] A third group around Ludger Vollmer had taken a middle position and stressed that, in the light of events in Yugoslavia, they were, in principle, ready to embrace a German engagement for peace with military means. However, they insisted on a clear line between peace-keeping and peace enforcement, i.e. combat missions. The former was acceptable, the latter not.[20] In the end, IFOR split the Greens down the middle: 22 parliamentarians voted for, 22 against, and five abstained.

The PDS was the only party that remained united around its pacifist convictions. All ex-communist MdBs voted against the German IFOR deployment in protest against the ongoing 're-militarisation' of German policy. The ulterior motive behind the NATO led IFOR, it was argued, was to strengthen NATO at the cost of the UN. It had nothing to do with concern for human rights and international law.[21]

IFOR demonstrated that the base of political support for out-of-area deployments of the Bundeswehr was becoming broader. The German left was in the process of reinterpreting the lessons of the past and the historical responsibility incurred by Germany's past crimes. As the new commitment to engagement instead of abstention gained ground, the Kohl doctrine, precluding the deployment of German soldiers in areas where the Wehrmacht had been during the Second World War, was gradually softened. By 1995 the doctrine still had its defenders among the Conservatives.[22] The Liberals, however, openly questioned its logic: 'Exactly because German soldiers were forced to break the law in the past, we, today, have a special obligation as a constitutional democracy to engage in the protection of peace internationally' (Ulrich Irmer, FDP).[23] The Social Democrats joined the criticism. The Kohl doctrine had been problematic from the outset, it was argued, 'because it entailed, that the crimes of the past precluded aiding today'(Günter Verheugen, SPD).[24]

SFOR

In November 1996, the German government contributed 3,000 soldiers to SFOR – the peacekeeping force that took over after IFOR. SFOR was authorised by the UN Security Council and charged with deterring a resumption of hostilities between the parties to the conflict in Bosnia, as well as supporting the civilian reconstruction of the area. The 30,000-member force was led by NATO and relied on NATO command and control structures. As had been the case with IFOR, all Germany's NATO partners as well as twenty-two non-NATO members contributed.[25]

With the SFOR deployment Germany shed the last vestiges of the Kohl doctrine. This time German peace keepers were deployed directly in Bosnia, not in neighbouring Croatia. The mission also marked the first deployment of German combat troops. A 1,500-strong, armoured German contingent, which formed part of the Franco-German brigade, was charged with security tasks.[26]

The deployment of this brigade illustrated a change of heart among German politicians. In the Fall of 1991 a French proposal to deploy the brigade as part of a WEU force for peacekeeping purposes in ex-Yugoslavia had been vigorously opposed by Defence Minister Volker Rühe, charging that the task of the brigade was to safeguard stability at the heart of Europe, not to serve as an 'expeditionary force'. By 1996, the tone had changed. The deployment of the brigade as part of SFOR was heralded as a symbol of good cooperation and partnership in Europe.[27]

In terms of mandate and deployment area, the German SFOR contribution ventured into areas that had earlier been off-limits, involving as it did the deployment of German combat troops directly in Bosnia. The Bundestag nevertheless endorsed the deployment with a broad majority on 13 December 1996: 499 parliamentarians voted in favour and ninety-three against.[28] When SFOR was up for renewal eighteen months later, it received the support of an even bigger majority. On 19 June 1998, 528 MdBs voted in favour, thirty-seven against, and eleven abstained.[29]

The SFOR debates revolved around the same points as the debate over

IFOR: the partners and the past, more and more parliamentarians argued, required a German engagement. Germany had a historically based moral obligation to engage for peace and human rights in Yugoslavia and the sequence of events had demonstrated that military means were, unfortunately, necessary.[30]

There was a measure of reluctance among Social Democrats and Greens to accept a further expansion of the possible uses of the Bundeswehr in out-of-area peace missions. But though SFOR transgressed earlier taboos and in several respects went further than IFOR, resistance was dwindling. This must be understood in the context of the translation of Germany's historical responsibility into activist terms. The logic of 'never again war' was to circumscribe Germany's military engagement as much as possible. As long as this precept held sway, each little expansion had to be pushed through against ingrained left-wing resistance.

After Srebrenica, a different logic took hold. Further extensions of Germany's military engagement in international peace efforts became acceptable in principle if they were perceived as necessary to halt or prevent large-scale ethnic violence or massive human rights violations. For many former pacifists the acceptance of IFOR had constituted the decisive and agonising leap into new territory. It entailed the fundamental decision to accept a German engagement for peace in Yugoslavia, which relied on military means. It entailed the abandonment of long-standing convictions and beliefs. The step from IFOR to SFOR was far less dramatic.

Kosovo and *Operation Allied Force*

In October 1998 German politicians took the final step on the road that led from military abstinence to full participation in out-of-area crisis management. Approving the contribution of fourteen German fighter jets to *Operation Allied Force* over Kosovo, a broad majority in the Bundestag endorsed the first participation ever of Bundeswehr soldiers in a combat mission – a mission that was not directly legitimised by the UN Security Council. Nevertheless, 500 MdBs voted in favour, sixty-two against, and eighteen abstained.[31]

In early 1998 violence started escalating in Kosovo – a Serb republic in which Kosovar Albanians constituted the population majority. Until 1989 the republic had enjoyed a high degree of autonomy. However, with the break-up of Yugoslavia, the Serb leader Slobodan Milosevic had altered the status of the area and brought it under the direct control of Belgrade, a move strongly opposed by the Kosovar Albanians.

As Serb police and army units cracked down on the Kosovo Liberation Army (KLA) in the spring of 1998, more than 300,000 Kosovars were forced to flee their homes. The UN Security Council expressed concern about excessive use of force by Serbian security forces and pressured the Belgrade government to initiate a political dialogue with the non-violent branch of Kosovo's independence movement – but to no avail.[32] Two rounds of negotiations between a Serb and a

Kosovar Albanian delegation at Rambouillet near Paris floundered, the last ending when the Serbs rejected a mediation proposal agreed to by the Kosovars.

Eventually, NATO threatened air strikes to stop the campaign of Serb security forces – strikes that did not have a UN mandate, though the NATO Council could refer to a number of earlier resolutions by the Security Council that called for an end to hostilities and set limits on the number of Serbian forces in Kosovo.[33] The absence of a clear UN mandate was cause for concern among German politicians across the political spectrum. However, the concern was overcome because the pattern of events provoked an unpleasant *déjà vu*: a succession of attempts to find a political solution floundered, Serb security forces appeared to deliberately target civilians, and a humanitarian catastrophe accompanied by a massive exodus of refugees from Kosovo seemed to be looming. The immediate instinctive reaction across the German political spectrum was: 'not a second Bosnia!'[34]

United by frustration and the feeling that too little had been done to prevent previous Balkan atrocities, the outgoing CDU/FDP government and the incoming SPD/Green Government joined forces in pledging for the Bundestag's approval of a German contribution to potential NATO air strikes.[35] Politicians from the CDU on the right to Green 'realos' on the left stressed the need to prevent a new humanitarian disaster and act as a reliable partner within Europe and NATO.[36] With special address to the doubters within their own ranks, SPD and Green leaders stressed Germany's historical responsibility to stand up against an impending genocide. In the debate prior, during, and after *Operation Allied Force*, this argument was brought into its final and starkest form – 'never again Auschwitz': 'Never again Auschwitz' warned the new foreign minister, Joschka Fischer, 'is the historical admonition to prevent what could develop into a genocide. This is – without claiming that the catastrophe in Kosovo is equal to Auschwitz – the reason for my position.'[37]

In 1995, German political leaders had taken pains to stress that the German IFOR contingent had not been sent to Croatia on a combat mission, that there would be no war fighting, and that there was no opponent. Whereas fifty-five Social Democrats had voted against IFOR, only twenty-one voted against *Operation Allied Force*. In 1995, the Green party's mainstream had drawn the line on acceptable Bundeswehr deployments at humanitarian missions. By October 1998 Joschka Fischer, former anti-Vietnam activist and a veteran of the German peace movement, had obtained the support of his party for the first combat mission in the history of the Bundeswehr.[38] The Greens who had split down the middle in the vote on IFOR approved *Operation Allied Force* with twenty-nine votes in favour, nine against, and eight abstentions.[39] At this point the PDS was the last political party still defending the absolute validity of a pacifist policy and the commitment never, under any circumstances, to deploy military means for other purposes than self-defence.[40]

Less than a year after the approval of German participation in air strikes against Serb forces, on 11 June 1999, it was once again underlined how far the

German consensus had moved since the beginning of the decade. With an overwhelming majority, the Bundestag endorsed the biggest ever out-of-area deployment of German ground troops – 8,000 – to KFOR, the Kosovo peace force deployed after the bombing campaign.[41]

In sum, between 1990 and 1995 the German left wing took a cautious step on the road that led from total abstinence to participation in international crisis management. Gradually and grudgingly the left came to accept a German contribution to UN blue helmet peacekeeping. Between 1995 and 1998, it took a more decisive step. German participation in peacekeeping and peace-enforcing missions relying on the use of military force had become acceptable. Until the mid-1990s it was still hotly disputed whether peace and political solutions could be furthered by military means. By the end of the decade this had become broadly accepted. It had also become accepted that Germany had a moral and historical obligation to engage in efforts to manage international crises together with its partners. Germany's international responsibility had been redefined and 'never again war' reinterpreted. Instead of obliging military abstention it was now believed that it obliged positive action to prevent violence, if necessary by the use of violence. The process culminated in 1999 with *Operation Allied Force* and the first ever participation of the Bundeswehr in a combat mission.

Tactical considerations or cultural change?

A realist might argue that when a German left-wing government pushed for German participation in *Operation Allied Force* in 1999 it was not due to moral convictions and cultural beliefs. It was due to tactical political considerations of a new governing coalition eager to prove its 'Regierungsfähigkeit' – its ability to govern and act as a responsible and reliable member of Western organisations. Had the new coalition balked, it might have undermined its influence in a number of European and international fora. In other words, a realist might suspect that it was not so much the weight of Germany's past as the weight of governmental responsibility that prompted the left wing to revise its view on Germany's role in international crisis management.

There is no doubt that an urge to prove 'Regierungsfähigkeit' played a role in connection with the vote on *Operation Allied Force*. The new incoming SPD/Green government, many of whose members were former vocal pacifists, presumably felt the need to reassure partners and neighbours that German security policy would be characterised by continuity.[42]

However, it could be argued, even if such considerations influenced the behaviour of the new government's leaders, that they were able to mobilise the rank and file only because the cultural beliefs of these politicians had already been challenged and revised. The decisive change in the voting pattern of the rank and file on the left occurred prior to the 1998 vote on *Operation Allied Force* and prior to the formation of the SPD/Green government. It occurred in 1995 when the Bundestag voted on IFOR in the wake of Srebrenica.

Prior to Srebrenica, clear majorities within both the SPD and the Green party had opposed any German out-of-area engagement that went beyond blue helmet peacekeeping. In the vote on Germany's contribution to IFOR – a force equipped with a robust mandate under Chapter VII of the UN Charter, legitimising the use of force in self- or mission defence – more than 75 per cent of the Social Democratic and half the Green MdBs came out in its favour. It is difficult to see why the urge to appear like responsible candidates for governmental power should have caused a decisive shift in the balance between opponents and proponents of an extended German role in international security at exactly that point – a point at which the Bundestag was only one year into its four-year election cycle.[43] Taking a culturalist approach, however, the timing of the shift in voting pattern makes sense: Srebrenica stripped German pacifists of the moral high ground and challenged fundamental moral convictions as well as operational beliefs on the German left. It forced an intellectual revision that eventually found external expression in the vote on IFOR.

Thus, even accepting that tactical considerations of the new left-wing government leaders played a role, it appears reasonable to assume that challenged and changing cultural beliefs and values were the crucial factors that made German participation in *Operation Allied Force* possible.

Result: a composite working consensus

Between the Gulf War and the Kosovo War Germany travelled the road from total abstinence to participation in international military crisis management, apparently on an equal basis with other major European powers – a process that culminated in the 1999 *Operation Allied Force*.

A close look at the German transformation, however, has indicated that different groups within Germany had different reasons to accept the change. The centre right had been driven by concern about Germany's influence and standing in international organisations such as NATO and the EU, as well as concern about the strength, coherence, and development prospects of these institutions – 'never again alone'. The German left wing came around in the wake of Srebrenica in 1995. These politicians were driven by a perceived historical German obligation to combat ethnic violence and massive human rights abuses – 'never again Auschwitz'.

The policy that emerged over the 1990s thus rested on an accommodation between rival views on why Germany needed to extend its role in international security. The possibilities, but also the limits of the working consensus between these rival schools of thought became apparent during the years following the Kosovo War, explored in Chapter 5.

Notes

1. Peter Schneider, 'Krieg und Frieden: Die Lehren von Sarajevo', *Die Zeit*, 18 June 1998.
2. John S. Duffield, *World Power Forsaken: Political Culture, International Institutions, and German Security Policy after Unification* (Stanford, CA: Stanford University Press, 1998), p. 213.
3. Richard Holbrooke, *To Stop a War* (New York: Random House, 1998), pp. 69–70.
4. Friedbert Pflüger, *Plenarprotokoll Deutscher Bundestag*, 13/76, p. 6663.
5. Volker Rühe, *Plenarprotokoll Deutscher Bundestag*, 13/74, p. 6447. See also Volker Rühe, interview with *Der Spiegel*, 16 November 1995. For expression of similar viewpoints, see Christian Schwarz-Schilling and Thomas Kossendey, *Plenarprotokoll Deutscher Bundestag*, 13/74, pp. 6453, 6466 and Wolfgang Schäuble, *Plenarprotokoll Deutscher Bundestag*, 13/76, p. 6640; Thomas Kossendey (CDU/CSU), *Plenarprotokoll Deutscher Bundestag*, 13/74, p. 6466; Klaus Kinkel, 'Deutsche Außen- und Sicherheitspolitik bei der internationalen Krisenbewältigung seit 1990', *Bulletin*, No. 98, 9 December 1997. For reactions to the Serb attack on Sarajevo's marketplace and the subsequent NATO bombing of the Serb artillery around Sarajevo, see 'BM des Auswärtiges Dr. Kinkel zu den Luftangriffen auf serbische Stellungen', *Stichworte zur Sicherheitspolitik*, 11/1995, pp. 13–14; Klaus Kinkel, 'Vor weitere Militäraktionen warne ich', interview with *Bild Zeitung*, 25 August 1995; Ulrich Irmer, *Plenarprotokoll Deutscher Bundestag*, 13/76, p. 6644; Theodor Waigel, *Plenarprotokoll Deutscher Bundestag*, 13/76, p. 6654; Rudolf Seiters, *Plenarprotokoll Deutscher Bundestag*, 13/74, p. 6435.
6. Günter Verheugen, *Plenarprotokoll Deutscher Bundestag*, 13/76, p. 6667; Karsten Voigt, *Plenarprotokoll Deutscher Bundestag*, 13/74, p. 6448; Karsten Voigt, *Plenarprotokoll Deutscher Bundestag*, 13/242, p. 22448.
7. Kabinettbeschluss, press release, Bundes Presse Amt, 26 June 1995.
8. See NATO Handbook, Chapter 5, p. 114, available at www.nato.int.
9. Friedrich W. Riechmann, 'Von Kroatien in die "Box"', in General Peter Goebel (ed.), *Von Kambodscha bis Kosovo: Auslandseinsätze der Bundeswehr* (Frankfurt am Main: Report Verlag, 2000), p. 154.
10. The German public, according to opinion polls, remained opposed to the Government's decision. An EMNID survey of 10 July 1995 revealed that whereas 40 per cent of the population supported the German contribution to IFOR, 56 per cent declared their opposition to sending German peace keepers to ex-Yugoslavia. EMNID survey, reprinted in *Stichworte zur Sicherheitspolitik*, 8/1995, p. 2.
11. For voting results see *Plenarprotokoll Deutscher Bundestag*, 13/76, pp. 6673–6675.
12. Helmut Kohl, 'Regierungserklärung', 6 December 1995, *Bulletin*, No. 19, 11 December 1995; Volker Rühe, interview with *Welt am Sonntag*, 11 June 1995.
13. Kossendey, *Plenarprotokoll Deutscher Bundestag*, 13/74, p. 6466; Friedbert Pflüger, *Plenarprotokoll Deutscher Bundestag*, 13/76, p. 6663; Theodor Waigel, *Plenarprotokoll Deutscher Bundestag*, 13/76, p. 6654.
14. Karsten Voigt, *Plenarprotokoll Deutscher Bundestag*, 13/74, p. 6448. See also Karsten Voigt, *Plenarprotokoll Deutscher Bundestag*, 13/242, p. 22448. See also Günter Verheugen (SPD), *Plenarprotokoll Deutscher Bundestag*, 13/76, p. 6667.
15. Rudolf Scharping, *Plenarprotokoll Deutscher Bundestag*, 13/76, p. 6635. See also 'Der Vorsitzende der SPD-Bundestagsfraktion Scharping zur deutschen Beteiligung an der Friedenstruppe für Bosnien', *Stichworte zur Sicherheitspolitik*, 12/1995, pp. 22–24.
16. The participation of German Tornados to provide air support for the IFOR troops if necessary caused some squabbling. A number of Social Democrats denounced the fighter jets as an offensive and redundant element. See the debate in the Bundestag, 30 November 1995, *Plenarprotokoll Deutscher Bundestag*, 13/76, pp. 6426–6472.
17. Gerd Poppe, *Plenarprotokoll Deutscher Bundestag*, 13/74, p. 6437.

18 Christa Nickels, *Plenarprotokoll Deutscher Bundestag*, 13/74, p. 6449.
19 Joschka Fischer, *Plenarprotokoll Deutscher Bundestag*, 13/76, p. 6657.
20 Ludger Volmer, *Plenarprotokoll Deutscher Bundestag*, 13/74, p. 6454. See also Hanns W. Maull, 'Germany and the Use of Force: Still a "Civilian Power"?', *Survival*, 42:2 (2000), p. 63.
21 Gregor Gysi, *Plenarprotokoll Deutscher Bundestag*, 13/76, p. 6647; Andrea Lederer, *Plenarprotokoll Deutscher Bundestag*, 13/74, p. 6443.
22 Volker Rühe, interview with *Der Spiegel*, 16 October 1995. See also Volker Rühe, interview with *Die Zeit*, 1 December 1995.
23 Ulrich Irmer, *Plenarprotokoll Deutscher Bundestag*, 13/76, p. 6645.
24 However, the dispatch of German soldiers to areas where the Wehrmacht had previously been was acceptable only to the Social Democrats if the parties to the conflict had explicitly agreed to their presence. Günter Verheugen, *Plenarprotokoll Deutscher Bundestag*, 13/74, p. 6434.
25 www.nato.int/sfor/sfor.about.htm.
26 Hans-Otto Budde, 'Gleiche Rechte und Pflichten – Die deutsche Beteiligung an SFOR', in Peter Goebel (ed.), *Von Kambodscha bis Kosovo: Auslandseinsätze der Bundeswehr* (Frankfurt am Main: Report Verlag, 2000), p. 166; 'Konflikt in ehemaligen Jugoslawien', *Stichworte zur Sicherheitspolitik*, 11/1996, p. 33.
27 Duffield, *World Power Forsaken*, p. 133; James Gow, *Triumph of the Lack of Will: International Diplomacy and the Yugoslav War* (New York: Colombia University Press, 1997), p. 161; Volker Rühe, 'Über den Kopf gewachsen', *Der Spiegel*, No. 16, 15 April 1996, p. 28.
28 For voting results, see *Das Parlament*, 20–27 December 1996, p. 1; Arthur Hoffmann and Kerry Longhurst, 'German Strategic Culture in Action', *Contemporary Security Policy*, 20:2 (1999), p. 38.
29 For voting results, see *Plenarprotokoll Deutscher Bundestag*, 13/242, p. 22451. See also Joschka Fischer, *Plenarprotokoll Deutscher Bundestag*, 13/242, p. 22431; Rudolf Scharping, *Plenarprotokoll Deutscher Bundestag*, 13/242, p. 22440; Günter Verheugen, *Plenarprotokoll Deutscher Bundestag*, 13/242, p. 22423; Uta Zapf, *Plenarprotokoll Deutscher Bundestag*, 13/242, p. 22443; 'Grosse Mehrheit für Verlängerung des Sfor-Einsatzes', *Frankfurter Allgemeine Zeitung*, 20 June 1998.
30 Joschka Fischer, *Plenarprotokoll Deutscher Bundestag*, 13/242, p. 22431; Klaus Kinkel, speech at 'Forum Bundeswehr und Gesellschaft', Berlin, reprinted in *Bulletin*, No. 47, 9 June 1997; Volker Rühe, 'Tagesbefehl an die Bundeswehr', *Bulletin*, No. 1, 2 January 1997; Rudolf Scharping, *Plenarprotokoll Deutscher Bundestag*, 13/242, p. 22440.
31 For voting results see *Plenarprotokoll Deutscher Bundestag*, 13/248, pp. 23161–23163.
32 United Nations Security Council Resolution 1199, available at www.un.int.
33 United Nations Security Council Resolutions 1199, 1203, available at www.un.int. For operational details about *Operation Allied Force*, see the website of the US Department of Defense, www.defenselink.mil/specials/kosovo. See also Ivo H. Daalder and Michael E. O'Hanlon, *Winning Ugly: NATO's War to Save Kosovo* (Washington, DC: Brookings Institution Press, 2000), p. 228.
34 'Regierungserklärung', reprinted in *Bulletin*, No. 22, 30 March 1998; Rudolf Scharping, 'Frieden und Stabilität in Europa', *Bulletin*, No. 6, 9 February 1999.
35 Joschka Fischer, cited in 'Grosse Mehrheit für Verlängerung des Sfor-Einsatzes', *Frankfurter Allgemeine Zeitung*, 20 June 1998; Klaus Kinkel, interview with *Fuldauer Zeitung*, 28 July 1998; Klaus Kinkel, *Plenarprotokoll Deutscher Bundestag*, 13/242, p. 22422; Rudolf Seiters, *Plenarprotokoll Deutscher Bundestag*, 13/242, p. 22429.
36 See debate in the Bundestag, 16 October 1998, *Plenarprotokoll Deutscher Bundestag*, 13/248, pp. 23127–23174; 'Breite Mehrheit im Bundestag für Beteiligung der Bundeswehr an einem Nato-Einsatz', *Frankfurter Allgemeine Zeitung*, 17 October 1998.

37 Joschka Fischer, interview with *Die Zeit*, 16/1999. See also 'Erklärung von Bundeskanzler Gerhard Schröder zur Lage in Kosovo', 24 March 1999, reprinted in *Bulletin*, No. 13, 30 March 1999; Fischer, *Die Zeit*, 25/1999; Joschka Fischer, interview with *Der Spiegel*, 18 October 1999; Johannes Rau, speech at the 38th Kommandeurtagung der Bundeswehr, Leipzig, 14 November 2000, reprinted in *Bulletin*, No. 76–1, 14 November 2000; Gerhard Schröder, 'Die Grundkoordinaten deutscher Außenpolitik sind unverändert', *Bulletin*, 83, 6 December 1999; Gerhard Schröder, *New York Times* 19 September 1999; Rudolf Scharping, *Die Zeit*, 8/1999; Helmut Schmidt, *Die Zeit*, 17/1999.

38 German left-wing intellectuals appeared less convinced than the left-wing politicians. If anything, the certainty of the recommendations of the past was gone. Few directly embraced the Kosovo bombings and even fewer directly rejected them. The main impression was one of ambivalence and perplexity. See Ernest-Otto Czempiel, 'Seltsame Stille', *Die Zeit*, 14/1999; Jürgen Habermas, 'Bestialität und Humanität', *Die Zeit*, 18/1999; Eric J. Hobsbawm, 'Die neuen Nationalismen', *Die Zeit*, 19/1999; 'Krieg der Köpfe', *Der Spiegel*, 15/1999.

39 More than half of the opponents to *Operation Allied Force* from within the government's own ranks stressed that they accepted in principle a German engagement for peace with military means. However, they opposed *Operation Allied Force* due to the absence of a clear UN mandate, thus disputing the legality rather than the moral and political legitimacy of the intervention. Eberhard Brecht, intervention during debate in the Bundestag, 16 February 2001, full transcript reprinted in *Die Zeit*, 20 February 2001; Ludger Volmer, *Plenarprotokoll Deutscher Bundestag*, 13/248, p. 23152; Gila Altmann, 'Erklärung zur Abstimmung', *Plenarprotokoll Deutscher Bundestag*, 13/248, p. 23173; Eberhard Brecht, 'Erklärung zur Abstimmung', *Plenarprotokoll Deutscher Bundestag*, 13/248, p. 23168; Winfried Nachtwei, Kerstin Müller, and Volker Beck, 'Erklärung zur Abstimmung', *Plenarprotokoll Deutscher Bundestag*, 13/248, p. 23167; Anlage 3, 'Erklärung zur Abstimmung', fifteen SPD members, *Plenarprotokoll Deutscher Bundestag*, 13/248, p. 23170.

40 Gregor Gysi, *Plenarprotokoll Deutscher Bundestag*, 13/248, p. 23145. See also Gerhard Zwerenz, *Plenarprotokoll Deutscher Bundestag*, 13/242, p. 22434.

41 For voting results, see *Plenarprotokoll Deutscher Bundestag*, 14/43, p. 3584. See also Fritz von Korff, 'Das deutsche Kontingent in einer Führungsrolle', in General Peter Goebel (ed.), *Von Kambodscha bis Kosovo: Auslandseinsätze der Bundeswehr* (Frankfurt am Main: Report Verlag, 2000), p. 174; Gerhard Neumann, intervention during debate in the Bundestag, 16 February 2001, full transcript reprinted in *Die Zeit*, 20 February 2001.

42 Revealingly, Joschka Fischer had rejected a November 1997 draft for a Green election programme – a programme which repeated the old Green claim that the Bundeswehr should be replaced by a civilian peace corps – as 'a program barring the way to governmental power'. Quoted in 'Grünes Konzept zur Sicherheits- und Außenpolitik führt Deutschland ins Abseits', IAP, November 1997, reprinted in *Stichworte zur Sicherheitspolitik*, 11/1997, p. 42. See also Rainer Baumann and Gunther Hellmann, 'Germany and the Use of Military Force: "Total War", the "Culture of Restraint", and the Quest for Normality', *German Politics*, 10:1 (April 2001); Gunter Hofmann, 'Wie Deutschland in den Krieg geriet', *Die Zeit*, 12 May 1999; Hanns W. Maull, 'Germany's Foreign Policy, post-Kosovo: Still a "Civilian Power"?', in Sebastian Harnisch and Hanns W. Maull (eds), *Germany as a Civilian Power? The Foreign Policy of the Berlin Republic* (Manchester: Manchester University Press, 2001), p. 117.

43 General elections had been held in October 1994.

5

Back to the Gulf: limits and possibilities of the new consensus

Introduction

Crises in Indonesia, the Balkans, Afghanistan, the Persian Gulf, and Congo demanded the world's and Germany's attention in the years after the Kosovo War. During these years, the limits and possibilities of Germany's composite consensus on the use of force became apparent. Troops were dispatched to as distant a place as East Timor, Indonesia; Germany contributed to a preventive peacekeeping mission in Macedonia, and in 2001 pledged almost 4,000 troops to aid US efforts in the war against the Taleban regime in Afghanistan. The two latter deployments, however, were accepted only grudgingly by the German left wing. With the 2003 Iraq War, the limit to Germany's new willingness to use force was breached. The German Chancellor issued an unconditional 'no' to any German participation in a prospective war against the regime of Saddam Hussein.

At first glance, Iraq might appear to have spelled the end to Germany's new military activism. Yet, while other countries prepared for war in the Gulf Germany, on US urging, took over the lead of the International Security and Assistance Force (ISAF), which had been put into place in Afghanistan after the war against the Taleban, and in June 2003 the German Bundestag with an overwhelming majority approved the contribution of Bundeswehr soldiers to the UN-mandated EU intervention, *Operation Artemis*, in Congo. Clearly, the willingness to use German military muscle had not disappeared.

This chapter shows how the limits and possibilities of Germany's willingness to use force flow from the composite nature of the working consensus – the coexistence of the precepts 'never again alone', 'never again Auschwitz', and 'never again war' and how the culturalist perspective helps account for aspects of Germany's new policy that appear puzzling from a realist's perspective.

East Timor

In a UN-organised referendum of 30 August 1999 a great majority of the people of East Timor expressed the wish for independence from Indonesia. Attempting to torpedo the independence movement militia groups, allegedly supported by the Indonesian military, launched a terror campaign against the population. A number of civilians were killed and around 400,000 people – approximately half the total population – fled their homes. A humanitarian disaster threatened.

A UN Security Council mission visited Jakarta and Dili – East Timor's major city – and managed to get the Indonesian government to commit to stop the violence in East Timor and accept the deployment of a UN force. The UN Security Council authorised a multinational force – INTERFET – on 12 September. Twenty-nine countries pledged troops to the 9,800-strong Australian-led force, among them the US, France, Italy, Great Britain, and Portugal. The task of INTERFET was to re-establish peace, protect civilians, permit the return of the refugees, and facilitate humanitarian assistance operations.[1]

During a September visit to the UN headquarters in New York, Foreign Minister Joschka Fischer pledged the contribution to INTERFET of a medical Bundeswehr unit consisting of 100 soldiers.[2]

In the parliamentary debates over this contribution, both Government and opposition invoked the partners and the past. In a by now well-known vein, it was stressed that Germany had a historical responsibility to resist genocide and excessive ethnic nationalism and to display solidarity with its European partners and the efforts of the UN.[3] The only dissenting voices came from the PDS, which called for a German civilian instead of a military engagement.[4]

Seen from a realist's perspective, Germany's military participation in the intervention in East Timor was highly unlikely. Germany had no historical connection to or direct interests in the area. Developments there could not conceivably impact Germany's security or economic well-being directly or indirectly. The decision to dispatch soldiers to the distant region was approved at a time when the Bundeswehr, in the unequivocal opinion of security experts from all political parties was already stretched to the limit by existing obligations in the Balkans, and Defence Minister Scharping cautioned that it would be preferable if a civilian aid organisation could undertake the task in East Timor.[5] Eventually, the deployment of the German contingent in East Timor, the furthest deployment of Bundeswehr soldiers ever, turned out to be an exercise complicated by the limited range of available air transportation capabilities. Though INTERFET was a relatively small deployment, it was logistically complicated and thus far from costless.

Nevertheless, INTERFET proved to be among the least controversial deployment of the Bundeswehr to date. When the Bundestag voted on 7 October, it received the support of an overwhelming majority of MdBs from all political parties excepting the PDS.[6]

This picture, puzzling from a realist's perspective, makes sense when seen against the backdrop of the domestic German logics of thinking about security.

The mission served to stop ongoing violence, prevent a potential genocide, and relieve a humanitarian disaster. Moreover, several of Germany's NATO and European partners had pledged troops to the Australian-led peace mission. INTERFET thus appealed simultaneously to both schools of thought underpinning Germany's composite consensus on out-of-area deployments – 'never again Auschwitz' and 'never again alone'.

Macedonia

The vote on East Timor demonstrated how the deployment of Bundeswehr soldiers in far-away crisis spots where developments could not possibly impact Germany had become politically possible. The crises in Macedonia, in contrast, proved much more divisive and illustrated the limits of what the new German consensus on international military engagements could achieve.

In March 2001, hostilities broke out in the former Yugoslav Republic of Macedonia as ethnic Albanian rebels clashed with police and army forces of the Macedonian government. The conflict, it was widely feared, might be the spark that set off a new Balkan debacle. The insurgency might cause Macedonia to disintegrate, rekindle Kosovar Albanian dreams of independence from Serbia or the creation of a 'greater Albania', and cause ripple effects in neighbouring Serbia, Albania, and Greece.

In June, EU and NATO diplomacy succeeded in forging a ceasefire as well as a political framework agreement between the parties – the rebels were to surrender their weapons in exchange for political reforms and improved minority rights. The Macedonian president requested the help of NATO in implementing the agreement. With the assent of both parties to the conflict a 1,000-strong NATO force (without a UN mandate) was dispatched to collect and destroy weapons and ammunition voluntarily turned in by the insurgents. The operation – *Operation Essential Harvest* – was to last thirty days and started on 26 August. Belgium, Canada, the Czech Republic, France, Greece, Italy, the Netherlands, Spain, Turkey, and Great Britain contributed militarily to the British-led force. The German government pledged two infantry companies, totalling 500 troops including 300 German soldiers already deployed in ex-Yugoslavia as part of KFOR.[7]

The follow-up mission, *Operation Amber Fox* was to guarantee the safety of civilian UN and OSCE observers who monitored the implementation of the agreed political reforms. It had been authorised by the UN Security Council but, like *Operation Essential Harvest*, it was a NATO-led operation. The task of the force was to asses the security environment for the civilian observers, provide them with relevant information, and, if necessary, function as an extraction force. Several NATO countries as well as France delivered military support, the major contributors being France, Italy, and Germany. The mission was scheduled to last three months and Germany, for the first time, was to take the position as lead nation. The general in command was German, as were most of the deployed soldiers – 600 out of a total of 1,000.[8]

In the parliamentary debates preceding the votes on *Essential Harvest* and *Amber Fox*, the government emphasised the need to live up to Germany's European and Atlantic responsibility and signal commitment to the further development and consolidation of a common European foreign and security policy.[9] Moral and historical reasons were also invoked. To vote 'no' to the missions in Macedonia, it was argued, was tantamount to voting 'yes' to a second Bosnia and reneging on Germany's historical responsibility to oppose aggression and violence against innocents. In the Yugoslavian succession wars, the Government stressed, the world community had acted too late to prevent the loss of scores of civilian lives. But in Macedonia there was a chance to stop such developments in their tracks by deploying military means as part of a broader, long-term political and economic strategy for stability in the area.[10]

While some Conservatives came out against the deployments, arguing that the government needed to allocate more funds to the already overstretched Bundeswehr before they could agree to additional obligations, most Conservatives and Liberals eventually gave their support to the government. In Macedonia the Europeans, through the Union's High Representative of foreign affairs, Javier Solana, had managed to speak with one voice in negotiating with the parties to the conflict. Both France and Great Britain had immediately pledged troops to the operations. The European efforts had the blessing of the US and both operations were carried out by relying on NATO planning and command capabilities. Thus *Operation Essential Harvest* and *Operation Amber Fox* symbolised both European and Atlantic security cooperation and appealed to the notions condensed in 'never again alone'.[11]

Among left wingers, in contrast, the case for intervention appeared less compelling. Earlier in the 1990s the then-CDU/FDP government had successfully invoked 'Europe' to generate support on the German centre left for a German contribution to peacekeeping operations in ex-Yugoslavia. Though leading Social Democrats and Greens attempted to repeat the trick and harness the positive notions surrounding European cooperation to the case for intervention in Macedonia, they were not successful.

Two factors thwarted their attempt. First, though the crisis concerned Europe far more than the US, NATO had nevertheless played a prevalent role in forging a ceasefire and a political agreement. This baited latent anti-NATO and anti-American feelings on the far left. Second, the humanitarian argument for dispatching soldiers was not convincing enough for German left wingers. Unlike *Operation Allied Force* and INTERFET, which both aimed to stop ongoing and large-scale human rights violations, the intervention in Macedonia was preventive. The case for military intervention was therefore emotionally less compelling, but also ran up against the notion that military means should only be used as a last resort. 'We do not', as a Liberal MdB put it, 'deploy for the sake of deployment itself'.[12]

Opposition from within the government's own ranks converged around the notion that it was not at all clear that events in Macedonia were poised to repeat the pattern from Bosnia, or that a military intervention was an efficient way of stabilising the area. This scepticism was not dispelled, though the proponents of intervention emphasised that it formed part of a comprehensive, long-term political strategy for peace. In the eyes of many left wingers, military means had been pushed to the fore as a first resort.[13]

The PDS, as usual, gave these suspicions their sharpest formulation: the German Government was attempting to build an 'international military reputation', NATO was positioning itself to become a 'global policeman,' and the intervention in Macedonia was driven by the ulterior motive to 'sideline' the UN in favour of NATO. NATO, it was claimed, had not so much been asked to help by the Macedonian government as it had placed pressure on the Macedonian Government to ask it to help.[14]

In the vote on *Essential Harvest* the government eventually gained the support of many Conservatives and Liberals. From within the government's own ranks, however, opposition was widespread. Nineteen Social Democrats and four Green MdBs went as far as to close ranks with the PDS and vote against the proposal of their own government. *Essential Harvest* was approved with 497 votes for and 130 against. Among all the cases of German participation in international crisis management that had been up for approval in the Bundestag, *Essential Harvest* provoked the strongest opposition.[15] In the vote on *Amber Fox*, which had a UN mandate, only ten SPD and Green MdBs abstained. Some of those who had voted 'no' to *Essential Harvest* approved on the grounds that once deployed it would most likely cause more harm than good to withdraw the peace keepers in the middle of the process they had been deployed to oversee. Though opposition was less evident in the latter vote, both deployments passed the Bundestag thanks only to the support of the Conservative and Liberal opposition.[16]

Reasoning along the lines of realist theory, the crisis in Macedonia ought to have generated a firm German willingness to contribute to a military intervention. Fighting had broken out in Germany's immediate neighbourhood and threatened to spill over and re-ignite hostilities in or among other Balkan countries. Already at the outbreak of the Yugoslavian succession wars in the early 1990s, Germany had been home to around 400,000 guest workers from the area, mainly Croats. Germany turned out to be the destination of choice for many of those forced to flee: out of a total of 700,000 refugees from ex-Yugoslavia, Germany had received approximately half.[17]

If Macedonia had fallen apart or set off a broader conflict it was certain to send new streams of refugees in Germany's direction – a point some proponents of the mission on the German centre right attempted to bring into play. Nevertheless, the missions, especially *Operation Essential Harvest*, proved more controversial and divisive than any other out-of-area engagement to which Germany had contributed after the Constitutional Court in 1994 had ruled such engagements constitutional.[18]

This pattern of opposition and support, however, makes sense when considering the two schools of thought within Germany's security culture. The engagement in East Timor appealed simultaneously to 'never again alone' and 'never again Auschwitz'. The engagement in Macedonia, in contrast, while clearly acceptable to the adherents of 'never again alone' appealed less to the notions condensed in 'never again Auschwitz'.

In sum, the missions in Macedonia approached the limits of what the new German consensus on the use of military means could sustain. The pro-active and preventive approach, where military means were deployed *ante factum*, was not palatable to everyone on the left and thus support for a German contribution was shaky even though the crisis, from a realist's perspective, should have produced a firm will to intervene.

Operation Enduring Freedom in Afghanistan

In response to the terror attacks on New York and Washington, DC on 11 September 2001, the US initiated a military campaign against the Afghan Taleban regime, *Operation Enduring Freedom*. The goal was to bring down a regime known to harbour terrorists and apprehend the perpetrators of 11 September. In response to the terror attacks the UN Security Council had passed a resolution unequivocally condemning terrorism and recognising the inherent right of any nation to 'individual or collective self-defence'.[19] The NATO Council, in a demonstration of solidarity with the US, invoked the Brussels Treaty's Article V – the collective defence clause.

In line with the rest of Europe, initial German reactions were characterised by shock and outrage. On 14 September more than a million Germans appeared at the Brandenburg Gate in Berlin to demonstrate their rejection of the attacks and solidarity with the victims. Chancellor Schröder declared Germany's unconditional solidarity with the US and personally visited Ground Zero in New York in early October to witness the destruction. When military actions ensued in Afghanistan initial German reactions contrasted sharply with the reactions to the Gulf War a decade earlier. All Germany's party leaders, excepting PDS' Gregor Gysi, came out in support of the American war.[20]

Great Britain and France, followed by Italy, pledged and dispatched ground, air, or naval units to support the US efforts. Australia, Canada, and Japan also contributed militarily to *Operation Enduring Freedom*.[21] The German government pledged to contribute 3,900 Bundeswehr soldiers, consisting of medical units, air transportation capabilities, naval patrolling vehicles, a counter-ABC unit, and a unit of 100 soldiers from the elite force 'Kommando Special Kräfte' to support the American efforts.[22]

However, what had initially appeared like a broad political coalition of support behind a German contribution, carried by a wave of sympathy with the US, soon began to fray. Civilian casualties and stray bombs hitting UN facilities rekindled German anti-war feelings. American rumblings about expanding the war on terrorism to other countries deemed to be part of President Bush's 'axis of evil' spurred fears in Germany of uncontrollable escalation, American irresponsibility, and unpredictable consequences for other parts of the world.

The residual of the German peace movement appeared to recover from its long post-Srebrenica shell shock. As a number of anti-war demonstrations were staged in major German cities the image of a trigger-happy and adventurous America re-emerged in the German public discourse. Unease with the US approach was not limited to the left wing. Commentators and politicians from across the political spectrum added their voices to the criticism of what in their eyes was an excessively unilateral and one-sidedly military approach to the problem of international terrorism.[23] The use of force, it was emphasised, might suppress problems such as international terrorism, drug trafficking, organised crime, proliferation of weapons of mass destruction, and religious fundamentalism in the short term. But in order to get to the root of all these problems long-term engagement and a comprehensive approach taking political, social, and economic aspects into account, was called for.[24]

In the November Bundestag debates over Germany's contribution to *Operation Enduring Freedom* the government faced fierce opposition from the PDS and widespread scepticism from within its own ranks in a context of growing public unease with American activities in Afghanistan.[25] To rally support behind the contribution, leading Social Democrats and Greens, echoed by the Conservative and Liberal opposition, invoked Germany's international responsibility and the requirements of partnership. They pointed to the UN Resolution, NATO's invocation of Article V, and the fact that all Germany's major European allies had contributed to the military campaign.

Simultaneously, however, it was stressed by parliamentarians from left to right that while Germany was obliged to stand by the US it was also obliged to lift its voice and speak up for multilateralism, cooperation, consultation, and comprehensive political and social measures to embed *Operation Enduring Freedom*. The concept of 'critical solidarity' emerged – a solidarity, it was emphasised, which should and could not mean an uncritical and unqualified acceptance of US concepts and conduct.[26]

Attempting to appease the critics among their own backbenchers, leading government members went out of their way to emphasise the broader humanitarian and civilian aspects of the proposed German contribution to the anti-terror campaign in Afghanistan. Together with numerous Liberals they promised that Germany would press for a 'new era of engagement' where the developed world would renew the efforts to close the 'poverty gap' between the North and the South, while stepping up intercultural dialogue between the West and the rest of the world to promote mutual understanding – ensuring that the war on terrorism did not degenerate into a 'clash of civilisations'. Only by means of a broad approach, it was argued, could terrorism be deprived of its foot soldiers.[27]

While the political, civil, and humanitarian efforts and intentions of the German government were thus put on display, the military content of the German contribution to *Operation Enduring Freedom* was played down and the potential combat role of German elite units evaded in the debate.[28] Initially the government looked set to gain the support of the centre right opposition parties. From within the government's own ranks, however, many MdBs kept rejecting the need for a military campaign. Instead, they called for 'police-actions' in the form of limited command raids to apprehend the terrorists.[29] As had been the case in the votes over Germany's contribution to crisis management in Macedonia, the German contribution to *Operation Enduring Freedom* was set to pass only by relying on the support of the opposition.

In order to preserve the government's foreign policy credibility in what was perceived as a crucial vote, Chancellor Schröder then decided to link the question to a vote of confidence. This eventually brought most of the doubters into line and in the vote 16 November only four Greens voted 'no'. More than twenty Social Democrats and Greens, however, emphasised that they rejected the military campaign and voted 'yes' only to save the government.[30]

At the other end of the political spectrum, the Chancellor's decision to call a vote of confidence caused Liberal and Conservative MdBs to vote against *Enduring Freedom* though simultaneously stressing their unequivocal support for the principle of delivering a German military contribution in Afghanistan. Eventually, the vote passed the Bundestag by only a narrow margin: 336 parliamentarians approved while 326 opposed.[31]

In the case of Afghanistan, the reactions of German policy makers once again make most sense when seen against the backdrop of the competing schools of thought within Germany's security culture. In light of the comprehensive involvement of all Germany's major partners, a German contribution to *Operation Enduring Freedom* was in tune with the precept 'never again alone'. The German centre right thus, in accordance with the culturalist expectation, was supportive of Germany's contribution – though the vote of confidence provoked most to vote 'no'. In *Operation Enduring Freedom*, however, military measures did not primarily serve a humanitarian purpose and the immediate consequences of the intervention was an escalation rather than a de-escalation of violence. Thus the German left proved hesitant to endorse the intervention. 'Never again war' re-emerged alongside 'never again Auschwitz' to compete for the allegiance of the centre left.

'No' to war in Iraq: a new assertive Germany?

The deployment in Afghanistan approached the limit of what the new German consensus could sustain. With the brewing crisis in Iraq and the tough talk of the hawks of the administration of American President George W. Bush, that limit was breached. Pre-emptive strikes against potential future threats carried out by coalitions of the willing did not sit well with either school of thought within Germany's security culture. Whereas the German centre right wobbled on the question of whether Germany in this case should stand by its long-time American ally, the leader of the centre left did not hesitate. Already in the summer of 2002, Chancellor Schröder as the first Western leader issued an unconditional 'no' to any German participation in a potential war against Iraq, even if the UN were to endorse it.[32]

In the debate over Afghanistan, Gerhard Schröder had worked against the current in forcing the German centre left to endorse a military contribution to the US-led campaign. In the case of Iraq, in contrast, he chose to ride the anti-war wave. Thus, prodded by the chancellor, who had put his office on the line to secure a German contribution to *Operation Enduring Freedom*, policy makers on the left dug in their heels during the run-up to *Operation Iraqi Freedom*, eventually launched in March 2003.

The bellicose US line, the chancellor charged, was ill considered. A war against Iraq would distract from the efforts to combat international terrorism and might lead to uncontrollable escalation and mass casualties. Further estrangement between the Arab world and the West would follow. Containment, not confrontation, Schröder argued, was the right strategy when dealing with Saddam Hussein – a strategy which, since 1991 had been successful in preventing renewed Iraqi aggression against its neighbours. Denouncing America's 'military adventurism' the chancellor promised that an SPD-led Germany would be a voice of reason and restraint.[33]

Domestically, the move was a triumph. The chancellor was facing general elections in September 2002 and had consistently trailed his Conservative challenger, Edmund Stoiber, in the polls. The chancellor's anti-war stance, however, indulged the SPD's disgruntled left wing and stopped the flight of votes from the SPD and Green Party to the only unreconstructed pacifist party – the ex-communist PDS. It tapped into widespread public unease with the new US line and permitted the chancellor to turn a looming defeat into a narrow victory.

Internationally, however, the re-elected Chancellor was in for a rude awakening. The chancellor's 'no' issued during an election speech in August 2002 was clearly attuned to a domestic audience. Presumably, the decision to oppose the US war had not involved the chancellor's closest foreign policy advisors, and the extent of American outrage had not been anticipated.[34] Initially, Germany had to face it alone. Soon, however, the German government managed to bring other country on board the anti-war coalition and as US–German relations kept deteriorating Europe split down the middle with countries such as the UK, Italy, and Denmark lining up behind the US, and others such as France and Belgium more sympathetic to the German point of view. This active counterbalancing of the American ally garnered with language about 'the end of check book diplomacy' and 'Germany's right to be consulted' was without precedent and might be interpreted as a sign that a new and more assertive Germany with more focus on German national interests was emerging.[35]

Another interpretation, however, is also possible. Arguably, when the German government in the Fall of 2002 was courting France and Russia it might have had less to do with a wish to assert the German position than with a culturally ingrained urge to avoid the international isolation the chancellor's electioneering had brought upon Germany. The countercoalition was arguably an attempt to save the day for 'never again alone' and indeed was invoked repeatedly by the leaders of the SPD/Green government to help justify their stance in confrontations with the domestic opposition, which fulminated against the Chancellor and asserted that Germany's international standing and influence had been sacrificed for the sake of ensuring the chancellor a second term in office.[36]

Further underlining that the German inclination towards international cooperation and integration was alive and well, the re-elected Government was soon found seeking to mend fences with its American ally. The US was permitted unrestricted use of its bases in Germany and German forces provided physical security for US military installations in Germany during the war. Moreover, Germany, on US urging, granted Iraq a $2.5 bn relief and engaged itself in various reconstruction activities and in the training of a new Iraqi policy force – training that took place in the United Arab Emirates.[37]

It is difficult to see why the German government should have offered such concessions against domestic protests if the ultimate aim of the 'no' was to assert Germany's independence from the US. Furthermore, if German leaders wished to launch a German or European alternative to US hegemony, it is perplexing that they largely refrained from exploiting and highlighting the fact that most of the warnings issued by Germany about the consequences of a war in Iraq eventually proved accurate. On the contrary, German policy makers emphasised the need to look ahead and cooperate in managing the escalating insurgency in Iraq and building a democratic Iraqi state.[38]

Making sense of the German stance on Iraq arguably requires that the analyst looks inside Germany at the composite nature of Germany's strategic culture. Surely, a chancellor with a track record of committing German troops to a variety of international peacekeeping operations was not moved by pacifist feelings when he issued his 'no' to Iraq. Yet, by choosing to run on an anti-war platform, the German chancellor tapped into widespread sentiments among the policy making elite of the centre left and the population at large. Thus, the reason why he was able to mobilise voters around this issue had to do with ingrained cultural belief. For a while, 'never again war' superseded 'never again Auschwitz' on the German left wing. At the same time, however, 'never again alone' remained alive and well, prompting the government to engage in apparently self-contradictory and illogical behaviour: ganging up with European countries against the US while at the same time attempting to repair relations with its American ally.

Surely, the notion that Germany had the right to have on opinion on how to deal with new security threats because Germany delivered an increasing contribution to international crisis management was emerging. Yet, despite what one might conclude from a quick glance, Iraq did not herald a new Germany emancipating itself from bonds and alliances. On the contrary, the counterbalancing of the US was arguably precisely an expression of the ingrained German inclination to avoid standing alone on important international issues.

From Iraq to Iraq: full circle?

An external observer might conclude, that Germany by 2003 had come full circle: from abstinence in the first Gulf War via a temporary change in its view on the use of military means, and back to a policy of abstinence when the second Gulf War broke out in 2003. The debate over *Operation Enduring Freedom* and Iraq featured a number of anti-war and anti-American themes recalling the debate over the first Gulf War in 1991. However, the Germany that said 'no' in 2002 was different from the Germany that said 'no' in 1990 and the will to engage German military might in international crisis spots had not disappeared.

Less than four months after *Operation Iraqi Freedom* had been launched without German soldiers the Bundestag voted 441 to thirty in support of a German contribution to the EU *Operation Artemis* in Congo. *Operation Artemis* was equipped with a robust UN mandate and its purpose was to stabilise a deteriorating security situation, protect the civil population of the area, and permit an existing UN peacekeeping force to be reinforced and expanded to match the situation. A number of Germany's EU partners contributed to the mission, including the UK and France, which functioned as the intervention's lead nation.

The debate over the German contribution – up to 350 soldiers, transportation capabilities, medical support, and a few officers attached to the multinational operational headquarters of the mission – was one of the least confrontational debates over a specific military interventions ever. The SPD/Green government, with the ease and skill that comes with practice, invoked the humanitarian need in Congo, the fact that innocent civilians were being killed and forced from their homes, the international responsibility of Germany, and the multilateral nature of the intervention.[39] Further to the left the only remaining pacifist party, the PDS, though voting against the deployment because it signalled a 'militarisation' of EU foreign policy, now conceded that 'no reasonable human being' could possibly object to the principle of using the Bundeswehr personnel and material to combat a humanitarian disaster if need be – only, it had to be under civilian leadership. Even to the pacifists, military means were no longer an unequivocal evil.[40]

At the other end of the political spectrum, among members of the CDU and CSU, the new-found left-wing willingness to deploy the Bundeswehr had in contrast become almost too much of a good thing. Nobody openly argued with the 'never again Rwanda' emphasised by the governing parties. Yet, some indicated that it might be time to slow down a bit and develop more clear and explicit notions of German national interests to guide the out-of-area decisions. 'Of course', argued Christian Schmidt from the CDU/CSU, 'avoiding a humanitarian catastrophe has to be a criteria that prompts us to consider an engagement'. 'However', he continued, 'we cannot simply conclude that no matter where it occurs, we need to go there'.[41]

Thus, by 2003 the German willingness to engage the Bundeswehr in out-of-area operations had become so rooted that the original proponent of expanding the role of the Bundeswehr – the Conservative party – while supporting the Congo deployment now cautioned the left wing, that it needed to learn to say 'no'.

The positions taken by Germany's major parties in the debate over Congo leave no doubt, that the Iraq War did not herald an end to the German military activism that emerged over the 1990s, a conclusion further supported by the fact that, while other countries were preparing for war in Iraq, Germany stepped up its military engagement in Afghanistan and in February took over the lead of the ISAF in Kabul, Afghanistan. Instead, the German abstention in Iraq simply highlighted the fact, that Germany, like most other 'normal' nations, had conditions for lining up – conditions flowing from the peculiar nature of Germany's strategic culture.

German reactions to the international crises of the years 1999–2003 indicated that broad political support behind an international military engagement hinged on whether the sets of notions and beliefs condensed in 'never again alone', 'never again Auschwitz', and 'never again war' were all taken into account. The analysis has indicated, that domestic support will materialise when it comes to engaging the Bundeswehr alongside the armed forces of major allies as a last resort in managing crises that entail large-scale ethnic violence or abuse of human rights. Such interventions will appear legitimate to politicians across the German political spectrum. The composite consensus, however, will not sustain a potential policy of unilateral deployments of the Bundeswehr outside of established organisational frameworks. It will also prove shaky where a German government seeks to engage the Bundeswehr before a variety of political, diplomatic, and economic strategies to manage a conflict had been given a chance, or if the military intervention does not serve a plausible humanitarian goal beside its political and military objectives. Such interventions will either jar with 'never again alone', bait residual anti-militarism and war Angst, and/or make it difficult to invoke 'never again Auschwitz' to mobilise support on the German left.

In other words, Germany will remain an active participant in the military management of international crises, but on a number of conditions. Unilateral deployments, military interventions to protect oil fields or sea lanes, pre-emptive strikes, or punitive action against rogue regimes will find limited support in Germany. Should a future German government attempt such engagements it will either fail to obtain support or have to embed the military policy in a substantial broad civilian and humanitarian engagement in the targeted area in order to keep the left flank of Germany's new composite consensus on board.

Making war or stopping it? New threats, pre-emption, and the American war on terrorism

As argued above, the German resistance to Iraq did not indicate that the German out-of-area policy had changed back to a policy guided by pacifism and reticence. What had changed compared to the 1990s, however, were the conditions under which engagement was expected to take place. Throughout the post-Cold War decade, Germany would be called upon to deploy peace keepers only after extensive diplomatic efforts had failed, only within broad multinational frameworks, and, excepting the Kosovo War, only in UN-mandated missions. Most importantly, the 1990s were years in which the armed forces of the Western world were rarely deployed to *make* war, but to stop it.

The strong American focus on the dual danger of terrorism and proliferation of weapons of mass destruction (WMD), emerging after the terrorist attacks on New York and Washington, DC, however, created a new operating environment.[42] The new emphasis on pre-emptive military strikes carried out by coalitions of the willing challenged the composite German consensus and did away with some of the circumstances that had helped appease the sentiments condensed in 'never again war'.

One might suspect that this would diminish the re-unified Germany's international military relevance before it was ever really consolidated. Not least, because the EU and the UN also increasingly emphasised the gravity of the new threats identified by the US and the need to tackle them preventively. The EU's Security Strategy of June 2003 listed terrorism and WMD proliferation together with regional conflicts, state failure, and organised crime as key threats against the Union's member states.[43] The report of the UN Secretary-General's High-Level Panel on Threats, Challenges and Change – a report supposed to establish the conceptual foundation for reform of the UN – identifies similar threats.[44] Both documents, moreover, recognize the need for preventive action, including, at times, the use of military force. The European Security Strategy echoes *The National Security Strategy of the United States* in insisting that the key threats to international security have to be tackled early on, that the threats are connected and mutually reinforcing: weak states and regional conflict complicate the combat against transnational terrorist organisations, some of which are known to harbour WMD ambitions, which might in turn be facilitated by organised international criminal networks, contributing to proliferation for economic gain. 'The first line of defense', the EU Security Strategy emphasises, 'will often be abroad ... Conflict prevention and threat prevention cannot start too early'.[45] The UN High-Level Panel likewise stresses the transnational and interdependent nature of the threats and the need to act preventively, at times with military means.[46]

However, though combating international terrorism and preventing the proliferation of WMD have risen to the top of the international agenda and although it has again become conceivable that Western military forces start wars, the cases in which they end them will arguably remain prevalent. The numerous moral, political, and practical problems entailed in pre-emptive and preventive wars will ensure that they remain few. Afghanistan, and particularly Iraq, amply illustrate the complications and costs of such operations.

The weeding out of even more pro-active language from the first version of the European Security Strategy considered by EU leaders in early 2003 indicates that the EU consensus is less keen on military pre-emption than the current US administration. The EU strategy still stresses civilian approaches and non-violent means of conflict resolution above all. The UN High-Level Panel likewise suggests a high bar for when the preventive use of military force should be considered legitimate. Pre-emptive or preventive use of force against a non-imminent threat can take place, it is emphasised, only if military action is the only reasonable response in the given situation. Furthermore, pre-emption must be based on credible evidence that the threat is real and can take place only with the approval of the UN Security Council (which the High-Level Panel urges to become more pro-active in light of the nature of the new threats).[47]

Finally, despite the current prominence of new threats and new responses, the type of peace-creating and peacekeeping interventions around which re-unified Germany's new consensus on international crisis management developed are as relevant as ever. Civil wars and ethnic violence threatening the lives and well-being of innocent civilians will continue to demand Western military action. Arguably, the fight against international terrorism will make these tasks even more pertinent than before. Weak states and regional wars no longer constitute a threat only to the directly affected populations and areas. With international terrorist networks on the lookout for new bases in the wake of their ouster from Afghanistan, weak and failing states have come to be perceived as more than a humanitarian concern in the Western World. They are increasingly seen as a security concern as well.[48]

In sum, threat perceptions and security policy priorities have changed. Yet, the new US emphasis on pre-emption, while posing a challenge to the coherence of Germany's composite consensus on the use of military force, has not made the German contribution to international crisis management politically impossible, as demonstrated by the engagement in Congo. Moreover, though Germany's composite consensus sets limits to what kind of missions are acceptable to Germany, this has not made a German out-of-area contribution irrelevant. On the contrary, the new focus on terrorism and WMD proliferation accentuates the need to end regional wars and stabilise failing states. Thus, the country which was dismissed by US hawks as part of 'old Europe' will remain an active participant in out-of-area crisis management and one of the biggest players on the international peacekeeping scene.[49]

Notes

1. See website of the United Nations, www.un.org/peace/etimor/UntaetB.htm.
2. A number of parliamentarians, including members of the government, protested against Fischer's approach. If individual members of the government could go ahead and pledge German troops to UN missions as Fischer had done in New York, the Bundestag had little choice but to follow suit or damage Germany's foreign policy credibility. It was important, they argued, to decide on a case-by-case basis and avoid slipping into an 'automatism' of German participation in UN peace missions. Walter Hirche, *Plenarprotokoll Deutscher Bundestag*, 14/61, p. 5427; Volker Neumann, *Plenarprotokoll Deutscher Bundestag*, 14/61, p. 5425.
3. Wolfgang Bötsch, *Plenarprotokoll Deutscher Bundestag*, 14/61, p. 547; Gernot Erler, *Plenarprotokoll Deutscher Bundestag*, 14/55, p. 4893; Joschka Fischer, interview with *Der Tagesspiegel*, 24 October 1999, reprinted in *Stichworte zur Sicherheitspolitik*, 10/1999, p. 9; Hermann Gröhe, *Plenarprotokoll Deutscher Bundestag*, 14/55, p. 4901; Walter Hirche, *Plenarprotokoll Deutscher Bundestag*, 14/61, p. 5427; Karl Lamers, *Plenarprotokoll Deutscher Bundestag*, 14/61, p. 5423; Volker Neumann, *Plenarprotokoll Deutscher Bundestag*, 14/61, p. 5426.
4. Carsten Hübner, *Plenarprotokoll Deutscher Bundestag*, 14/61, p. 5428. For voting results, see *Plenarprotokoll Deutscher Bundestag*, 14/61, p. 5437.
5. Rudolf Scharping, *Plenarprotokoll Deutscher Bundestag*, 14/61, p. 5431. See Chapter 7 for an elaborate analysis of the force projection capability of the Bundeswehr and the problems encountered in handling the new international tasks of the 1990s.
6. In uncontroversial votes the Bundestag votes by hand raising and the *Plenarprotokoll* simply records whether a proposal was passed or rejected, together with a commentary. The vote on East Timor passed with approval of 'the great majority of the house against the vote of the PDS and a few members of the CDU/CSU, FDP, and SPD', *Plenarprotokoll Deutscher Bundestag*, 14/61, p. 5437.
7. 'Antrag der Bundesregierung', Bundestags-Drucksache 14/6830, reprinted in *Stichworte zur Sicherheitspolitik*, 8/2001, pp. 16–19; 'Task Force Harvest Mission', available at NATO's web site, www.afsouth.nato.int.
8. 'Neuer Bundeswehreinsatz in Mazedonien beschlossen', at www.bundesregierung, de/dokumente/Artikel/ix.55736.1499.htm.; 'Task Force Fox', at NATO's web site, www.afsouth.nato.int.
9. Gernot Erler, interview with *Die Zeit*, 8 May 2001; Gerhard Schröder, *Plenarprotokoll Deutscher Bundestag*, 14/184, p. 18203; Christian Sterzing, *Plenarprotokoll Deutscher Bundestag*, 14/184, p. 18207.
10. Gernot Erler, *Plenarprotokoll Deutscher Bundestag*, 14/190, at www.bundestag.de; Joschka Fischer, *Plenarprotokoll Deutscher Bundestag*, 14/184, p. 18178; Wolfgang Gerhardt, *Plenarprotokoll Deutscher Bundestag*, 14/184, p. 18184; Kerstin Müller, *Plenarprotokoll Deutscher Bundestag*, 14/184, p. 18195; Peter Struck, *Plenarprotokoll Deutscher Bundestag*, 14/184, p. 18192; Gert Weisskirchen, *Plenarprotokoll Deutscher Bundestag*, 14/184, p. 18186.
11. Angela Merkel, *Plenarprotokoll Deutscher Bundestag*, 14/184, p. 18194; Volker Rühe, *Plenarprotokoll Deutscher Bundestag*, 14/184, p. 18181; Volker Rühe, *Plenarprotokoll Deutscher Bundestag*, 14/190, at www.bundestag.de. A number of Conservatives and Liberals exploited the Macedonia debate to object to continuous drops in the defence budget and, while expressing support for *Operation Essential Harvest* and *Operation Amber Fox*, voted against the deployments in protest. The Government budgetary priorities, they claimed, were harming Germany's capability of being a good partner and handling tasks such as that in Macedonia. Jörg van Essen, interview with *Die Zeit*, 2 July 2001; Herbert Kremp, 'Erste NATO-Soldaten in Mazedonien erwartet', *Die Welt*, 17 August

2001; 'Keine halben Nato-Sachen', *Die Welt*, 21 August 2001; *Plenarprotokoll Deutscher Bundestag*, Anlage 1–7, 9–12, 16–20.
12 Wolfgang Gerhardt (FDP), *Plenarprotokoll Deutscher Bundestag*, 14/184, p. 18184. See also Gernot Erler (SPD), *Plenarprotokoll Deutscher Bundestag*, 14/190, at www.bundestag.de; Christian Schmidt (CDU/CSU), *Plenarprotokoll Deutscher Bundestag*, 14/190, at www.bundestag.de.
13 See declarations by SPD members who voted 'no' to *Operation Essential Harvest*, *Plenarprotokoll Deutscher Bundestag*, 14/184, Anlage 8, pp. 18215, Anlage 27, p. 18226; 'Streit in der SPD um Mazedonieneinsatz der Bundeswehr', *Die Zeit*, 27 July 2001.
14 Wolfgang Gehrcke, *Plenarprotokoll Deutscher Bundestag*, 14/184, p. 18185; Gregor Gysi, *Plenarprotokoll Deutscher Bundestag*, 14/184, p. 18199.
15 Appendix D provides an overview of the analysed cases of German participation in out-of-area crisis management, the auspices under which they were carried out, other participating nations, and the voting results from the German Bundestag.
16 For voting results, see *Plenarprotokoll Deutscher Bundestag*, 14/184, pp. 18210–18212 and *Plenarprotokoll Deutscher Bundestag*, 14/190, at www.bundestag.de.
17 Great Britain and France, in contrast, received only respectively 6,000 and 16,000 refugees from Yugoslavia over the first half of the 1990s. General Peter Goebel, 'Beteiligung der Bundeswehr am Wiederaufbau in Bosnien-Herzegowina', in General Peter Goebel (ed.), *Von Kambodscha bis Kosovo: Auslandseinsätze der Bundeswehr* (Frankfurt am Main: Report Verlag, 2000), p. 317.
18 Klaus Kinkel, *Plenarprotokoll Deutscher Bundestag*, 13/248, p. 23130; Christian Schmidt, *Plenarprotokoll Deutscher Bundestag*, 13/74, p. 6462; Gerhard Schröder, *Plenarprotokoll Deutscher Bundestag*, 14/184, p. 18201; Theodor Waigel, *Plenarprotokoll Deutscher Bundestag*, 13/76, p. 6655; Guido Westerwelle, *Plenarprotokoll Deutscher Bundestag*, 14/184, p. 18197.
19 United Nations Security Council Resolution 1368, 12 September 2001. Available at the UN website, www. un.org.
20 Stephen F. Szabo, *Parting Ways: The Crisis in German-American Relations* (Washington, DC: Brookings Institution Press, 2004), p. 17.
21 'Operation Enduring Freedom – Deployments', available at www.globalsecurity.org.
22 Beschlussempfehlung der Bundesregierung, Drucksachen 14/7296, Presse und Informationsamt der Bundesregierung; Hans-Jürgen Leersch, 'Kämpfen statt zahlen ist diesmal die deutsche Devise', *Die Welt*, 2 October 2001, p. 2.
23 Josef Joffe, 'Feldzug gegen Unbekannt', *Die Zeit*, 66/2001; Berthold Kohler, 'In Reserve', *Frankfurter Allgemeine Zeitung*, 9 October 2001, p. 1; Fritz Kuhn, interview with *Die Welt*, 18 November 2001; Theo Sommer, 'Allein ist der Starke hilflos', *Die Zeit*, 66/2001; Theo Sommer, 'Wir trauern mit', *Die Zeit*, 38/2001; Peter Struck, *Plenarprotokoll Deutscher Bundestag*, 14/202, at www.bundestag.de.
24 Michael Glos, *Plenarprotokoll Deutscher Bundestag*, 14/202, at www.bundestag.de; Friedrich Merz, *Plenarprotokoll Deutscher Bundestag*, 14/202, at www.bundestag.de; Gerhard Schröder, *Plenarprotokoll Deutscher Bundestag*, 14/202, at www.bundestag.de; 'Scharping fordert weltweite Solidarität gegen den Terror', *Die Welt*, 4 October 2001, p. 2; 'Wo stehen die Bundestagsparteien?', *Die Welt*, 9 October 2001. The perception of a difference between German and American concepts about crisis management was not born with *Operation Enduring Freedom*. Most of the points brought up in the Bundestag debates over the German contribution in Afghanistan had been raised earlier by a range of German politicians, analysts, and commentators. See for example Egon Bahr, 'Ein Protektorat wird selbstständlich', *Die Zeit*, 23/2000, pp. 6–7; Ernst Otto Czempiel, 'Seltsame Stille', *Die Zeit*, 14/1999; Daniel Cohn-Bendit, 'Wir werden die Welt verbessern', *Die Zeit*, 50/2000; Gernot Erler, *Die Zeit*, 11/2001; Joschka Fischer, Speech to the Council of Foreign Relations, New York, 5 November 1999; Josef Joffe, 'Weltmacht USA', *Die Zeit*,

09/2001; Herbert Kremp, 'Wir brauchen belebenden deutschen Eigenwillen', *Die Welt*, 29 May 2000, p. 5; Helmut Schmidt, 'Die NATO gehört nicht Amerika', *Die Zeit*, 17/1999; Gerhard Schröder, 'Deutsche Russlandpolitik – europäische Ostpolitik', *Die Zeit* 15/2001; Karsten D. Voigt, *The Discussion of a European Security and Defence Policy: Labor Pains of a New Atlanticism*, www.auswaertiges-amt.de.

25 In the immediate aftermath of the attacks on the US, German public opinion, according to an EMNID survey, approved of full German support, including military support, for the US: 65 per cent favoured full German support, 27 per cent rejected a military contribution. By the time of the vote in the Bundestag, however, public support had dropped somewhat and surveys showed a majority against a German military participation. EMNID survey reprinted in *Die Welt*, 15 October 2001.

26 Gernot Erler, *Plenarprotokoll Deutscher Bundestag*, 14/190, at www.bundestag.de; 'Fischer warnt vor Krieg der Zivilisationen', *Die Welt*, 16 October 2001; Wolfgang Gerhardt, *Plenarprotokoll Deutscher Bundestag* 14/184, p. 18184; Joffe, 'Feldzug gegen Unbekannt'; Klaus Kinkel, *Plenarprotokoll Deutscher Bundestag* 14/190, at www.bundestag.de; Berthold Kohler, 'In Reserve', *Frankfurter Allgemeine Zeitung*, 9 October 2001, p. 1; Fritz Kuhn, interview with *Die Welt*, 18 November 2001; Johannes Rau, 'Wir müssen den Terrorismus bekämpfen', *Die Welt*, 15 October 2001; Rudolf Scharping, interview with *Die Zeit*, 15 September 2001; Christian Schmidt, *Plenarprotokoll Deutscher Bundestag* 14/190, at www.bundestag.de; Tina Stadlmeyer, 'Grüne stimmen für Militäreinsätze', *Financial Times Deutschland*, 8 October 2001, p. 12; Theo Sommer, 'Allein ist der Starke hilflos', *Die Zeit*, 66/2001; Theo Sommer, 'Wir trauern mit', *Die Zeit*, 38/2001; Peter Struck, *Plenarprotokoll Deutscher Bundestag*, 14/202, at www.bundestag.de.

27 'Fischer warnt vor Krieg der Zivilisationen', *Die Welt*, 16 October 2001; Klaus Kinkel (FDP), *Plenarprotokoll Deutscher Bundestag*, 14/190, 27 September 2001, at www.bundestag.de; Karl Lamers, 'Schwarze Löcher in der Weltpolitik müssen verschwinden', *Financial Times Deutschland*, 8 October 2001, p. 15; Johannes Rau, 'Wir müssen den Terrorismus bekämpfen', *Die Welt*, 15 October 2001; Rudolf Scharping, interview with *Die Zeit*, 15 September 2001; Tina Stadlmeyer, 'Grüne stimmen für Militäreinsätze', *Financial Times Deutschland*, 8 October 2001, p. 12.

28 Joschka Fischer, intervention during debate in the Bundestag, 26 September 2001, reprinted in *Bulletin*, No. 64–2, 2001; Kerstin Müller, *Plenarprotokoll Deutscher Bundestag*, 14/202, at www.bundestag.de; Gerhard Schröder, *Plenarprotokoll Deutscher Bundestag*, 14/202, at www.bundestag.de; Peter Struck, *Plenarprotokoll Deutscher Bundestag*, 14/202, at www.bundestag.de; Heidemarie Wieczorek-Zeul, *Plenarprotokoll Deutscher Bundestag*, 14/202, at www.bundestag.de.

29 Wolfgang Gerhardt, *Plenarprotokoll Deutscher Bundestag*, 14/202, at www.bundestag.de. See also Jochen Buchsteiner, 'Three Green Parliamentarians in George Bush's Court', *Frankfurter Allgemeine Zeitung*, 9 October 2001, p. 2; 'Grüne-Spitze unterstützt US-Angriff auf Afghanistan', *Die Welt*, 9 October 2001; 'Ja zum Kriegseinsatz spaltet grüne Basis', *Frankfurter Allgemeine Sonntagszeitung*, 18 November 2001, pp. 1–2.

30 See Anlage 6, *Plenarprotokoll Deutscher Bundestag*, 14/202, at www.bundestag.de; Steffi Lemke, *Plenarprotokoll Deutscher Bundestag*, 14/202, at www.bundestag.de; Rüdiger Veit, declaration on behalf of 15 SPD members of the Bundestag, *Plenarprotokoll Deutscher Bundestag*, 14/202, at www.bundestag.de.

31 For voting results, see *Plenarprotokoll Deutscher Bundestag*, 14/202, at www.bundestag.de. For Conservative reactions see Anlage 6, *Plenarprotokoll Deutscher Bundestag*, 14/202, at www.bundestag.de.

32 Gerhard Schröder, 'Rede von Bundeskanzler Gerhard Schröder zum Wahlkampfauftakt', 5 August 2002, Hannover, (Opernplatz), p. 8, at www.spd.de/servlet/PB/show/1019520/ Schr%F6der%20Rede%20WahlkampfauftaktHannover.doc (accessed on 8 February 2005).

33 Szabo, *Parting Ways*, p. 23.
34 Szabo, *Parting Ways*, pp. 23, 137.
35 Piotr Buras and Kerry Longhurst, 'The Berlin Republic, Iraq, and the Use of Force', *European Security*, 13:3 (2004), pp. 242–243.
36 'Hundertjähriges Chaos', interview with Antje Vollmer (Greens), *Die Zeit*, 05/2003; 'Irak: Union wirft Regierung Täuschungsmanöver vor', *Die Welt*, 23 December 2002; 'Krieg und Wahlkampf', *Die Welt*, 21 December 2002; 'Schröder hat Europa gespalten', interview with Edmund Stoiber (CSU/CDU), *Die Zeit*, 14/2003; Daniel Friedrich Sturm, 'Schäuble fordert zu Irak-politik klaren Positionen im Sicherheitsrat', *Die Welt*, 3 January 2003.
37 'German Role in Afghanistan Gains US Praise', *Germany Info*, 11 August 2003, at www.germany-info.org/relaunch/politics/new/pol_isaf_nato.html (accessed on 21 December 2004).
38 Nikolaus Blome and Torsten Krauel, 'Gerhard und George', *Die Welt*, 26 February 2004; 'Die Krise, die Europa eint', interview with Gerhard Schröder, *Die Zeit*, 14/2003; John Vincour, 'Berlin Says Europeans Need Close Bond to US', *International Herald Tribune*, 17 July 2004; Hubert Wetzel, 'Bush und Schröder wägen Interessen ab', *Financial Times Deutschland*, 25 February 2004.
39 Peter Struck (Minister of Defence), *Plenarprotokoll Deutscher Bundestag. Stenographischer Bericht*, 51. Sitzung, Berlin, 18 June 2003, p.2; Joschka Fischer (Minister of Foreign Affairs), *Plenarprotokoll Deutscher Bundestag. Stenographischer Bericht*, 51. Sitzung, Berlin, 18 June 2003, p. 9; Andreas Weigel (SPD), *Plenarprotokoll Deutscher Bundestag. Stenographischer Bericht*, 51. Sitzung, Berlin, 18 June 2003, p. 15.
40 Petra Pau (PDS), *Plenarprotokoll Deutscher Bundestag. Stenographischer Bericht*, 51. Sitzung, Berlin, 18 June 2003, p, 19.
41 Christian Schmidt (CDU/CSU), *Plenarprotokoll Deutscher Bundestag. Stenographischer Bericht*, 51. Sitzung, Berlin, 18 June 2003, p. 24.
42 *National Strategy for Combating Terrorism*, The White House, Washington, DC, February 2003; *The National Security Strategy of the United States*, Washington, DC, The White House, September 2002.
43 *A Secure Europe in a Better World: European Security Strategy*. Document proposed by Javier Solana and adopted by the Heads of State and Government at the European Council in Brussels on 12 December 2003, p. 9.
44 *A More Secure World: Our Shared Responsibility*. Report of the Secretary-General's High-Level Panel on Threats, Challenges and Change (New York: United Nations, 2004).
45 *A Secure Europe in a Better World*, p. 11.
46 *A More Secure World*, pp. 1–3.
47 *A More Secure World*, p. 64.
48 Ken Menkhaus, 'The Security Paradox of Failed States', *National Strategy Forum Review*, 12:3 (Spring 2003); Ulrich Schneckener, *Transnationale Terroristen als Profiteure fragiler Staatlichkeit*, Berlin: SWP-Studie, Stiftung Wissenschaft und Politik, Deutsches Institut für Internationale Politik und Sicherheit, May 2004.
49 Auslandseinsätze – aktuelle Zahlen der im Ausland eingesetzten Soldaten, at www.bundeswehr.de/forces/einsatzzahlen.php (accessed on 8 December 2004).

PART III

The Bundeswehr: willing and able?

Over the decade that followed unification, German politicians became willing to engage German military might in international crisis management – provided Germany's partners were involved and the intervention served a clear humanitarian purpose. A fundamental redefinition of Germany's international military role had thus taken place. Part III of this book turns to the instrument for carrying out Germany's new policy – the Bundeswehr. It analyses whether the German armed forces were willing and able to engage in international crisis management, and how German soldiers approached the task.

Chapter 6 analyses how German soldiers, despite increased risk to life and limb, remarkably quickly came to accept the new international tasks and how they were willing to work as part of a multinational military coalition as required in out-of-area operations. It also looks at the approach of German soldiers to the new tasks and points to the distinctly civilised cast of the Bundeswehr's international efforts.

Chapter 7 looks at how the Bundeswehr, which throughout the 1990s remained structured and equipped for territorial defence, struggled to dispatch and sustain ever greater number of troops abroad. While pointing to problems arising from the current composition and funding of the Bundeswehr, the chapter explains how Germany is in the midst of implementing a military reform that will enhance the ability to participate in international crisis management.

6

The Bundeswehr: a force for good?

Introduction

The Gulf War and the break-up of Yugoslavia shattered the German centre left's belief in a world progressing towards pacific settlement of conflicts and peaceful coexistence within and among nations. The end of the Cold War did not herald less violent conflict. On the contrary, it brought more. In parallel, the Bundeswehr's personnel experienced how the disappearance of the external enemy did not decrease their professional risk. On the contrary, it seemed to increase it. Just as the existential threat to Germany vanished, German soldiers had to come to terms with deployments in distant conflicts with no evident impact on the life and welfare of Germans. Initially, some balked.

This chapter tells the story of how an improved public image – the image of a civilised and internationalist Bundeswehr – nevertheless prompted a quick adaptation to the new tasks. It also shows how this image, though fashioned and promoted by political entrepreneurs eager to make out-of-area engagements acceptable to the German left, actually to a large extent corresponded to the culture and approach of deployed German units.

From reluctant warriors to content peace keepers

The Bundeswehr was conceived as a passive instrument of German foreign and security policy. Rather than engaging in actual war fighting, its Cold War task was to help maintain the delicate balance of nuclear deterrence – to be ready to fight in order not to have to fight. As the Cold War remained 'cold' in Europe the Bundeswehr in effect was an army that never knew anything but peace. Thus, the prospect of actual fighting, wounding, or death was not imminent in the day-to-day life of German armed forces.[1] But as Germany's role in international crisis management increased during the 1990s, this ceased to be the case.

As argued in Chapter 2, a handful of the Bundeswehr's top leaders had been among the original proponents of an extended German role in international security. Geostrategic developments, international loyalties, and the logic of institutional self-preservation had prompted them to lobby quietly for this extension. But the new international role was met with scepticism from the ranks. As the Kohl government in 1991 prepared to dispatch German elements of NATO's ACE Mobile Force to Turkey – a NATO member – some soldiers refused the assignment, arguing that they had pledged to defend Germany, but not to be deployed in far-flung trouble spots.[2]

A debate ensued within the armed forces over the geographical extension of the duties entailed in the oath of military service. Particularly officers of the older generation leaned to a restrictive interpretation of the pledge to 'faithfully serve the Federal Republic of Germany, and bravely defend the rights and freedoms of the German people'. The political controversy surrounding out-of-area deployment also dampened the enthusiasm of many officers within a military organisation where the primacy of the political system is normally strictly observed. Indeed, as the political skirmishes grew less acrimonious and the Constitutional Court in 1994 gave its blessing to out-of-area deployments, open resistance to the new mandate receded.[3]

In 1995, the Institute of Social Science of the Bundeswehr (SOWI) surveyed the opinion of 1,200 professional soldiers and longer-serving volunteers, deployable in international missions, on the issue of out-of-area deployment in UN-mandated missions (Table 6.1).[4]

The survey indicated that a majority of German soldiers had accepted the

Table 6.1 Percentage willingness within different Bundeswehr ranks to accept international deployment in UN-mandated missions

	Officer cadet	NCO[a]	Senior NCO or NCO specialist	Lieutenant	Captain	Field grade officer (Major–Colonel)	Average
Willing to accept OOA deployment	77	56	46	51	73	65	54
Only peacekeeping missions	8	28	36	15	7	10	27
Not willing	1	5	4	4	1	5	4
Depends[b]	14	11	14	31	19	20	15

Source: G. M. Meyer and S. Collmer, *Zum UN-Einsatz bereit? Bundeswehrsoldaten und ihr neuer Auftrag* (Sozialwissenschaftliches Institut der Bundeswehr: Wiesbaden, 1997).
Notes: [a] NCO = Non-Commissioned Officer. [b] The respondent in this category made their consent conditional on one or more factors such as a clear mandate and time frame, public support, a multinational framework, or personal conviction of the rightness of the mission.

new mandate. Only 4 per cent were not willing to be deployed internationally while more than 50 per cent indicated that they were. However, almost one-third of the respondents in 1995 insisted on a distinction between peacekeeping missions and other international missions such as peace enforcement or combat missions. They were willing to participate in the former, but not the latter.

On the surface, this might appear as a major obstacle to Germany's participation in out-of-area deployments. It became increasingly clear during the 1990s that the line between peacekeeping and peace enforcement could be difficult to draw. To permit flexibility in coping with fluid and unpredictable environments, peacekeeping forces from UNOSOM II in Somalia to *Operation Artemis* in Congo were equipped with robust mandates under Chapter VII of the UN Charter – mandates permitting the peace keepers to use force if necessary to protect themselves, their mission, or third parties. By the mid-1990s one-third of the German soldiers surveyed in effect indicated that they were unwilling to accept such missions. As Chapter 7 shows, the Bundeswehr did struggle with personnel shortcomings in certain areas critical to international force projection during the latter half of the 1990s.

The SOWI survey, however, also revealed a generational trend, suggesting that the number of soldiers insisting on a clear distinction between peacekeeping and peace enforcement was set to decline. Among the young officer cadets and captains – the next generation of field grade and staff officers – only between 7 and 8 per cent insisted on a distinction between peacekeeping and other international crisis management operations and less than 1 per cent were unwilling to accept international deployment.

Overall, the survey depicted a Bundeswehr that was, by the mid-1990s, already set to come to terms with the transformation from territorial defence to out-of-area crisis management – findings that were confirmed by the observations and impressions of military and educational leaders.[5]

In light of the increased risk to the life and limb of German soldiers, this quick adaptation may at first sight appear surprising. Considered more closely, however, it becomes clear that on a number of accounts the new task entailed a welcome change. It improved the image of the armed forces both in Germany and abroad, and gave German soldiers a convincing new *raison d'être*.

A military identity crisis

In post-war Germany, the right of a modern nation-state to possess, not to say use, national armed forces was challenged to an extent that found no parallel in other European countries. The Bundeswehr was born amid the vocal protests of intellectuals, pacifists, and left-wingers and regarded with scepticism by the populace at large. Though most Germans gradually came to accept that Germany needed to contribute to the Western Alliance, it was an acceptance devoid of enthusiasm and even at the height of the Cold War, public and political indifference towards the armed forces was palpable. The yearly parliamentary debate on the military spending bill and the presentation of the report of the Wehrbeauftragte – the parliamentary ombudsman for military affairs – routinely generated tepid interest. But beyond that, it normally took a scandal, such as revelations of Nazi sympathies or right-wing extremism among the ranks, to generate broader political and public attention – and on these occasions, self-evidently, mostly negative attention.[6]

With the implosion of the Soviet threat the Bundeswehr lost its major *raison d'être*. German politicians from left to right came to perceive the stabilisation and rebuilding of East and Central Europe as the best possible investment in German security.[7] This called for economic assistance, political engagement, and help in building civil societies and democratic institutions – tasks in which the Bundeswehr had no role to play.[8]

Soon, voices from the left started questioning to what extent Germany needed armed forces at all. The Green party demanded the military budget cut to zero or transferred into a budget for conversion of military assets into civilian uses. The Bundeswehr, they argued, should be replaced by a civilian peace corps for fighting ecological and humanitarian disasters.[9] The ex-communists suggested that Germany should take the lead in total and global disarmament. Germany, it was claimed, needed neither foreign soldiers nor her own to protect her security.[10] The Social Democrats called for deep cuts in force numbers and some proposed to turn the German military into a militia of the Swiss kind. Between 1990 and 1991 the number of conscientious objectors jumped from 74,000 to 151,000 and eventually climbed to approximately 170,000 before stabilising. The defence budget, on the contrary, kept declining.[11]

In sum, the end of the Cold War faced national armed forces across the Western world with the question of how to re-define their role. But for the Bundeswehr, whose legitimacy was shakier in the first place, the lack of an external enemy posed a particularly great challenge. Under siege from the left, at the loss for a convincing role, and regarded with widespread indifference by the public and the political mainstream, a creeping identity crisis took hold within the Bundeswehr.[12]

A new *raison d'être* and an improved image

For German soldiers, the new international deployments brought a change for the better. In spite of the increased personal risk, many soldiers perceived peacekeeping as more rewarding than the Cold War task of deterrence. Before 1990, success could be measured only on a non-event – the absence of a Soviet attack. The new mandate, on the contrary, permitted the soldiers to see and feel immediate and concrete results of their efforts.[13] The tasks of de-escalating skirmishes between hostile groups, ensuring the arrival of humanitarian aid, and contributing to civilian reconstruction provided meaningful and rewarding experiences. When asked to explain their motivation for participating in UNOSOM II, IFOR, SFOR, and KFOR, 'making a difference' was the reason German soldiers most frequently gave.[14]

German soldiers also found their esteem growing among their NATO peers. Before the end of the Cold War, the Bundeswehr had been regarded as a 'soft' and inexperienced garrison army by some officers from allied armed forces with more field experience.[15] In the perception of German officers and commanders, this view changed during the 1990s as the performance of deployed German units permitted the Bundeswehr to prove itself as 'part of the team'.[16]

Furthermore, the interest of the domestic media exploded as the Bundeswehr, together with peace keepers from other nations, served in Somalia and ex-Yugoslavia. More than 400 journalists visited the 1,700 German soldiers deployed in Somalia. German IFOR, SFOR, and KFOR contingents enjoyed similar attention.[17]

Deployed units also received visits from community leaders, organisational representatives, and politicians, to the initial surprise and lasting delight of the soldiers, unfamiliar with such positive attention.[18] Towards the end of the 1990s the soldiers who had started out on the 1990s struggling to justify their existence enjoyed overwhelmingly positive press and an improved public image.[19]

The notions about the Bundeswehr, as expressed in the political discourse, also became markedly more positive. As the out-of-area debate intensified in the early 1990s, designations such as 'attack-force', 'intervention-force', and 'war-fighting force' – terms of highly negative connotations in Germany – became common currency.[20] In the wake of Srebrenica, however, things changed. A group of Conservative security experts successfully promoted the notion that the military could serve as a force for good, protecting unarmed civilians against aggressors and warmongers.[21]

This image was first introduced in the debate over Germany's contribution to IFOR where the government of Helmut Kohl, attempting to garner broad political support for the first engagement of German ground troops in Yugoslavia, took great effort to play down the military aspects of the mission. The expression 'deployment abroad' was discarded in favour of 'service for peace'. The German soldiers were characterised as 'soldiers for peace' and the German contribution to IFOR as an engagement for 'humanity, and solidarity'.[22] Social Democratic security experts, supportive of IFOR, were quick to pick up on the suggestion that the military could be a force for good. Echoing the Government, they pointed out that German soldiers were not sent to Yugoslavia to fight a war, but to protect the peace. IFOR was characterised as 'the police force of a global order based on peace and the rule of law'.[23]

The image of a civilised military was further honed in the debate over SFOR. German peace keepers were described by security experts from both ends of the political spectrum as politically well-informed, diplomatically skilful, and culturally sensitive.[24]

Eventually, sympathy grew even on the far left. When parliamentary speaker of the Greens, Jürgen Trittin, appeared among other demonstrators in 1998 waving 'soldiers are murderers' banners, he came under fire from his own party.[25] The parliamentary group introduced a resolution paying homage to the Bundeswehr for its 'service for peace' in ex-Yugoslavia and its efforts in rebuilding the civilian and social structures of the area.[26] The famous Tucholsky quote that 'soldiers are murderers', which had served as a rallying cry for German pacifists for years, was no longer acceptable.[27]

By the mid-1990s, calls for demolishing the Bundeswehr died down and politicians from left to right now almost competed to express their appreciation of the Bundeswehr's international 'engagement for peace and human rights'.[28] Germany's security elite had succeeded in defining an active of role for the Bundeswehr that did not smack of past militarism. Thus, whereas the existence of German armed forces used to remind the Germans of a collective trauma – the militarism of the past – or a collective nightmare – a Soviet attack and nuclear annihilation – the 1990s saw positive and progressive connotations take over.

In sum, the new international tasks of the Bundeswehr entailed an increased danger to German soldiers. Yet, those duties provided the Bundeswehr with a new convincing raison d'être and soon earned the Bundeswehr positive attention and recognition both at home and abroad. Already by the mid 1990s a majority among German soldiers had come to accept out-of-area deployments. The increased political willingness to engage in international crisis management was thus matched by a willingness within the armed forces to perform the new task.

The Bundeswehr: internationalist and civilised?

The question remains as to what extent the political image of an internationalist and civilised Bundeswehr matched the reality. This section looks at the attitude of the Bundeswehr personnel towards international cooperation, the next two subsections analyse the approach of deployed German units to see if the political image of 'civilised' peace keepers was accurate.

Internationalism and multinational military coalitions
International peacekeeping interventions in the 1990s were without exception carried out by multinational coalitions, among other things, to ensure their international legitimacy. For Germany, multinationalism was not just a political, but also a constitutional requirement, as established by the Constitutional Court in its 1994 ruling.[29]

The Bundeswehr was from the outset an alliance army. To heed concerns at home and abroad it was constructed as an organisation that could function only in an alliance framework. Moreover, numerous bi-national and multinational joint military ventures had, since the 1960s, made German armed forces the most integrated among the forces of all major states. The Danish–German LANDJUT was established in 1962, the French–German Brigade in 1988, the Eurocorps, composed by military units from Germany, France, Belgium, Spain, and Luxembourg, in 1992, a German–American and an American–German corps were established in 1993, a German–Dutch corps in 1995, and in 1999 LANDJUT was converted into a joint Danish–German–Polish corps. Only one Bundeswehr corps – the IV in Potsdam – was not by the end of the 1990s integrated in a multinational or bi-national corps.[30]

The notion of multinational military cooperation was thus not new to German soldiers. But until the end of the Cold War, military multinationalism had affected only a limited number of officers who served in integrated NATO staffs.[31] International peacekeeping forces – excepting the Franco-German brigade deployed as part of SFOR – did not involve a mixture of soldiers from different nations beneath the battalion level. The international deployments of the 1990s nevertheless entailed that more German soldiers and commanders than ever interacted with colleagues from the armed forces of partner countries on a daily basis. This placed higher demands on their ability to accommodate different military cultures and required further adaptation on part of the Bundeswehr.[32]

In the early 1990s some Bundeswehr leaders expressed concern that the democratic German military practices based on 'inner leadership' and 'citizen in uniform' would suffer under the pressure to harmonise within multinational units. Perceived differences between, for example, French and German military practices caused occasional friction. German peace keepers complained about what they experienced as a more formalistic and hierarchical French attitude, as well as French problems with the German concept of 'Auftragstaktik' – delegation tactics – according to which the commander indicated the goal but left the subordinate some room to determine the means.[33]

Nevertheless, toward the decade's end, most German field commanders were very favourable towards the concept of multinationality. Practical problems, they claimed, had proved surmountable by means of mutual goodwill and flexibility. It was also stressed how the presence of multinational units could actually enhance the effectiveness of peacekeeping by demonstrating the determination and unity of the international community to potential trouble makers. Simultaneously, German officers argued, it provided an example of how old enemies – Europe's major states – could overcome their past and turn antagonism into cooperation.[34]

Internationalism was not just an elite phenomenon. It prevailed throughout the Bundeswehr's ranks. A 1991 survey of the German personnel assigned to the Franco-German brigade revealed that 85 per cent of the soldiers, 82 per cent of the non-commissioned officers (NCOs), and 97 per cent of the field grade and staff officers evaluated the cooperation as a very positive thing. A 1997 survey of Bundeswehr personnel assigned to the Dutch–German corps indicated that 61 per cent of the soldiers, 86 per cent of the NCOs, and 84 per cent of the grade officers were very positive towards the common venture.[35]

Finally, the educational approach and daily practices of Bundeswehr institutions also reflected and promoted internationalism. The German defence academy in Hamburg hosted numerous foreign officers and actively sought to further international and intercultural understanding.[36]

In sum, regardless of occasional friction between the culture and approach of German armed forces and the armed forces of other countries, German soldiers were overwhelmingly positive towards multinationalism and willing to work as part of an international team, as required by the task of out-of-area crisis management. The political image of an internationalist Bundeswehr was not just a political construct or left-wing dream, but had a firm grounding in reality.

The Bundeswehr, reconstruction, and humanitarian efforts

The same was arguably true regarding the other part of the new political image of the Bundeswehr: the image of 'civilised' soldiers displaying empathy, diplomatic skills, democratic values, and engagement in civil and humanitarian activities. Throughout the 1990s, deployed German units without exception engaged extensively in both humanitarian and civilian tasks, supported by and in cooperation with non-governmental organisations (NGOs), the Ministry of Foreign Affairs, the Ministry of the Interior, the Ministry of Development Aid, and the Ministry of Economic Affairs.[37]

The German UNOSOM II field hospital treated more than 10,000 Somalis, and German medical personnel assisted local doctors in the hospitals of Belet Weyne with operations and ambulant treatment of local patients. The population was supplied with purified drinking water, wells were re-established, and irrigation and infrastructure improved.[38] In Bosnia-Herzegovina, German IFOR and SFOR soldiers rebuilt bridges and roads. In Kosovo, German soldiers assisted in reconstructing water supply and electricity systems, fire departments, and local hospitals. In cooperation with the United Nations High Commissioner for Refugees (UNHCR), Bundeswehr units distributed aid packages, reconstructed houses and apartments, and organised start-up help for local businesses.[39] In East Timor, civilians and locals were treated in the military hospital run by German soldiers. In Afghanistan, the Bundeswehr played a crucial role in creating, training, and equipping a local police force for Kabul. In cooperation with NGOs, German soldiers also engaged in reconstructing the social infrastructure of the city, making sure that schools were rebuilt and teachers hired and paid. In the North-Eastern part of Afghanistan, Germany was leading two so-called Provincial Reconstruction Teams (PRT) with the purpose of providing security and contributing to reconstruction.[40]

While military leaders stressed that the soldiers' primary task was to create a safe environment in which civilian organisations could go about the humanitarian aid work, they also pointed to the security pay-off from direct military engagement in reconstruction. Such an engagement, they contended, defused latent aggressions and discontent directed against the peace keepers.[41]

Testifying to the scope of the military's civilian and humanitarian engagement, a number of NGOs only half in jest started complaining that the Bundeswehr was driving them out of business. On a more serious note, it was also argued that blurring the line between military forces and civilian NGOs would endanger the latter by making them targets of forces resisting the international military engagement in a given area. Moreover, the reconstruction efforts of the Bundeswehr were criticised by the development community for being excessively focused on short term impact and insufficiently on long-term sustainability. As a sign that such concerns were being heeded, the Bundeswehr's PRTs in Afghanistan were constructed to grant civilian personnel a greater say and ensure a clear distinction between civilians and soldiers.[42]

Treading lightly: the approach of German peace keepers

'Creative, politically insightful, diplomatic, open minded and culturally sensitive': these may not be the first adjectives springing to the mind of an external observer when thinking about soldiering. Yet, this is how German military leaders described the ideal peace keeper – a description corresponding closely to the image of civilised soldiers that dominated the German political discourse throughout the late 1990s.[43]

There are no systematic comparative studies of the style of German, British, French, and American peacekeepers. Thus, strong conclusions about whether the German style was singular are not warranted. However, in the perception of a number of political–military elites in Berlin, Paris, and Washington, the Bundeswehr took an approach that differed from the approach of the forces of other big countries, particularly the US. German soldiers tended to be more communicative and responsive to the locals and they cultivated a less assertive and forceful style.[44]

It is also a fact, that when setting up the Bundeswehr's pre-deployment training programmes, modelling them on British and French pre-deployment programmes had been deliberately avoided. High-ranking military officials explained this choice as a consequence of not wishing to import what was perceived as 'a certain neo-colonial arrogance' and a 'somewhat trigger-happy approach'. Instead, the training and education programmes of Austria and Finland – two small countries with no colonial background, but extensive UN experience – served as an inspiration. The official goal was 'firm but friendly' peacekeeping, a non-offensive approach, and the treatment of local populations with consideration and respect.[45] Indeed, over the course of the 1990s there was not a single incident in which German peace keepers were being accused of excessive use of force even though the sensitivity and alertness towards transgressions were probably higher in German society than anywhere else due to the German history of excessive militarism.[46]

Up until 1998, Bundeswehr units were not deployed directly in high-tension areas. This might explain why German peace keepers apparently took a 'soft' approach. German units could afford to be friendly and had more time to engage in humanitarian and civilian activities because the hard-core military tasks were less demanding. Yet, the 'civilised' approach continued to characterise German peace keepers after they took over tasks and zones as demanding as those of British and French peace keepers in Bosnia-Herzegovina, Kosovo, and Kabul, Afghanistan.[47]

Seen against the backdrop of the peculiar post-war ethos and self-perception of German armed forces, it appears plausible that German soldiers should take a particularly non-forceful and civilised approach. As argued in Chapter 2, the founding fathers of the Bundeswehr deliberately sought to hedge against the return of excessive militarism and to exorcise the cult of the warrior from German military thinking. They were intent on resurrecting the armed forces without resurrecting the legacy of a 'state in the state'. When it came to military training, soldierly ideals, and culture, the effort to prevent the past from returning was given equal, if not more, attention than the Bundeswehr's efficiency as a military machine.[48]

The democratic and civilised values of the Bundeswehr were challenged on two different accounts over the 1990s: both instances, however, lead to a reconfirmation of these values. In 1997 a string of revelations regarding right-wing extremist incidents within the Bundeswehr placed a question mark over the military's the democratic and civilised values.[49] The Ministry of Defence immediately launched an action plan which entailed more political education of soldiers and conscripts, increased critical focus on German military history, and the hiring of external advisors to support military commanders in identifying and dealing with potential problems among their troops. Simultaneously, on the insistence of the Social Democrats and the Greens, the Bundestag's Defence Committee initiated an independent investigation, which ran from January through June 1998.

The result of the inquiry eventually led politicians from across the political spectrum to declare their confidence in the democratic culture and constitutional allegiance of the Bundeswehr.[50] Some politicians charged that 'inner leadership' had been neglected by the Conservative government, permitting 'pockets' of people of right-wing views to establish themselves in the military. But by early 1998 no German politician, excepting members of the PDS, seriously questioned the full democratic commitment of the German military leadership or suspected the army of being a breeding ground for right-wing extremism.[51]

This conclusion is confirmed by looking at table 6.2, showing the number of Bundeswehr right-wing extremist incidents – use or display of right-wing symbols, language, or propaganda, and in a few cases physical violence – reported to or disclosed by the Wehrbeauftragte over the latter half of the 1990s.[52]

Table 6.2 also shows the rank and number of soldiers involved in right-wing incidents between 1996 and 2000. It illustrates how the overwhelming majority

Table 6.2 Number of soldiers from different ranks within the Bundeswehr involved in right-wing extremist incidents, 1994–2000

	1996	1997	1998	1999	2000
Total number of soldiers involved	44	229	240	133	135
Number of conscripts and NCOs[a]	32	214	216	111	114
Number of officers	12	13	20	11	19
Number of field grade officers	0	2	4	1	2

Source: *Jahresbericht 1997 der Wehrbeauftragte des Deutschen Bundestages, 1990, 1996, 1997, 1998, 1999, 2000.*
Note: [a] NCO = Non-Commissioned Officer.

of the soldiers involved were from the lower ranks. According to the *Bundesamt für Verfassungsschutz* – the German office for protection of the Constitution – the number of people inclining towards right-wing extremist views in German society at large doubled between 1991 and 1999. Societal trends almost automatically show up within the Bundeswehr due to the yearly intake of conscripts.[53] Thus, arguably, the increased number of incidents beginning in 1997 reflected a general societal trend and not a phenomenon originating in the Bundeswehr. Moreover, within an organisation of almost 300,000 military personnel, the percentage involved in wrongdoing remains small, even with the increase that came in 1997.

Yet, the official civilised self-perception of German armed forces was also challenged on a different front during the 1990s. Within the Bundeswehr, the new era and the new task of international crisis management made the old debate about the content of soldiering and the meaning of 'inner leadership' flare up.[54] Harking back to the conservative and traditionalist officers who during the 1950s and 1960s had resisted the reforms conceived by the Himmerod group, some officers disputed the 1990s political image of civilised peace keepers. The requirements of military efficiency in the post-Cold War geo-strategic environment, they argued, posed limits to the desirable level of democratisation and civilisation within the armed forces. The image of an intellectually sophisticated and interculturally sensitive soldier was out of touch with reality. This kind of soldier, it was charged, would not be able to prevail over unscrupulous warlords and armed criminals in messy and unpredictable crises areas. To permit the Bundeswehr to fill its new role, the focus of training ought to be instead on combat and fighting power and on classical soldierly virtues such as courage, comradeship, and character.[55]

The traditionalists eventually proved to be in the minority. 'Inner leadership' and 'citizen in uniform' were reconfirmed in all the major studies and documents by the German security establishment between 1991 and 2003.[56] The notion that the new tasks required Germany to alter the culture of German armed forces was rejected. On the contrary, it was emphasised how effective crisis management called for more than combat power and technical proficiency and how the ideals of the founding fathers of the Bundeswehr were more in tune with the requirements of the day than ever.[57] These ideals were reflected in the

Bundeswehr's educational focus and arguably confirmed by the attitude and feedback of German officers: political education and information occupied a central space in the pre-deployment courses for German peace keepers, a focus that was welcomed and appreciated by the soldiers.[58]

In sum, lacking any comprehensive studies, the evidence about the style of German peace keepers is necessarily incomplete and does not warrant any firm conclusions. However, seen against the background of the post-war ethos, self-perception, and educational concepts of the Bundeswehr it seems plausible that German soldiers at large should take a non-offensive and 'civilised' approach to military crisis management. The cult of the warrior was weak or absent within the Bundeswehr and the focus on political and historical education and democratic values strong. To complement this apparently non-offensive style, deployed German units also engaged extensively in humanitarian and civilian tasks, and engagement which, in the perception of German commanders, enhanced the effectiveness and safety of German peace keepers.

Summary

Over the course of the 1990s a political majority came to accept German participation in out-of-area crisis management. In spite of some initial scepticism, Bundeswehr personnel soon accepted the new international tasks. With those duties, German soldiers found a new convincing *raison d'être*, together with increased popularity both at home and abroad. Serving in an organisation permeated by internationalist attitudes, German soldiers also proved willing to work as part of an international military coalition, as required in out-of-area deployments.

Towards the mid-1990s, political notions about the Bundeswehr started changing and traditionally sceptical and negative attitudes gave way to the image of a 'civilised soldier' engaged for peace and human rights in the world's trouble spots. The political image of a civilised military apparently corresponded to the actual approach and self-perception of German peace keepers. The civilised ethos that had become ingrained over the post-war era and educational concepts with a strong emphasis on political education arguably inclined Germans to a civilised and non-offensive style.

Notes

1 In 1970, the Social Democratic defence minister – Helmut Schmidt – with the 1970 *White Book* found it necessary to remind the soldiers that a situation in which they would have to do what they were trained to do – fight – could not be completely excluded: 'Even in the age of deterrence the possibility cannot be excluded that the soldier must fight.' *Weißbuch 1970*, Bundesministerium der Verteidigung, Bonn. See also Michael Steger-de Wiljes, professional Bundeswehr soldier, quoted in Andreas Molitor, Sabine Rückert,

Stefan Willeke, Stefan Merx, and Michael Schwellen, 'Aus Dienst wird Ernst', *Die Zeit*, 15/1999.

2 *Legitimitätsfragen bei Auslandseinsätze der Bundeswehr*, Zentrum Innere Führung, Koblenz, Arbeitspapier, 3/1996, p. 10; General Peter Goebel (ed.), *Von Kambodscha bis Kosovo: Auslandseinsätze der Bundeswehr* (Frankfurt am Main: Report Verlag, 2000), p. 14.

3 *Legitimationsfragen bei Auslandseinsätze der Bundeswehr*, Arbeitspapier, 3/1996, Zentrum Innere Führung, Koblenz; Major General Hans-Christian Beck, *Anforderungen an die Erziehung in den Streitkräften vor dem Hintergrund ihrer aktuellen und künftigen Aufgaben*, Zentrum Innere Führung, Koblenz, April 1999, p. 9; Goebel, *Von Kambodscha bis Kosovo*, p. 18; General Harald Kujat, interview in *Der Tagesspiegel*, 26 November 2000; General Klaus Naumann, 'Die Bundeswehr steht für Frieden und Freiheit', *Europäische Sicherheit*, 1/1996; Rolf Wenzel (Chairman of German Soldiers' Union), interview with Südwestfunk, 22 April 1993, 1.20 p.m. Helmut Willmann, cited in 'Heeresinspekteur warnt vor Kürzungen', *Die Welt*, 19 June 1997.

4 Longer-serving volunteers were conscripts voluntarily prolonging their term of service with thirteen months to a total of twenty-three months. In contrast to conscripts serving a regular term, they were deployable in international operations. There are no surveys indicating the willingness of officers to accept deployment in non-UN-mandated missions. By 2000 most officers seemed to be of the opinion that if a mission was carried out by a multinational coalition of states and if it had the approval of the Bundestag, it was to be considered a legitimate mission. Author's interview, 'Forum Bundeswehr und Gesellschaft', Berlin, October 2001 and Defence Academy of the Bundeswehr, Hamburg, October, 2001.

5 Major General Hans-Christian Beck, *Identität und Professionalität des deutschen Soldaten*, Zentrum Innere Führung, Koblenz, 1999, p. 27; Helmut Jermer, 'Innere Führung – auf den Punkt gebracht', in Oskar Hoffmann and Andreas Prüfert, *Innere Führung 2000* (Baden-Baden: Nomos Verlagsgesellschaft, 2001), p. 51; Rüdiger Moniac, 'Der Kampfeinsatz gehört zum neuen Berufsalltag', *Die Welt*, 22 September 1998; Gero von Randow and Constanze Stelzenmüller, 'Zivis fürs Grobe', *Die Zeit*, 12/2000; Rolf Wenzel, interview with SüdWestFunk, 22 April 1993, 1.20 p.m.

6 Hans Rattinger, 'The Federal Republic of Germany: Much Ado About (Almost) Nothing', in Gregory Flynn and Hans Rattinger (eds), *The Public and Atlantic Defense* (London: Rowman & Allanheld, 1985), p. 108.

7 Detlef Bald, *Militär und Gesellschaft 1945–1990* (Baden-Baden: Nomos Verlagsgesellschaft, 1994), pp. 114–115; Katrin Fuchs, *Die Architektur einer neuen europäischen Sicherheitsordnung*, press release, 25 September 1991; Hans-Dietrich Genscher, 'Kontinuität und Wandel: Moderne Außenpolitik in der Perspektive 2000', in Hans-Dietrich Genscher (ed.), *Nach vorn gedacht: Perspektiven deutscher Außenpolitik* (Bonn: Bonn aktuell, 1987), p. 9; Klaus Kinkel, 'Die Außenpolitik der Bundesrepublik Deutschland nach der Wiedervereinigung', *Europäische Sicherheit*, 1/1993, p. 14; *Weißbuch 1994*, Bundesministerium der Verteidigung, Bonn, p. 39.

8 Franz H.U. Borkenhagen, *Außenpolitische Interessen Deutschlands: Rolle und Aufgabe der Bundeswehr* (Bonn: Bouvier Verlag, 1997), p. 200; Dieter Dettke, 'Civil Foreign Policy: German Domestic Constraints and New Security Arrangements in Europe', in Beverly Crawford (ed.), *The Future of European Security*, University of California Center for German and European Studies, University of California at Berkeley, Research Series, No. 84, 1992, pp. 251, 253; Volker Rühe, speech to the Rheinisch-Westfälischen Handwerkerbundes, 12 January 1993, reprinted in *Bulletin*, No. 6, 18 January 1993.

9 Angelika Beer, 'Antimilitärische Verständnis der Grünen', *Europäische Sicherheit*, 4/1996, p. 6; Vera Wollenberger, *Plenarprotokoll Deutscher Bundestag*, 12/41, p. 3366; Berthold Meyer and Roberto Zadra, *Die Grünen und List Verdi – Sicherheitspolitische Alternativen für Europa?* (Munich/Hamburg: Lit. Verlag, 1992).

10 Decision of the 2nd PDS party convention, PDS Pressedienst, 12 July 1991, p. 11.
11 Borkenhagen, *Außenpolitische Interessen Deutschlands*, p. 200; SPD, *Stellungnahme der Kommission Sicherheitspolitik beim SPD-Parteivorstand zur sicherheitspolitischen Verantwortung der Bundesrepublik Deutschland*, press release, 17 May 1991; Dieter Heisterman (SPD), *Plenarprotokoll deutscher Bundestag*, 12/41, p. 3362. See Chapter 7 for more details on the defence budget.
12 Alfred Biehle (Wehrbeauftragter), *Plenarprotokoll Deutscher Bundestag* 12/41, p. 336, Goebel, *Von Kambodscha bis Kosovo*, p. 18; Volker Rühe, 'Abschluss der humanitären Hilfsaktion für Somalia', *Bulletin*, 19, 25 March 1993; Rolf Wenzel (Chairman of the German Solders' Union), interview with Südwestfunk, 22 April 1993, 1.20 p.m.
13 Frank Buchholz, 'Ernstfall Frieden – Ernstfall Krieg', in Paul Klein and Andreas Prüfert, *Militärische Ausbildung Heute und in der Zukunft* (Baden-Baden: Nomos Verlagsgesellschaft, 1994), p. 49; General Klaus Naumann, *Die Bundeswehr in einer Welt im Umbruch* (Berlin, 1994), p. 68.
14 Beck, *Identität und Professionalität des deutschen Soldaten*, p. 28; Hans-Otto Budde (Commander of the French–German SFOR brigade), 'Gleiche Rechte und Pflichten – Die deutsche Beteiligung an SFOR', in General Peter Goebel (ed.), *Vom Kambodscha bis Kosovo: Auslandseinsätze der Bundeswehr* (Frankfurt am Main: Report Verlag, 2000), p. 173; Friedrich W. Riechmann (Commander of the German IFOR contingent), 'Von Kroatien in die "Box"', in Peter Goebel (ed.), *Vom Kambodscha bis Kosovo: Auslandseinsätze der Bundeswehr* (Frankfurt am Main, Report Verlag, 2000), p. 163.
15 Author's interviews, Ifri, Paris, July 2001, and 'Forum Bundeswehr und Gesellschaft', Berlin, October 2001. See also Beverly Crawford and Jost Halfmann, 'Domestic Politics and International Change: Germany's Role in Europe's Security Future', in Beverly Crawford (ed.), *The Future of European Security*, University of California Center for German and European Studies, University of California at Berkeley, Research Series, No. 4, 1992, p. 217; Molitor, Rückert, Willeke, Merx, and Schwellen, 'Aus Dienst wird Ernst'; Craig Whitney, 'Gulf Fighting Shatters Europeans' Fragile Unity', *New York Times*, 25 January 1991, p. A7.
16 Budde, 'Gleiche Rechte und Pflichten', p. 168; Dieter Leder (Commander of a German minesweeping unit in the Gulf in 1990–91), 'Internationale Minenräumoperationen im Arabischen Golf', in General Peter Goebel (ed.), *Vom Kambodscha bis Kosovo: Auslandseinsätze der Bundeswehr* (Frankfurt am Main: Report Verlag, 2000), p. 43; Riechmann, 'Von Kroatien in die "Box"', p. 165.
17 Holger Kammerhoff (Commander of the German UNOSOM II contingent), 'Unter Blauhelm am Horn von Afrika', in General Peter Goebel (ed.), *Vom Kambodscha bis Kosovo: Auslandseinsätze der Bundeswehr* (Frankfurt am Main: Report Verlag, 2000), p. 133.
18 Budde, 'Gleiche Rechte und Pflichten – Die deutsche Beteiligung an SFOR', p. 172; Riechmann, 'Von Kroatien in die "Box"', p. 165.
19 Constanze Stelzenmüller, 'Die Reform-Armee', *Die Zeit*, 20/2000. See also Molitor, Rückert, Willeke, Merx, and Schwellen, 'Aus Dienst wird Ernst'; Randow and Stelzenmüller, 'Zivis fürs Grobe'; Peter Schneider, 'Krieg und Frieden: Die Lehren von Sarajevo', *Die Zeit*, 18 June 1998; Michael Schwellen, 'Hilfe, die Helfer sind gekommen', *Die Zeit*, 19/1999.
20 Ulrich Briefs, *Plenarprotokoll Deutscher Bundestag*, 240/12, p. 21205; Gregor Gysi, *Plenarprotokoll Deutscher Bundestag*, 13/76, 1995, p. 6649; See also debate in the Bundestag, 15 January 1993, *Plenarprotokoll Deutscher Bundestag*, 12/132, 12/101.
21 This is evident in the interventions of MdBs from all parties, excepting the PDS, in Bundestag debates on security policy or military matters occurring towards the late 1990s. See, for example, *Plenarprotokoll Deutscher Bundestag*, 14/58, pp. 5225–5235 and *Plenarprotokoll Deutscher Bundestag* 13/242, especially pp. 22428–22429 and p. 22431.

22 Ulrich Irmer, *Plenarprotokoll Deutscher Bundestag* 13/76, p. 6644. See also Klaus Kinkel, press release, Bundes Presse Amt, 26 June 1995; Klaus Kinkel, *Deutscher Bundestag Plenarprotokoll*, 13/242, p. 22421; Klaus Kinkel, *Plenarprotokoll Deutscher Bundestag*, 13/74, p. 6429; Friedbert Pflüger, *Plenarprotokoll Deutscher Bundestag*, 13/76, p. 6663; Volker Rühe, *Plenarprotokoll Deutscher Bundestag*, 13/74, p. 6445; Volker Rühe, interview with ADR, 30 November 1995, reprinted in *Stichworte zur Sicherheitspolitik*, 12/1995, p. 25; Volker Rühe, interview with *Bild am Sonntag*, 2 July 1995; Rudolf Seiters and Thomas Kossendey (CDU/CSU), *Deutscher Bundestag Plenarprotokoll*, 13/74, pp. 6437, 6465. As the Bundeswehr's Inspector General, Klaus Naumann, publicly insisted that the German IFOR soldiers were deployed in a 'Kampfauftrag' (in a combat mission) he was forced to resign by Defence Minister Volker Rühe. Klaus Naumann's successor, Hartmut Bagger, before taking up his post in February 1996 stressed that IFOR was '*a priori* a *no* combat mission'. Hartmut Bagger, Inspector General of the Bundeswehr, interview with *Außenpolitik*, 19 December 1995, reprinted in *Stichworte zur Sicherheitspolitik*, 12/1995, pp. 21–22.

23 Rudolf Scharping, *Plenarprotokoll Deutscher Bundestag*, 13/76, p. 6634; Günter Verheugen, *Plenarprotokoll Deutscher Bundestag*, 13/76, p. 6666; Karsten Voigt, *Plenarprotokoll Deutscher Bundestag*, 13/74, p. 6448.

24 Gerd Höfer, SPD, *Plenarprotokoll Deutscher Bundestag*, 14/58, p. 5232; Bundespresident Johannes Rau, speech at the 38th Kommandeurtagung der Bundeswehr, Leipzig, 14 November 2000, reprinted in *Bulletin*, No. 76–1, 14 November 2000; Walter Kolbow, *Plenarprotokoll Deutscher Bundestag*, 13/242, p. 22445; Volker Rühe (CDU/CSU), *Plenarprotokoll Deutscher Bundestag*, 13/242, p. 22435; Rudolf Scharping, interview with *Die Zeit*, 'Ein sanfter Mann fürs Militär', *Die Zeit*, 13/1999; Gerhard Schröder, 'Weil wir Deutschlands Kraft vertrauen', Government Declaration to the Bundestag, 10 November 1998, reprinted in *Bulletin*, 11 November 1998; Gerhard Schröder, speech in Berlin, 23 May 2000, reprinted in *Bulletin*, No. 30–1, 26 May 2000; Günter Verheugen, *Plenarprotokoll Deutscher Bundestag*, 13/242, p. 22423.

25 Rüdiger Moniac, 'Grünen streiten über Verhältnis zum Militär', *Die Welt*, 20 June 1998.

26 See *Plenarprotokoll Deutscher Bundestag*, 13/242, especially p. 22428. For Green MdBs denouncing Trittin's behaviour, see pp. 22428–22429, 22431.

27 Joschka Fischer, *Plenarprotokoll Deutscher Bundestag*, 13/76, p. 6657; Werner Schulz, *Plenarprotokoll Deutscher Bundestag*, 13/242, p. 22437.

28 See interventions from across the political spectrum, *Plenarprotokoll Deutscher Bundestag*, 14/58, pp. 5225–5235.

29 François Heisbourg, *Emerging European Power Projection Capabilities*, GCSP-RAND Workshop Paper, Geneva, 15-16 July 1999, p. 6, available at Columbia International Affairs Online, www.ciaonet.org/conf/hef01/; *The Strategic Defence Review White Paper*, UK Ministry of Defence, July 1998, p. 23.

30 *Corps Concept 1 (German/Netherlands)*, Münster, Section Press and Information 1(GE/NL) Corps, 2001; W. Feld, 'Franco-German Military Cooperation and European Unification', *Journal of European Integration*, 12: 2–3 (1989), p. 154; François Heisbourg, *European Defense: Making it Work*, Chaillot Paper, 42, Institute for Security Studies of the WEU, Paris, September 2000, p. 30.

31 *Bestandsaufnahme: Die Bundeswehr an der Schwelle zum 21. Jahrhundert*, Bundesministerium der Verteidigung, Bonn, May 1999, p. 24.

32 Paul Klein, 'Multinationale Streitkräfte: Modell für die Zukunft oder bereits wieder Vergangenheit?', in Paul Klein and Dieter Walz (eds), *Die Bundeswehr an der Schwelle zum 21. Jahrhundert* (Baden-Baden: Nomos Verlagsgesellschaft, 2000), p. 173; F. V. Rosen, *Soldatenbeteiligung in integrierten Stäben*, SOWI, Beiträge zu Lehre und Forschung, 2/1999, p. 12.

33 German commanders would for, example, find that higher-ranking French officers could

not be directly approached, and soldiers would regret that the relatively informal interaction between the ranks of the Bundeswehr was absent in the French army. Author's interviews, Defence Academy of the Bundeswehr, Hamburg, October 2001.

34 General Hartmut Bagger, *Bundeswehr-aktuell*, 2 February 1997, p. 7; Hans-Otto Budde (Commander of the French–German SFOR brigade), cited in Rüdiger Moniac, 'Vorgelebte Versöhnung', *Die Welt*, 2 July 1997; Jermer, 'Innere Führung – auf den Punkt gebracht', p. 58; Leder, 'Internationale Minenräumoperationen im Arabischen Golf', p. 44; Kammerhoff, 'Unter Blauhelm am Horn von Afrika', p 128; Klein, 'Multinationale Streitkräfte', p. 178; Fritz von Korff (Commander of the Multinational Brigade South, KFOR), 'Das deutsche Kontingent in einer Führungsrolle', in General Peter Goebel (ed.), *Vom Kambodscha bis Kosovo: Auslandseinsätze der Bundeswehr* (Frankfurt an Main: Report Verlag, 2000), p. 182; Geoffrey van Orden, 'The Bundeswehr in Transition', *Survival*, 33: 4 (1991), p. 360; Frank Ropers, 'Embargo-Überwachung in der Adria', in Peter Goebel (ed.), *Vom Kambodscha bis Kosovo: Auslandseinsätze der Bundeswehr* (Frankfurt an Main: Report Verlag, 2000), pp. 116, 119; General Klaus Naumann, cited in 'Die Bundeswehr steigt in die Bezirksklasse ab', *Die Welt*, 28 July 1999; Admiral Wellershoff, cited in 'Reserven kann man nicht wieder herbeisaubern', *Die Welt*, 24 July 1999.

35 Klein, 'Multinationale Streitkräfte', p. 179.

36 Different national or religious holidays, dietary prescriptions, and religious practices, for example, were accommodated in the daily practices of the academy and in the armed forces as such. Author's interviews, Defence Academy of the Bundeswehr, Hamburg, October 2001. See also Gonne Garling, 'Die heile Welt der Kleinen an der Führungsakademie', *Die Welt*, 22 November 2000; Jermer, 'Innere Führung – auf den Punkt gebracht', p. 59.

37 Website of the German Ministry of Defence, www.bundeswehr.de.

38 Kammerhoff, 'Unter Blauhelm am Horn von Afrika', p. 133.

39 Korff, 'Das deutsche Kontingent in einer Führungsrolle', pp. 181–182. For further accounts of the Bundeswehr's civilian and humanitarian activities, see reports of the *Wehrbeauftragte des Deutschen Bundestages*, 1997–2000; Javier Solana, cited in 'NATO-Chef: Bundeswehr hat großartige Arbeit geleistet', *Bild am Sonntag*, 23 March 1997, p. 4.

40 Author's interviews, Defence Academy of the Bundeswehr, Hamburg, October 2001, Chancellery and Ministry of Defence, Berlin, March 2002. See also www.bundeswehr.de.

41 Kammerhoff, 'Unter Blauhelm am Horn von Afrika', p. 133; Riechmann, 'Von Kroatien in die "Box"', p. 163.

42 Molitor, Rückert, Willeke, Merx, and Schwellen, 'Aus Dienst wird Ernst'; Peter Viggo Jakobsen, *PRTs in Afghanistan: Successful but not Sufficient*, DIIS Report, 6 (Copenhagen: Danish Institute for International Studies, 2005); Randow and Stelzenmüller, 'Zivis fürs Grobe'; Schwellen, 'Hilfe, die Helfer sind gekommen'; Stelzenmüller, 'Die Reform-Armee'; Constanze Stelzenmüller, 'Hebammen in Uniform', *Die Zeit*, 39/2004; Schneider, 'Krieg und Frieden: Die Lehren von Sarajevo'.

43 Hartmut Bagger, 'Der Generalinspekteur der Bundeswehr zur Allgemeine Wehrpflicht am 15.5.1996 Paris', press release BMVg, 5 May 1996, reprinted in *Stichworte zur Sicherheitspolitik* 6/1996, pp. 38–40; Beck, *Identität und Professionalität des deutschen Soldaten*, p. 22; Wilfried von Bredow and Gerhard Kümmel, *Das Militär und die Herausforderung globaler Sicherheit*, SOWI-Arbeitspapier, No. 119, Strausberg, September 1999, p. 24; Oberst Kratschmer, cited in Hans-Jürgen Leersch, 'Leere Kassen machen den Soldaten das Leben schwer', *Die Welt*, 14 September 1999; Manfred Lange (Head of planning, command centre of the Bundeswehr), 'Die Bundeswehr auf dem Weg ins 21. Jahrhundert', *Europäische Sicherheit*, 10/2000, pp. 24–25; General Klaus Naumann, cited in 'Generalinspekteur Naumann zur Lage der Bundeswehr nach dem Karlsruher Urteil', *Frankfurter Rundschau*, 2 August 1994; General Klaus Reinhardt, in 'Letzter

Ausweg Berufsarmee', *Süddeutsche Zeitung*, 6 August 2001, p. 2; General Klaus Reinhardt, cited in 'FDP stellt Wehrpflicht in Frage – Truppe hält dagegen', *Berliner Morgenpost*, 28 July 2001, p. 2.
44 Author's interviews, Institut Français des Relations Internationales (ifri), Paris, June 2001; 'Forum Bundeswehr and Gesellschaft', Berlin, October 2001, Defence Academy of the Bundeswehr, Hamburg, October 2001; German Embassy, Washington, DC, November 2001. See also Naumann, 'Die Bundeswehr steht für Frieden und Freiheit'; Ropers, 'Embargo-Überwachung in der Adria', p. 117.
45 Author's interview, Defence Academy of the Bundeswehr, Hamburg, October 2001. With one exception – the small elite unit *Kommando Spezialkräfte* (KSK) established in 1996. KSK was modelled on the British elite unit SAS and trained in common exercises with the British soldiers. Bundesministerium der Verteidigung, *Auftrag Kommando Spezialkräfte (KSK)*, at www.deutschesheer.de/C1256B6C002D670C/vwContentFrame/N2582A8G 725PTILDE (accessed on 5 January 2005); 'Deutsche Elitesoldaten bereiten sich in Oman auf den Einsatz vor', *Die Welt*, 27 November 2001; Friedrich Kuhn, 'Im freien Fall ins Krisengebiet', *Die Welt*, 29 March 1997; Martin S. Lambeck, 'Erster Einsatz der Bundeswehr-Elitetruppe', *Die Welt*, 16 June 1998.
46 Together with French and Italian KFOR troops German soldiers were, however, accused of being excessively timid in quelling riots in Kosovo in March 2004. Human Rights Watch, *Failure to Protect: Anti-Minority Violence in Kosovo, March 2004*, Human Rights Watch Report, 16: 6 (D), July 2004 at http://hrw.org/reports/2004/kosovo0704/ (accessed on 6 January 2004).
47 Author's interview, Ministry of Foreign Affairs and Chancellery, Berlin, March 2002.
48 Gordon A. Craig, *The Politics of the Prussian Army 1640–1945* (London: Oxford University Press, 1979); Martin Kitchen, *A Military History of Germany: From the Eighteenth Century to the Present Day* (London: Weidenfeld & Nicolson, 1975).
49 In March 1997, a group of uniformed conscripts attacked four foreigners in the German town of Detmold. Later the same year four videotapes of anti-Semitic and right-wing extremist content, apparently shot by soldiers in the years 1990, 1993, 1994, and 1996, respectively, were discovered. In August 1997 two conscripts committed arson against a home for asylum seekers and in December the same year it was revealed that the German Defence Academy in 1995 had invited a person of suspected right-wing sympathies to give a lecture on 'The Expulsion of Ethnic Germans from the Königsberg area in the wake of World War II'. *Jahresbericht 1997 der Wehrbeauftragte des Deutschen Bundestages*, section 3.1.
50 Walter Kolbow, *Plenarprotokoll Deutscher Bundestag*, 13/244, p. 22768. Thomas Kossendey, *Plenarprotokoll Deutscher Bundestag*, 13/244, p. 22753; Günther F. Nolting, *Plenarprotokoll Deutscher Bundestag*, 13/244, p. 22750.
51 Angelika Beer, *Plenarprotokoll Deutscher Bundestag*, 13/244, p. 22747; Peter Zumkley, *Plenarprotokoll Deutscher Bundestag*, 13/244, p. 22745.
52 German politicians and security experts generally regarded the reports of the Wehrbeauftragte as solid and reliable accounts of the inner condition of the Bundeswehr.
53 *Jahresbericht 1998 der Wehrbeauftragte des Deutschen Bundestages*, section 3.2; *Jahresbericht 1999 der Wehrbeauftragte des Deutschen Bundestages*, p. 10; *Jahresbericht 2000 der Wehrbeauftragte des Deutschen Bundestages*, p. 9.
54 See, for example, the debate pages of *Truppenpraxis* during the years 1991 and 1992.
55 Major General Johann Adolf Graf von Kielmanssegg, 'Der Krieg ist der Ernstfall', *Truppenpraxis*, 3/1991. See also Michael J. Inacker, 'Die mentale Ausrichtung von Streitkräften', *Europäische Sicherheit*, 10/1995, p. 5; Helmut Willmann, *Leadership: Der militärische Führer im Einsatz – Forderung für Erziehung und Ausbildung*, Bundesministerium der Verteidigung, Bonn, 25 June 1998.
56 See, for example, *The Bundeswehr Advancing Steadily into the 21st Century: Cornerstones*

of a Fundamental Renewal, Bundesministerium der Verteidigung, Bonn, 14 June 2000; Eckwerte für die konzeptionelle und planerische Weiterentwicklung der Streitkräfte, Generalinspekteur der Bundeswehr, Bonn, 23 May 2000; Gemeinsame Sicherheit und Zukunft der Bundeswehr, Bericht der Kommission and die Bundesregierung, Berlin, 23 May 2000. See also Jermer, 'Innere Führung – auf den Punkt gebracht', p. 41.

57 Rudolf Hamann, lecturer, Defence Academy of the Bundeswehr, 'Abschied vom Staatsbürger in Uniform', in Paul Klein and Dieter Walz (eds), *Die Bundeswehr an der Schwelle zum 21. Jahrhundert* (Baden-Baden: Nomos Verlagsgesellschaft, 2000), p. 74; Andreas Prüfert, 'Politische Bildung mit und für Soldaten – Ein tragfähiges Handlungskonzept für die Zukunft', in Oskar Hoffmann and Andreas Prüfert, *Innere Führung 2000* (Baden-Baden: Nomos Verlagsgesellschaft, 2001), p. 127; Günter Steinhoff, 'Nicht nur Wissen – GE-wissen ist gefragt', in Oskar Hoffmann and Andreas Prüfert, *Innere Führung 2000* (Baden-Baden: Nomos Verlagsgesellschaft, 2001), pp. 34, 36–37.

58 According to a SOWI survey conducted in 1995, covering 1,200 professional soldiers and longer-serving volunteers, 88 per cent expressed a 'strong' or 'medium' interest in politics and international politics. The number of respondents expressing a 'strong' interest increased with rank. Among the field grade officers, for example, 82 per cent were strongly politically interested. Sabine Collmer, 'Neuer Auftrag – neue Soldaten?', in Paul Klein and Dieter Walz (eds), *Die Bundeswehr an der Schwelle zum 21. Jahrhundert* (Baden-Baden: Nomos Verlagsgesellschaft, 2000), pp. 134–135. See also Beck, *Identität und Professionalität des deutschen Soldaten*, pp. 16–18; *Bestandsaufnahme: Die Bundeswehr an der Schwelle zum 21. Jahrhundert*, Bundesministerium der Verteidigung, Bonn, May 1999, p. 17; Inspector General Hans Peter von Kirchbach, 'Neue Herausforderungen an die Ausbildung des Heeres in der Zukunft', in Oskar Klein and Andreas Prüfert, *Militärische Ausbildung Heute und in der Zukunft* (Baden-Baden: Nomos Verlagsgesellschaft, 1994), p. 41.

7

The Bundeswehr's projection capability

Introduction

The 1990s saw a widening gap between the new German political willingness to deploy military might out-of-area, on the one hand, and German force planning, on the other. Though ever-greater numbers of troops were dispatched to ever more distant theatres, Germany's security policy elite remained committed to force structures tailored for defensive territorial defence. With increasing difficulty the gap was straddled by German troops on the ground in Africa, the Balkans, and Afghanistan.

The year 2000 saw the launch of a series of military reforms, gradually bringing German defence planning more into line with the requirements of international deployments – requirements including the ability to mobilise and deploy troops on short notice to distant areas, the ability to function in multinational military coalitions, the disposal of joint service command and control equipment compatible with the equipment of Germany's major security partners, and a general equipment profile permitting the Bundeswehr to participate in the whole range of acceptable missions, including those fought mainly by relying on precision ammunition and laser guided bombs (such as *Operation Allied Force* in Kosovo). Despite the ongoing reforms, however, Germany, in contrast to major allies such as France, the UK and the US, maintains conscription instead of professionalising, dedicates less of the military budget to investment in new equipment, and has less centralised and smaller joint service planning and command capabilities than its partners.

This chapter analyses whether Germany's peculiar defence policy choices and priorities impair Germany's ability to contribute to out-of-area crisis management within multinational military coalitions.

German force structures

For forty years the Bundeswehr was a territorial defence organisation with stable structures and one clear primary task: forward defence of West Germany in case of a Soviet attack. The end of the Cold War transformed the geostrategic basics of Europe. The security establishment of most Western European countries eventually concluded that the future task of their armed forces would not be to defend homeland borders against a conventional enemy, but instead to manage regional crises in Europe's neighbourhood as well as in more distant parts of the world.[1]

During the second half of the 1990s both France and Great Britain embarked on military reforms to create smaller, more professional, and more mobile forces. British force planning aimed to create the ability to deploy and sustain around 25,000 ground troops in a war-fighting mission anywhere in the world, or alternatively be able to deploy around 12,000 soldiers indefinitely in a peacekeeping operation and another 12,000 for six months in a war-fighting mission. For short expeditionary missions, the British armed forces would be able to field close to 50,000 ground troops with necessary navy and air force back-up, as they eventually did during the 2003 military campaign in Iraq.[2]

The British force goals functioned as a model for the French military reforms announced in 1996. The French reform suspended conscription and downsized the armed forces from about 400,000 (excluding the gendarmerie) to around 250,000. Following the British model, all French forces were in principle crisis reaction forces and the aim was to be able to project and sustain up to 50,000 ground troops with navy and air force back-up units in an international mission. In both the British and French military planning, force projection became the priority.[3]

Germany, in contrast, retained the territorial defence priority well into the 1990s, and throughout the decade German forces remained structured mainly for traditional homeland defence rather than for projection.

In 1992, the Bundeswehr was divided into a Main Defence Force (MDF) for territorial defence and a Crisis Reaction Force (CRF) for out-of-area peacekeeping. The CRF was kept on a higher level of readiness than the MDF and had a higher proportion of professional soldiers (around 80 per cent professionals supplemented by longer-serving volunteers).[4] However, totalling 50,000 soldiers, it amounted to less than 14 per cent of Germany's standing forces.

Based on the rotation principle used by most Western militaries (six-month intense pre-deployment training, six-month deployment, six-month low-intensity training and recuperation), Germany should in principle have been able to project up to 12,000 ground troops with navy and air force back-up units – less than half the targeted French and British projection goals. The real number was lower due to logistical and material shortcomings, as discussed below. The MDF, totalling 320,000 soldiers, remained the backbone of the Bundeswehr. 'Our armed forces', as Defence Minister Gerhard Stoltenberg explained, 'are first and foremost main defence forces for the defence of Germany within a NATO framework'.[5]

The homeland defence priority was reconfirmed in the 1994 *White Book* and with the 1995 'Bundeswehr Personnel Structure Model', which maintained the size of the CRF at 50,000 troops.[6] By the year 2000, almost 85 per cent of Germany's standing forces were still maintained on a low level of readiness and earmarked for territorial defence. Table 7.1 shows these force structures in the year 2000.

Table 7.1 German force structures, 2000

	Army	*Air force*	*Navy*	*Total*
CRF	37,000	12,300	4,300	53,600
MDF	191,300	64,100	23,800	279,200
Total	228,300	76,400	28,100	332,500

Source: The Military Balance 1999–2000, London: IISS, 2000.

German politicians and members of the security establishment defended the territorial defence priority in political and strategic terms. Germany's main role, they argued, was to provide stability at the centre of Europe, not to dispatch troops worldwide. A defensive citizen's army firmly rooted in German society, not a projection force, was what Germany needed.[7] As the biggest continental member of the NATO alliance, they further argued, Germany had a special obligation to maintain a territorial defence capability, a reservist system, and an augmentation capability in case of a re-emerging threat to Western Europe.[8] They argued that France and Great Britain could permit themselves to downsize, professionalise, and project their forces only because Germany gave priority to territorial defence and ensured that NATO retained a credible collective defence capability.[9]

Thus, even though the German political consensus of the 1990s gravitated towards accepting a role in international peace missions, this did not entail an agreement to transform the Bundeswehr into a projection force. There was no political desire for revamping German force structures along the lines laid out by France and Great Britain.

Projection problems

Whereas the Bundeswehr remained structured for territorial defence, Germany's international military obligations grew over the 1990s. Germany contributed 4,000 troops to IFOR in 1996, 3,000 troops to SFOR in 1997, around 8,000 troops to KFOR beginning in 1999, and almost 4,000 troops to *Operation Enduring Freedom* in 2001. When the Bundestag in June 2003 approved a German contribution to *Operation Artemis* in Congo, Germany already had close to 9,000 peace keepers engaged around the world.[10]

Based on a six-month rotation principle, the force structures shown in Table 7.1 should have permitted Germany to meet these commitments. Logistically and materially, however, the Bundeswehr was ill equipped to engage in missions outside the European theatre. Having traditionally been able to rely on the civilian infrastructure of Germany, the Bundeswehr's strategic lift and long-distance transportation capabilities were limited. Its weapon systems were tailored to counter a massive Soviet onslaught, and many were too heavy to be used for peacekeeping purposes and cumbersome to transport over longer distances. There was also a shortage of personnel with skills critical to force projection. In reality, therefore, the deployable and sustainable number of troops was much lower than 12,000.

The 1991 deployment of German elements of NATO's ACE Mobile Force to Turkey was achieved only by leasing commercially operated Ukrainian aircraft to transport troops and equipment.[11] To sustain the 1993 contribution to UN peacekeeping efforts in Somalia, medical facilities for out-of-area operations, long-distance ground transportation capabilities, air conditioning units, and uniforms suited for the desert environment had to be borrowed or leased from allies.[12]

As deployments grew bigger and more militarily demanding, a lack of up-to-date communication equipment became problematic. The German IFOR and SFOR contingents experienced problems because they did not possess modern digital and integrated command, control, and communication capabilities (c3 capabilities). The software used by German commanders was not harmonised, causing communication and coordination problems, and the Bundeswehr's analogue communication system, Autoko II, fell short of the need for quick data and fax transmissions. German KFOR units had to struggle with similar problems.[13]

The Bundeswehr also struggled with an acute shortage of specialised personnel in areas of critical importance to force projection – logistics, communication, and medical supply. This placed extraordinary strain on officers in those areas. Some had to rotate in and out of international deployment with intervals as short as four months. Efforts to educate more personnel were initiated, but complicated by the frequent need to deploy the instructors themselves.[14]

Due to continued defence budget cuts, the military leadership was forced to authorise 'controlled cannibalisation' of the specialised personnel and equipment of the MDF units to keep deployed units operational. During the latter half of the 1990s, this gave rise to difficulties within the MDF. In numerous units within all three services, less than half the equipment was operational, adversely affecting the level of readiness, training, and education. The German basing system mixed units from the MDF and the CRF in garrisons across Germany. The negative impact of cutbacks in training and exercises therefore affected both troops assigned to territorial defence and the CRF units in their pre-deployment preparation phase.[15]

In sum, the attempt to straddle old structures and new tasks placed extreme strain on the German armed forces. 'The Bundeswehr with its current personnel structure and equipment profile', the Wehrbeauftragte warned in 1999, 'is stretched to the breaking point'.[16]

Reviews and reform

By the late 1990s, the problems could no longer be ignored by the German security elite and the responsible government, no matter how committed to territorial defence. Upon its elevation to power in the fall of 1998, the new SPD/Green government initiated a broad review process. It commissioned a high-level group of individuals – the 'Commission on Common Security and the Future of the Bundeswehr' headed by the former German president, Richard von Weizsäcker – to assess future military needs and propose defence reforms.[17] In parallel, the Ministry of Defence produced its own report under the Inspector General of the Bundeswehr, Hans-Peter von Kirchbach. The results of both reports were presented in May 2000. In May 2003 a new set of Defence Policy Guidelines was issued, and in January 2004 a detailing of new force structures in 'Road signs for the new course' (*Wegmarken für den neuen Kurs*).[18]

To improve Germany's ability to fill its new international military role, and to keep in line with its partners, the Weizsäcker report suggested, it was necessary to reverse the logic of force planning. Instead of preparing first and foremost for territorial defence, the report suggested, future efforts should be geared primarily towards force projection – as they were in France and Great Britain. The report recommended a tripling of the size of the CRF and an increase in the proportion of professional soldiers from approximately 55 per cent to 85 per cent.[19]

While suggesting a similar force projection capability, neither the review from the Ministry of Defence nor Defence Minister Rudolf Scharping's reform program in *The Bundeswehr Advancing Steadily into the 21st Century: Cornerstones of a Fundamental Renewal* (hereafter, *Cornerstones*) heeded the recommendation to formally reverse the logic of force planning. *Cornerstones* reiterated that national territorial defence was the core mission of the German armed forces.[20] It was only with the new Defence Policy Guidelines of May 2003 that the most likely task of the Bundeswehr – out-of-area deployments – formally came to determine the German force planning, illustrating the longevity of an outdated post-war defence policy choice that had become an ingrained part of German strategic culture.[21]

Cornerstones, the 2003 Defence Policy Guidelines, and 'Road Signs for the New Course' gradually moved Germany towards the French and British reform models. They outlined the government's vision for the future size, structure, composition, and equipment profile of the Bundeswehr, and laid out defence reforms to be implemented between the year 2000 and 2006.[22]

The size of the Bundeswehr is currently being reduced from 332,500 to

242,500 troops. The differentiation between a low-readiness MDF and a high-readiness CRF has been dropped. Instead, German armed forces will be divided into a 35,000-strong 'intervention force' dedicated to multinational high-intensity operations within an EU or NATO frame. A 70,000-strong 'stabilisation force' will be available for operations of low or medium intensity. The intervention and stabilisation forces will be supported by 137,500 soldiers responsible for the performance of sovereign and national territorial tasks – guaranteeing the integrity of the German territory, gathering military intelligence, performing basic logistical tasks, medical support, and military training.[23]

Table 7.2 shows the expected size and structure of the Bundeswehr when the reform has been fully implemented. Based on a six-month rotation principle, these force structures will permit Germany to deploy and sustain a total of 50,000 ground troops in out-of-area missions for up to one year. If fully realised, these force goals would bring Germany into line with French and British projection capabilities.

Table 7.2 Projected force structure by 2010[a]

	Army	Air force	Navy	Total
Professionals	112,000	47,000	19,000	178,000
Short-Service Volunteers[b]	21,000	3,200	2,800	27,000
Conscripts	39,000	9,800	1,200	50,000
Standing force	172,000	60,000	23,000	255,000

Source: The Bundeswehr – Advancing Steadily into the 21st Century: Cornerstones of a Fundamental Renewal, Bundesministerium der Verteidigung, Bonn, 14 June 2000.
Notes: [a] Further changes are currently being worked out on the basis of 'Road Signs for the New Course'. Thus Table 7.2 shows the approximate distribution of personnel and size of the services and as of early 2005 the number of professionals was slightly higher and that of conscripts slightly lower. [b] Short-Service Volunteers are conscripts who choose to extend their period of service up till twenty-three months beyond the compulsory ten months.

Cornerstones and the Defence Policy Guidelines also outlined a re-equipment programme aimed at enhancing the Bundeswehr's ability to participate in international crisis management. Heavy equipment tailored for armoured warfare and national defence is currently being scaled back to free up funds for acquisition of newer and lighter platforms.[24] The top priorities are to improve Germany's strategic lift capability for projecting troops and equipment beyond Europe, to introduce new c3 facilities permitting Germany to participate in combined and joint operations, and improve the Bundeswehr's reconnaissance capabilities crucial for both military effectiveness and force protection.[25]

In sum, the German security policy elite long resisted an open break with the force structures and force planning of the era of defensive territorial defence. Yet, finding themselves with military obligations in the Balkans and elsewhere of the same magnitude as the obligations of other major European states, they eventually embarked on a reform of German force structures bringing them closer to those of France and Great Britain. At the same time, however, Germany remained different on a number of accounts – in particular, conscription, and funding – as discussed below.

Conscription: bulwark against the past or military deadweight?

It is commonly accepted throughout the Western world that conscripts for moral, political, and practical reasons cannot be asked to risk life and limb in conflicts far from their homelands. The technically advanced equipment of modern armed forces also makes it difficult to train them adequately for such missions within a relatively short compulsory term of military service. Thus, during the 1990s, all of Germany's major allies professionalised their armed forces or announced their intention to do so. Even in France – the birthplace of the 'citizens' army' – the changed geostrategic landscape of the post-Cold War world prompted the suspension of conscription in 1996.[26]

The number of conscripts serving in the Bundeswehr was scaled down over the 1990s and the length of the term of service was reduced.[27] According to the plans laid out in 'Road Signs for the New Course', the number of conscripts will be reduced further between 2000 and 2010 to 47,500 (out of which the Ministry of Defence estimates that one-third will be longer-serving volunteers), and the period of compulsory service will be reduced from ten to nine months.[28] But upon the completion of the current reform, conscripts will still make up a significant percentage of total standing forces.

When the Bundeswehr was created in the 1950s, there were several reasons why a conscript-based organisation was the only viable option. First, universal male military service was necessary to raise a force of sufficient size to counter a massive conventional Soviet threat. Second, conscription was indispensable as a means to assuage the fear and distrust of German armed forces both at home and abroad. Conscription was to root the Bundeswehr firmly in the democratic values of the FRG, while reassuring neighbours and domestic anti-militarists of the defensive character of Germany's military potential.[29]

The fundamental distrust that dominated especially French attitudes towards Germany at the time of re-armament abated during the course of the Cold War. To be sure, German unification and the assertive German diplomacy and eventual early recognition of Croatia and Slovenia demonstrated that historical anxieties were not dead. Nevertheless, towards the end of the decade calls for a greater German military role in managing security in and around Europe had become far more frequent than public display of concern about Germany's power potential.[30]

Domestic distrust of the armed forces likewise abated over time. As shown in Chapter 6, the international humanitarian and civilian engagement of the Bundeswehr improved its image even on the far left, and by the end of the decade – the vision of a freewheeling military pushing for out-of-area adventures had lost its grip on most German minds.[31]

Eventually, German defence analysts, Liberal politicians, and a handful of Social Democrats started calling for a suspension of the draft. The absence of a clear threat to German territory, they argued, made the political legitimacy of conscription dubious.[32] Moreover, it was pointed out, the structure and composition of German armed forces were out of step with Germany's most important partners and did not correspond to the new threat environment. In a world where the job of the armed forces was to manage international crises and instabilities instead of defending homeland borders, they charged, conscription constituted a military deadweight. The new era called for a downsizing and professionalisation of the Bundeswehr.[33]

The PDS and forces within the Green party likewise called for abolishing the draft, though for quite different reasons. Far from aiming for enhanced German projection capabilities, the left wingers over the longer term wished to demilitarise Germany altogether and transform the Bundeswehr into a civilian peace corps. The abolition of conscription was seen as the first step in that direction.[34]

Conscription, however, was defended by the leaders of Germany's big parties and by members of the security establishment with arguments akin to the ones used to explain Germany's territorial defence priority: Germany's major military mission, it was argued, was to ensure stability at the centre of the continent. A fully professional projection force would therefore make little sense.[35] As this argument was overtaken by the 2003 Defence Policy Guidelines, other arguments were emphasised. Conscription, it was suggested, made for a more 'intelligent army' by allowing the Bundeswehr to draw on the diverse skills represented by the inducted young men. Moreover, it formed an indispensable link between the armed forces and the German people, keeping the Bundeswehr in touch with all segments of society.[36]

Finally, German politicians are also likely to have had pragmatic reasons to defend the draft. By 1999, 170,000 young men had chosen to serve in the alternative civilian service instead of in the Bundeswehr. The consequences for already strained public budgets if the federal government instead had to hire professional social workers are easy to imagine. Furthermore, politicians at the state level lobbied against the downsizing, and base closures entailed in the conversion to a professional army.[37]

Conscription, international crisis management, and terrorism

There is little doubt that conscription to some extent limits Germany's ability to contribute to international crisis management, as claimed by its critics. It is generally assumed that operational units deployed in an out-of-area contingency require the back-up of domestic service support units manned by twice the number of deployed troops. Regular conscripts might fill domestic support roles, however, arguably less effectively than professional soldiers. Furthermore, a certain proportion of the professional soldiers will be tied up as instructors and therefore unavailable for deployment. Yet, even if accepting that the future belongs to international conflict and crisis management, there are reasons why sticking to conscription might remain the best choice for Germany.

First, though the image of the Bundeswehr improved during the 1990s a diffuse anti-militarism remains a feature of German society. The ability of German armed forces to attract high-quality volunteers is still likely to fall short of the ability of nations with a less problematic military past. Presently, around 50 per cent of German officers are recruited from the pool of conscripts. Among them are young men with Gymnasium educations who, according to the German military leaders, might never have decided to embark on a military career in the absence of conscription.[38]

Second, though a massive conventional attack on the German homeland is unlikely, the increasing likelihood of large-scale terrorism creates new homeland security needs. It is becoming accepted in a number of Western countries that the military might be called upon to support the civilian authorities in case of an attack where the need for personnel exceeds what civilian authorities can mobilise or there is a demand for specialist equipment.[39]

In the immediate wake of 11 September, the New York National Guard mobilised more than 4,000 soldiers providing security, medical, and engineering services. In the following weeks almost 10,000 Reserve and National Guard troops were called up to aid the rescue and clean-up efforts and provide security against further attacks.[40] Natural disasters, such as the floods in Central Europe in the summer of 2002, may likewise require the ability to mobilise substantial number of troops to support the civilian authorities. Some tasks, such as patrolling and physical protection of potential terrorist targets, could require long-term military commitment of personnel.

For countries such as Germany with no Home Guard, such tasks might place undue strain on the professional military, already pressed to meet international needs. Conscripts and the reservist system that goes with conscription might thus be the best way of ensuring the capacity to meet homeland security needs. Though political and legal hurdles to deploying the Bundeswehr at home remain, conscripts would arguably also be considered less objectionable to a number of people than the deployment of professional soldiers.

Moreover, there is much to indicate that, for Western European countries, the deployment of troops abroad increases the terrorist threat to the homeland by creating anger among minorities at home or by bringing the country to the attention of international terrorist groups active in the deployment area.[41] Against this backdrop, it could be argued that Germany's conscript system, far from impeding Germany's ability to contribute to international crisis management, is actually a long-term precondition for sustaining an international presence and at the same time protecting citizens at home.

In sum, by 2000, a majority within Germany's political and military elite retained a number of cultural and practical reasons to defend conscription. This sets Germany apart from its major Western partners and arguably compromises the effectiveness of the Bundeswehr's international engagements. However, instead of seeing conscription as a major practical impediment to Germany's international military engagements, it could be regarded as a political precondition for upholding an international presence in the future. Since Germany has no Home Guard, conscription might be the best way to ensure the capability to engage internationally while maintaining security at home – provided, of course, German policy makers are willing to accept that the Bundeswehr has a role to play in homeland security.

The budget squeeze

While the armed forces of all major Western states had to live with declining defence budgets during the 1990s, the Bundeswehr was particularly hard hit. As the German government struggled to cope with the costs of unification, the defence budget, as shown in Table 7.3, dropped from more than 53 bn DM in 1990 to around 47 bn DM in 2005 (23.9 bn Euro). Table 7.4 shows how Germany was throughout the 1990s lagging behind all its major partners regarding defence spending as percentage of gross domestic product (GDP).

Germany's allies expressed their concern over this development on several occasions. US Defence Secretary William S. Cohen and his successor Donald Rumsfeld used the annual *Wehrkunde* conference (an annual high-level security policy forum for policy makers and experts) in Munich to urge Germany to increase its defence budget. The French security establishment also called on

Table 7.3 The German defence budget, 1990–2000, bn DM

Year	1990	1992	1995	1998	2000	2001	2005
Defence budget	53.4	52.7	47.5	46.7	47.33[a]	46.86	46.7

Source: IAP-DIENST Sicherheitspolitik Nr. 7/Juli 2001.
Note: [a] From 2000 onwards, the Bundeswehr did not, as in previous years, obtain extra funding to cover the costs of operations in the Balkans. From 2000, 2bn DM are earmarked to cover these costs. In the wake of the terrorist attack on the US on 11 September 2001, the Bundestag passed a spending bill granting the Bundeswehr and extra 1.5 bn DM yearly. The real sum available to cover personnel costs, procurement, investment, R&D, maintenance, etc. will thus amount to approximately 46.2 bn DM from 2001 onwards.

Table 7.4 Defence expenditure as per cent of GDP[a], 1990–2003

	Average 1990–94	Average 1995–99	1997	1998	1999	2003
Germany	2.1	1.6	1.6	1.5	1.5	1.4
US	4.7	3.3	3.3	3.1	3.0	3.2
France	3.4	2.9	2.9	2.8	2.7	2.6
UK	3.9	2.8	2.7	2.7	2.6	2.4
Italy	2.1	1.7	1.7	1.7	1.7	1.5

Note: [a] *Defence Expenditures of NATO Countries (1980–2000)*, available at www.nato.int.

Germany to change its spending habits and align its military budget more closely with the French and British budget to obtain a more equitable intra-European burden sharing.[42]

Defence expenditure as percentage of GDP is a politically charged number and in this respect significant to Germany's standing as a partner. However, it is not in itself a measure of the quality or modernisation level of armed forces and thus of Germany's ability to contribute to international crisis management. The key point, instead, is the composition of the defence budget and particularly the share going towards investment. Defence experts generally assume that in order to keep a modern force running and technologically up-to-date one-third of the military budget should go towards covering personnel costs, one-third towards maintenance and operations (M&O), and one-third towards investment (i.e. research and development (R&D), testing, and procurement of new equipment). The investment share is an indicator of the modernisation level of the force, the share going towards maintenance and operations indicates the level of operational readiness and training.[43]

In line with these assumptions, German military leaders cite 30 per cent as the ideal investment level – a level that West Germany on average maintained during the Cold War.[44] However, as shown in Table 7.5, the investment part of the German budget has since 1991 consistently fallen below this target.

The development shown in Table 7.5 resulted from the continued German preference for a relatively large territorial defence organisation and from the continued commitment to conscription. While the defence budget kept falling personnel costs remained largely fixed throughout the 1990s; necessary savings had to be taken out of the budget's investment share.

Table 7.5 Percentage distribution between the expenditure categories: investment, maintenance & operations (M&O), and personnel in the German defence budget, 1990–2005

	1990	1991	1992	1994	1995	1996	1998	2000	2001	2005
Investment	32.17	26.90	23.91	21.09	21.68	22.33	23.73	24.33	23.93	25.5
M&O	22.81	23.06	24.58	25.52	25.45	24.92	25.27	24.87	24.36	24.3
Personnel	45.02	50.04	51.51	53.39	52.87	52.75	51.00	50.80	51.71	50.2

Source: www.bundeswehr.de/ministerium/haushalt/bild_ausgabenentwicklung01.htlm, www.bmvg.de/ministerium/haushalt/index.php.

In the short term, the prospect of a major increase in the German military budget seems unlikely regardless of the colour of the German government: Germany is currently fighting to bring a federal budget deficit under control. Increased funds for investment in new equipment have thus to come from reduced personnel costs.

The reforms underway will remedy part of the investment shortfall. Between 2000 and 2006, the total strength of the Bundeswehr will decline from 332,500 to approximately 255,000. The defence budget has been frozen at the nominal 2001 level (see Table 7.3). However, according to the Ministry of Defence rationalisations in the defence administration, downsizing of the civilian administration, new private–public partnerships (PPPs) in maintenance, logistics, and telecommunications services, together with a sell-off of redundant military property and equipment, should permit an injection of extra 2 bn DM per year into the investment part of the budget. This will increase the investment share to around 28 per cent. The structural composition of the defence budget is thus set to improve.[45]

However, investment will still not reach the critical 30 per cent mark cited by German military leaders, and the total size of the budget will most likely not honour the financial minimum requirement quoted by military top leaders for implementing the reform – a yearly sum of 49 bn DM.[46]

Interoperability with partners

Most organisations and institutions wish for better funding most of the time. Most of the time they are also right to point out that more money would permit them to do a better job. The Bundeswehr is no exception. The crucial question is not how much is desirable, but how much is enough. The question is what the practical consequences of the German 'underinvestment' are when it comes to Germany's ability to contribute to crisis management in cooperation with its major Western partners.

International crisis management has throughout the 1990s been carried out by multinational military coalitions, and Germany is constitutionally obliged never to act outside of such frameworks. In practice, Germany has most frequently acted within a NATO framework and almost always together with nations such as France, Great Britain, the US, and, at times, Italy. German forces must therefore maintain a level of modernisation that allows them to stay interoperable with the armed forces of these countries.

For all types of out-of-area operations, but particularly for higher-end tasks, interoperable command and communication equipment is crucial both in order to coordinate between coalition forces and to protect the safety of the troops by permitting swift and secure transfer of information, requests, and commands. In more demanding missions such as *Operation Allied Force* in Kosovo or *Operation Enduring Freedom* in Afghanistan, fought according to a low-loss and low-collateral damage strategy, full participation also requires the disposal of precision ammunition such as laser-guided bombs.[47] As outlined on p. 129, the Bundeswehr re-equipment programme ascribes priority to the introduction of new command and control equipment and to the acquisition of precision ammunition.

A cross-national comparison of investment shares of national defence budgets shows that Germany is trailing all its major Western partners, with the exception of Italy. Table 7.6 shows investment as a percentage of total defence expenditure in Germany, France, UK, US, and Italy between 1990 and 2003.[48]

Table 7.6 Percentage of total defence budget dedicated to investment (minus investment in military infrastructure), 1990–2003

	Average 1990–94	Average 1995–99	2000	2001	2003
Germany	13.5	11.8	13.5	14.0	14.0
US	25.1	26.2	21.9	25.7	27.6
France	–	21.3	18.9	19.4	20.6
UK	21.0	24.8	25.7	24.2	23.5
Italy	16.3	12.9	14.3	10.3	12.7

Source: *Defence Expenditures of NATO Countries*, available at www.nato.int/docu/pr/2003/table5.pdf (accessed on 11 January 2005). Numbers may differ from those given by national authorities due to different definitions of defence expenditure. NATO's definition of investment, for example, does not include investment in infrastructure.

Comparing the sum invested to the force size in the US, France, Great Britain, and Italy indicates a wide modernisation gap between Germany and its three most important security partners. Against the background of such numbers, defence analysts and observers have warned that unless the German government changes its military spending habits or dramatically reduces the size of German armed forces, the Bundeswehr will in a few years time no longer be interoperable with the forces of its major allies. Germany will still be able to deliver a contribution to humanitarian and peacekeeping missions. However, they argue that a lack of modern c3 equipment will make the Bundeswehr an inadequate partner in militarily demanding missions.[49] Since the line between peacekeeping and peace enforcement has proven harder and harder to draw during the 1990s, Germany may in effect be deemed an inadequate partner even in missions that do not from the outset appear like high-risk operations.

Arguably, however, the warnings about imminent non-interoperability are exaggerated. First, the German navy and air force are proportionally smaller and the army proportionally bigger than the French, British, and American armies.[50] Between the three services, the army is the least capital-intensive. The 'top-down' approach and Table 7.7 thus overestimates the modernisation differential between Germany and its Western partners.

Table 7.7 Investment relative to number of active soldiers, 2003

	Defence budget (bn Euro)	Investment (I) (bn Euro)	Active soldiers	I/active soldiers
Germany	30.9	4.3	285,000	15.1
US	299.2	82.5	1,558,000	52.6
France	40.2	8.3	356,000	23.3
UK	37.4	8.8	214,000	41.1
Italy	24.4	3.1	325,000	9.5

Source: *Defence Expenditures of NATO Countries, Distribution of Total Defence Expenditures by Category, Armed Forces – Annual Average Strength*, all available at www.nato.int (accessed 11 January 2005). Numbers may differ from those given by national authorities due to different definitions of defence expenditure.

Second, modernisation levels are seldom uniform throughout the armed forces of any country. The Bundeswehr leadership gave preferential treatment to the CRF in equipment and procurement matters through most of the 1990s and is set to continue a targeted modernisation of those Bundeswehr units most likely to be assigned to out-of-area deployment within an international coalition.[51] In practice, this means that Germany will be able to deploy some units that measure up to French and British forces, but that Germany will be unable to fully modernise all Bundeswehr units.

Finally, though the re-equipment of the Bundeswehr with new, lighter and technologically more advanced weapon systems has proceeded slowly, some of the existing equipment procured to counter the Soviet threat has proved well adapted to the new international tasks. The German mine-sweeping capability, for instance, is bigger than both the French and the British and has been in demand in connection with several international missions since the mid-1990s.[52] The German navy also has a significant off-shore and coastal patrolling capability, originally conceived for deployment in the Baltic Sea. This capability has turned out to provide a mixture of mobility and robustness that makes it well suited for international sea embargo monitoring and enforcement. Germany's so-called 'flying hospitals' – military aircraft fitted with advanced medical equipment – also filled a crucial medical support role in *Operation Enduring Freedom* as well as for the ISAF, currently deployed in Kabul, Afghanistan.[53] It is thus very unlikely that a situation will occur in which Germany will be incapable of delivering a meaningful contribution to an international peace mission, including the more demanding types.

The critics, however, are right in the sense that, based on current financial planning the Bundeswehr will not be able to live up to the force projection target of *Cornerstones* and 'Road Signs for the New Course'. It has been estimated that the German defence budget would have to grow by 2.5 per cent each year between 2000 and 2006 alone to make up for the backlog in investment accumulated during the 1990s, even when the force size reduction currently in implementation is taken into account.[54] Yet, as mentioned above, the defence budget has been frozen at the 2001 level and military spending is likely to maintain a relatively low priority in the German political cultural context.

In sum, the Bundeswehr is currently underfunded and its average level of modernisation will remain below that of French, British, and American armed forces for the foreseeable future. This, however, will not render Germany incapable of delivering a real contribution to international crisis management. Nor will it make all parts of German armed forces non-interoperable with the armed forces of major allies. Instead, Germany will over the coming years be able to contribute to the whole range of peacekeeping and enforcing operations – but with fewer troops than the 50.000 quoted in *Cornerstones*.

Command structures

Up until German reunification in 1990, the Bundeswehr was the only defence force in the world with no joint service planning or command capabilities. The air force and the navy had small service operational command headquarters but the army had no command structures above the corps level. The Ministry of Defence was not organised to exercise broad operational control or conduct independent planning. The highest ranking German officer – the Inspector General – was not included in the military chain of command, and the inspectors of the three individual services reported directly to the Minister of Defence. The Inspector General's personal staff (Führungsstab der Streitkräfte) was also not structured for joint service planning or command, but charged with more mundane tasks of coordination in matters of personnel, training, equipment, and force planning.[55]

When the Bundeswehr was created in the 1950s, the resurrection of a German General Staff would have been unacceptable, both at home and abroad. From a military point of view it also remained unnecessary since German troops would be deployed only in the case of a collective defence contingency within a NATO framework. Thus, they would be able to rely on NATO command structures and planning capabilities.

The need for enhanced national command capabilities initially arose in 1990, as Germany took over responsibility for the territorial integrity of the new Eastern states. The two-plus-four Treaty for German unity did not allow for the stationing of military units integrated in NATO structures in these states until Soviet withdrawal had been completed.[56] The emerging political consensus around out-of-area deployments, however, also accentuated the need to establish national capabilities for planning and conducting smaller joint-service military operations. Though Germany most frequently deployed troops in a NATO framework, and thus remained able to rely on NATO assets, this was not always the case. The French-led EU *Operation Artemis* in Congo, for example, was planned and conducted without relying on NATO structures. To permit Germany to participate in, or lead, such missions, a greater national planning capability would be necessary. Europe was indeed to be invoked by proponents of a stronger central Bundeswehr organisation in the late 1990s.[57]

The domestic German aversion to anything that smacked of military centralisation, however, remained. When Social Democrat Egon Bahr in 1992 floated a proposal for a modest central military analysis and planning unit consisting of fifteen–twenty strategic analysts, he was met with widespread rejection. And when the CDU/FDP government in the same year proposed to centralise the Bundeswehr's operational control structures to permit Germany to conduct smaller joint-service operations, the opposition protested. Left-leaning politicians and editors conjured up the ghost of the Prussian General Staff and accused a conspiracy of 'reactionary politicians and dangerous officers' of striving for world power status for Germany.[58]

Eventually the CDU/FDP government proceeded with very modest and incremental changes. The operational command capabilities of navy and air force were expanded, and in 1994 a small Army Operations Command (Heeresführungskommando) was set up in Koblenz. For the first time in the Bundeswehr's history, it gained the ability to conduct nationally controlled army operations above the corps level.[59] In 1995 a joint service command (Einsatzführungskommando) was set up in Potsdam, and a small central planning and operational command centre (Führungszentrum) was set up within the existing joint staff in the Ministry of Defence. Throughout the 1990s the Bundeswehr leadership thus relied on pragmatic ad hoc arrangements to handle international peace missions involving more than one Bundeswehr service. Normally, the service that provided the biggest contribution in terms of deployed personnel also provided the operational headquarters. Most frequently, joint planning and command fell to the Army Operational Command in Koblenz.[60]

The 'Führungszentrum' was still being developed by the end of the decade and thus relied on the individual services for essential staff work. It was designed to handle only relatively small deployments. It was not tailored for independent large-scale national projection, but for the small- and medium-sized deployments typically required by multinational crisis management. The reform currently underway aims further to streamline and strengthen the central command and control organisation of the Bundeswehr. The Inspector General has been given additional responsibilities for the execution of joint-service out-of-area missions as chairman of a new Joint Operations Command (Einsatzrat). The Joint Operations Command will in the future be in charge of planning Bundeswehr operations abroad and the operations commander will in future report directly to the Bundeswehr Inspector General.

In sum, the Bundeswehr's central planning and command capabilities remain less powerful than those of major Western partners. Yet, German abilities were sufficient to plan and carry out the smaller- and medium-sized deployments (KFOR with 8,000 troops being the largest) typically required by multinational crisis management missions. Meanwhile, the most imminent cultural reason why Germany did not wish to have a centralised military organisation – distrust of the armed forces – has faded. It thus appear reasonable to assume that the central organisation of the German armed forces will keep developing in the direction of those of its major partners.

Summary

Germany's defence policy priorities diverged from those of its allies throughout the 1990s. When it came to the structure, composition, and organisation of the Bundeswehr, Germany remained committed to the Cold War choice of a military organisation of a defensive cast. Germany's major partners, in contrast, embarked on reforms aimed on enhancing their international force projection capabilities.

Old force structures and old equipment caused problems for the Bundeswehr throughout the 1990s as it attempted to meet the new requirements of out-of-area deployments. German UNOSOM II, IFOR, SFOR, and KFOR units had to rely on a good deal of flexibility and improvisation and Germany frequently had to borrow or lease the necessary equipment to project and sustain these units abroad.

By 2000, German elites, based on a pragmatic reassessment of Germany's new international obligations, belatedly accepted the need to adjust Germany's military priorities. The reform currently underway aims to augment the projection capability of German armed forces and creates an equipment profile better suited for international crisis management. However, as the chapter has argued, the military budget squeeze and the backlog in investment entails that the number of German troops that can be equipped and trained for international deployment will fall short of this target.

Beside the territorial defence priority, eventually adjusted in 2003, Germany's political and military elite throughout the 1990s maintained a commitment to conscription. While setting Germany apart from France, the UK, and the US, conscription arguably does not fundamentally hamper Germany's ability to perform new international tasks. On the contrary, it could be argued, conscription might in future prove a crucial factor permitting Germany to engage abroad while maintaining the security of the homeland against new threats such as large-scale terrorism.

Moreover, the territorial defence priority, the commitment to conscription, and the aversion to a centralised military structure were all linked to a historically founded and culturally rooted distrust of the armed forces. These cultural notions set narrow limits to potential uses of the Bundeswehr. However, even if some of the military priorities to which they gave rise have remained, these notions themselves gradually changed in conjunction with the reinterpretation of the past that took place over the 1990s. The Bundeswehr is not yet ideally equipped or structured to participate in out-of-area contingencies. But the cultural aversion that led German elites to reject a German projection capability is fading. When this underlying development is taken into account, it seems less significant whether the current reform can be fully implemented within existing financial limits or whether the Bundeswehr in the short and medium term will technologically lag behind the armed forces of some of its partners. The long-term trend seems clear: Germany's willingness to contribute to international peace missions – and along with it its practical ability to do so – are on the rise.

Notes

1 *Reform of French National Defense*, Embassy of France in the US, 12 June 2001, p. 2, available at www.info-france-usa.org; Ronald Tiersky, 'French Military Reform and NATO

Restructuring', *Joint Force Quarterly*, 15 (Spring 1997), pp. 6–7; *The Strategic Defence Review*, London, 1998, pp. 7–11.

2 UK Ministry of Defence, *The Strategic Defence Review White Paper*, July 1998, pp. 21–22; *UK Regular Forces and Civilian Personnel Strengths at 1 April 2002*, SCPS1 Monthly Publication, Ministry of Defence, London, available at www.dasa.mod.uk.

3 *Reform of French National Defense*, p. 4, available at www.info-france-usa.org; Tiersky, 'French Military Reform and NATO Restructuring', p. 6; 'Zu den geplanten Veränderungen in den französischen Streitkräften', *Stichworte zur Sicherheitspolitik*, 5/1996, pp. 2–7.

4 All CRF units were assigned to multinational units and thus did not, as some left-leaning and Liberal critics charged, constitute a national projection capability. CRF units were assigned, respectively, to NATO's ACE Mobile Force (AMF), NATO's Rapid Reaction Corps (RRC), and the Eurocorps. *Konzeptionelle Leitlinie*, Bundesministerium der Verteidigung, Bonn, 1994. Reprinted in *Stichworte zur Sicherheitspolitik*, 9/1994.

5 Gerhard Stoltenberg, press release, Bundesministerium der Verteidigung, Bonn, 19 February 1992.

6 *Weißbuch 1994*, Bundesministerium der Verteidigung, Bonn, April 1994, p. 88; John S. Duffield, *World Power Forsaken: Political Culture, International Institutions, and German Security Policy after Unification* (Stanford, CA: Stanford University Press, 1998), p. 154.

7 Angelika Beer, cited in 'CSU und Grüne gegen Interventionsarmee', *Die Welt*, 10 May 2000; General Klaus Naumann, 'Zuverlässiger Instrument in den Händen der Politik', *Frankfurter Rundschau*, 27 October 1995; Volker Rühe, 'Berufsarmee lockt die Söldner-Typen', *Neue Ruhr Zeitung*, 7 May 1997; 'Union fürchtet um Wehrpflicht und warnt vor Eingrifftruppe', *Die Welt*, 24 May 2000.

8 Hartmut Bagger, 'Wir haben genug Wehrpflichtige', *Stuttgarter Nachrichten*, 23 January 1997; Duffield, *World Power Forsaken*, p. 154. Volker Rühe, cited in 'Unklarheiten in der deutsch-französischen Sicherheitspolitik', *Frankfurter Allgemeine Zeitung*, 2 March 1996 and 'Nach 2002 brauchen wir den Euro-Fighter', *Frankfurter Allgemeine Sonntagszeitung*, 3 March 1997.

9 The German reservist system in principle would permit the Bundeswehr to be augmented to more than twice its peacetime size. *Weißbuch 1994*, Ministerium der Verteidigung, Bonn, April 1994, p. 128. See also Peter Hintze, 'Zur Diskussion eine Abschaffung der allgemeinen Wehrpflicht', *Mittagsmagazin*, 8 August 1997; Günther Nolting, 'Noch eine Reform ist jetzt nicht sinnvoll', *Bonner Rundschau*, 9 August 1997; Volker Rühe, 'Rolle Deutschlands im zusammenwachsenden Europa und der Beitrag der Bundeswehr', *Bulletin*, No. 91, 14 November 1996; Volker Rühe, cited in 'BM der Verteidigung Rühe zur Fragen der Bundeswehr und deutscher Sicherheitspolitik', *Die Welt*, 24 November 1996.

10 Website of the German Ministry of Defence, www.bundeswehr.de

11 Karl Kaiser and Klaus Becher, 'Germany and the Iraq Conflict', in Nicole Gnesotto and John Roper (eds), *Western Europe and the Gulf* (Paris: Institute for Security Studies of the WEU, 1992), p. 63.

12 Duffield, *World Power Forsaken*, p. 159.

13 General Peter Goebel (ed.), *Von Kambodscha bis Kosovo: Auslandseinsätze der Bundeswehr* (Frankfurt am Main: Report Verlag, 2000), p. 20; Inspector General Hans Peter von Kirchbach, 'Soldaten können nicht Frieden herbeibringen und nicht die Köpfe ändern', *Berliner Zeitung*, 29 December 1999; General Klaus Naumann, *Erfahrungen aus dem Kosovo-Einsatz*, Führungsakademie der Bundeswehr, Hamburg, Akademie-Information, Sonderheft, August 1999, p. 45; Hans-Heinrich Weise, 'Erfahrungen aus dem Einsatz der Bundeswehr auf dem Balkan', *Europäische Sicherheit*, 11/2000, p. 12.

14 *Jahresbericht 1997 der Wehrbeauftragte des Deutschen Bundestages*, section 13.3; Franz-Josef Meiers, 'A German Defence Review?', in Gordon Wilson (ed.), *European Force Structures*, Paris: Institute for Security Studies of the WEU, Occasional Paper, 8, May 1999, p. 31.

15 *Die Bundeswehr der Zukunft: Sachstand der Reform 1. Juni 2001*, Bundesministerium der Verteidigung, p. 10, available at www.bundeswehr.de; *Jahresbericht 1999 der Wehrbeauftragte des Deutschen Bundestages*, p. 17; Volker Rühe, *Plenarprotokoll Deutscher Bundestag*, 13/74, p. 6447.
16 *Jahresbericht 1999 der Wehrbeauftragte des Deutschen Bundestages*, p. 7. See also Henning Bartels, 'Modernisierung und Ausrüstung unserer Streitkräfte', *Europäische Sicherheit*, 5/2001, pp. 31–48; *Bestandsaufnahme: Die Bundeswehr an der Schwelle zum 21. Jahrhundert*, Bundesministerium der Verteidigung, Bonn, May 1999; Albert Dinke, 'Nicht die Bundeswehr ist in der Sinnkrise – die ganze Gesellschaft ist es', *Europäische Sicherheit*, 7/1993, p. 325; *Jahresbericht 1996 der Wehrbeauftragten des Deutschen Bundestages*; *Jahresbericht 1997, 1998, 1999*, available at www.bundestag.de; Lt Gen. Willmann, interview with *Süddeutsche Zeitung*, 3 March 1999.
17 *Gemeinsame Sicherheit und Zukunft der Bundeswehr*, Bericht der Kommission and die Bundesregierung, Berlin, 23 May 2000.
18 *Defence Policy Guidelines*, Bundesministerium der Verteidigung, Berlin, 21 May 2004; *Eckwerte für die konzeptionelle und planerische Weiterentwicklung der Streitkräfte*, Generalinspekteur der Bundeswehr, Bonn, 23 May 2000, pp. 34–36; *Wegmarken für den neuen Kurs*, Bundesministerium der Verteidigung, reprinted in *Stichworte zur Sicherheitspolitik*, No. 1, January 2004, pp. 18–23.
19 The arguments for maintaining conscription are, according to the Commission, that Germany remains a continental power and therefore must preserve an augmentation capability, and that the conscript system has proven valuable in recruiting professional soldiers of high quality from the pool of conscripts. *Gemeinsame Sicherheit und Zukunft der Bundeswehr*, Bericht der Kommission und die Bundesregierung, Berlin, 23 May 2000.
20 *The Bundeswehr Advancing Steadily into the 21st Century: Cornerstones of a Fundamental Renewal*, Bundesministerium der Verteidigung, Bonn, 14 June 2000, p. 29.
21 *Defence Policy Guidelines*, p. 4.
22 *Eckwerte für die konzeptionelle und planerische Weiterentwicklung der Streitkräfte*, pp. 34–36; *The Bundeswehr Advancing Steadily into the 21st Century*. Changes in personnel structures are being phased in over a period of ten years to avoid major disruptions and layoffs. For broader reactions to the plan, see 'Bundeswehr & Gesellschaft', a special section of *Welt am Sonntag*, 7 October 2001; 'CDU will eine Atlantische Charta', *Frankfurter Allgemeine Zeitung*, 29 September 2001, p. 2; 'Das ist insofern tough', *Die Zeit*, 12/2001; Gernot Erler and Peter Zumkley, cited in 'Union fürchtet um Wehrpflicht und warnt vor Eingrifftruppe', *Die Welt*, 24 May 2000; FDP, *Bundeswehr 2000*, Berlin, 23 March 1999; Matthias Geis, 'Der Verteidigungsminister muss jetzt beweisen, dass er die Armee wirklich erneuern will', *Die Zeit*, 22/2000; Wolfgang Hoffmann, 'Bundeswehr: Das wird teuer!', *Die Zeit*, 43/2000; Günther F. Nolting, 'So muss die Bundeswehr aussehen!', *Die Welt*, 19 May 2000; Gerhard Schröder, speech at reception of the report 'Gemeinsame Sicherheit und Zukunft der Bundeswehr', reprinted in *Bulletin* No. 30–1, 26 May 2000; Constanze Stelzenmüller, 'Druck von allen Seiten', *Die Zeit*, 37/1999.
23 *The Bundeswehr Advancing Steadily into the 21st Century*, p. 25; *Wegmarken für den neuen Kurs*, p. 20.
24 *The Bundeswehr Advancing Steadily into the 21st Century*, pp. 22–24.
25 *Defence Policy Guidelines*, p. 20; *Material- und Ausrüstungskonzept für die Streitkräfte der Zukunft*, Bundesministerium der Verteidigung, Berlin, March 2001, p. 29; Meiers, 'A German Defence Review?', p. 24.
26 *Reform of French National Defense*, p. 2, available at www.info-france-usa.org; Tiersky, 'French Military Reform and NATO Restructuring', pp. 6–7.
27 *Konzeptionelle Leitlinie*; *The Bundeswehr Advancing Steadily into the 21st Century*, section 4.2, para. 61.

28 *The Bundeswehr Advancing Steadily into the 21st Century*, p. 26; *Wegmarken für den neuen Kurs*, p. 22.
29 Gordon A. Craig, *The Politics of the Prussian Army 1640–1945* (London: Oxford University Press, 1979); Martin Kitchen, *A Military History of Germany: From the Eighteenth Century to the Present Day* (London: Weidenfeld & Nicolson, 1975).
30 Alain Richard, speech at 'Berliner Dialog – Internationale Sicherheit', Berlin, 3 July 2001. Author's interview, Institut Français des Relations Internationales (ifri), and editorial office of *Le Monde*, Paris, July 2001.
31 Thomas Kossendey, *Plenarprotokoll Deutscher Bundestag*, 13/244, p. 22753; Günther F. Nolting, *Plenarprotokoll Deutscher Bundestag*, 13/244, p. 22750; Peter Zumkley and Angelika Beer, *Plenarprotokoll Deutscher Bundestag*, 13/244, pp. 22745, 22747; Walter Kolbow, *Plenarprotokoll Deutscher Bundestag*, 13/244, p. 22768.
32 'FDP fühlt sich bei Wehrpflicht bestätigt', *Süddeutsche Zeitung*, 8 August 2001, p. 6; 'FDP stellt Wehrpflicht in Frage – Truppe hält dagegen', *Berliner Morgenpost*, 28 June 2001, p. 2.
33 Rainer K. Huber and Bernhard Schmidt, *The Challenge for Defense Reform in Europe*, The Potomac Papers, May 2000; Meiers, 'A German Defence Review?', p. 23. For the FDP position, see *Zukunftsfähigkeit der Bundeswehr sichern – Wehrpflicht aussetzen*, Bill introduced by the FDP parliamentary group in the Bundestag on 10 October 2000, available at www.fdp.de; Rainer Brüderle, 'Die Wehrpflicht ist von Gestern', *Der Tagesspiegel*, 14 August 1997; Jürgen Köppelin, 'Rühe kann der FDP Debatte um Wehrpflicht nicht verbieten', *Thüringer Allgemeine Zeitung*, 9 August 1997, p. 32; Guido Westerwelle, *Bundeswehr Einsatz II: FDP für uneingeschränkte Solidarität/Aussetzung der Wehrpflicht gefördert*, 12 November 2001, www.fdp.de. For the views of the SPD defectors, see Klaus Lennartz, 'Wehpflicht ganz abschaffen', *Express*, 7 January 1997; Heiko Mass, 'Relikt des Kalten Krieges', *Süddeutsche Zeitung*, 8 August 2001; Manfred Opel, 'Plädoyer für eine moderne und flexible Freiwilligenarmee', *Frankfurter Rundschau*, 20 August 1997, pp. 49–52; Manfred Opel, 'Wehrpflicht hilft nicht gegen moderne Waffen', *Sonntagsblatt*, 29 August 1997, p. 55; Renate Schmidt, cited in 'Hier kommt die Berufsarmee!', *Die Welt*, 7 August 2001; Michael Stürmer, 'Abschied von der Wehrpflicht', *Die Welt*, 8 August 2001; Constanze Stelzenmüller, 'Deutschland braucht eine von Grund auf erneuerte Bundeswehr', *Die Zeit*, 20/2000; *Die Zeit*, 19 February 1993, p. 5; *Tagesspiegel*, 24 January 1993, p. 6.
34 Angelika Beer, 'Antimilitärische Verständnis der Grünen', *Europäische Sicherheit*, 4/1996, p. 6; Decision of the 2nd PDS party convention, PDS Pressedienst, 12 July 1991, p. 11; 'Kleinere Bundeswehr ohne Wehrpflicht: Gutachten der Friedensinstitute', *Frankfurter Allgemeine Zeitung*, 11 June 1997, p. 7.
35 Hans-Dietrich Genscher 'Die Bundeswehr ist eine Armee mitten im Volk', *General Anzeiger*, 12 August 1997; Klaus Kinkel, 'Bundeswehr braucht Ruhe und Planungssicherheit', *Die Welt*, 11 August 1997, p. 2; Klaus Kinkel, 'Deutsche Außen- und Sicherheitspolitik bei der internationalen Krisenbewältigung seit 1990', *Bulletin*, 9 December 1997; Theo Sommer, 'Wehrpflicht oder Berufsheer?', *Die Zeit*, 10/1996.
36 Hartmut Bagger, 'Der Generalinspekteur der Bundeswehr zur Allgemeine Wehrpflicht am 15.5.1996 Paris', press release, Ministry of Defence, Bonn, 5 May 1996, reprinted in *Stichworte zur Sicherheitspolitik*, 6/1996, pp. 38–40; Karl Feldmeyer, 'Mehr Geld gibt es nicht', *Frankfurter Allgemeine Zeitung*, 18 November 1997; Peter Hintze, 'Zur Diskussion eine Abschaffung der allgemeinen Wehrpflicht', *Mittagsmagazin*, 8 August 1997; Manfred Lange, 'Die Bundeswehr auf dem Weg ins 21. Jahrhundert', *Europäische Sicherheit*, 10/2000, pp. 24–25; Nolting, 'Noch eine Reform ist jetzt nicht sinnvoll'; Otto Hauser, 'Ende der Wehrpflicht – Beginn der Dienstpflicht?', *Europäische Sicherheit*, 4/1994, p. 179; General Klaus Reinhardt, in 'Letzter Ausweg Berufsarmee', *Süddeutsche Zeitung*, 6 August 2001, p. 2; Volker Rühe, 'Mogelpackung Schröder', *Focus*, 18 August 1997; Volker Rühe,

'Die Bundeswehr hat alle die Probleme der Gesellschaft auch', *Süddeutsche Zeitung*, 28 August 1997; Volker Rühe, cited in 'BM der Verteidigung Rühe zur Fragen der Bundeswehr und deutscher Sicherheitspolitik', *Die Welt*, 24 November 1996; Volker Rühe, 'Rolle Deutschlands im zusammenwachsenden Europa und der Beitrag der Bundeswehr', *Bulletin*, No. 91, 14 November 1996; Volker Rühe, cited in 'Rühe: Ich halte an der Wehrpflicht fest', *Westdeutsche Allgemeine Zeitung*, 20 May 1997; Volker Rühe, 'Berufsarmee lockt die Söldner-Typen', *Neue Ruhr Zeitung*, 7 May 1997; Volker Rühe, interview with *Westdeutschen Allgemeinen Zeitung*, 25 November 1997; Stürmer, 'Abschied von der Wehrpflicht'; Michael Wolffsohn, 'Wie wichtig ist für uns die Wehrpflicht?', *Bild*, 10 June 1997. For the official positions, see www.spd.de and www.cdu.de. See also 'Allgemeine Wehrpflicht', available at www.cdu.de/politik-a-z/sicherheit/kap21.htm; 'Die Wehrpflicht steht nicht zur Disposition', *Die Welt*, 13 January 2000.

37 'Huber: Bundeswehr trägt auch zur Strukturpolitik bei', *Die Welt*, 19 June 2000; *Jahresbericht 2000 der Wehrbeauftragte des deutschen Bundestages*, p. 24.

38 Bagger, 'Der Generalinspekteur der Bundeswehr zur Allgemeine Wehrpflicht am 15.5.1996 Paris', pp. 38–40; Lange, 'Die Bundeswehr auf dem Weg ins 21. Jahrhundert', pp. 24–25; General Klaus Reinhardt, in 'Letzter Ausweg Berufsarmee', *Süddeutsche Zeitung*, 6 August 2001, p. 2.

39 Anja Dalgaard-Nielsen, 'Homeland Security and the Role of the Armed Forces: A Scandinavian Perspective', in Heiko Borchert (ed.), *Mehr Sicherheit – Weniger Souveränität* (Hamburg: Verlag E. S. Mittler & Sohn, 2004); *Defence Policy Guidelines*, p. 5.

40 Lynn E. Davis, 'Defining the Army's Homeland Security Needs', in Lynn E. Davis and Jeremy Shapiro (eds), *The US Army and the New National Security Strategy*, Santa Monica: RAND, 2003, p. 68.

41 The attacks in Madrid on 11 March 2003 were presumably carried out in order to force a Spanish withdrawal from Iraq. Several other coalition members have been threatened with similar attacks. The deployment of Western forces in Afghanistan has also been a cause of anger among some extremist groups.

42 Jean-Michel Boucheron, cited in 'Paris übt Kritik an deutschem Verteidigungsetat', *Financial Times Deutschland*, 1 August 2001, p. 11; Daniel Coats, cited in 'USA warnen Deutschland', *Berliner Zeitung*, 2 August 2001, p. 1; Alain Richard, speech at 'Berliner Dialog – Internationale Sicherheit', Berlin, 3 July 2001 and speech at 'Forum Bundeswehr und Gesellschaft', Berlin, 2 October 2001, reprinted in 'Bundeswehr & Gesellschaft', a special section of *Welt am Sonntag*, 7 October 2001, p. 7; Lord Robertson and Alain Richard, speech at 'Forum Bundeswehr und Gesellschaft', reprinted in 'Bundeswehr & Gesellschaft', a special section of *Welt am Sonntag*, 7 October 2001, pp. 1, 7; 'Skeptische Blicke der Partner auf den Reformer Scharping', *Die Welt*, 9 June 2000.

43 David C. Gompert, Richard L. Kugler, and Martin C. Libicki, *Mind the Gap: Promoting a Transatlantic Revolution in Military Affairs* (Washington, DC: National Defense University Press, 1999); Reiner K. Huber, 'Die Erneuerung der Bundeswehr', *Europäische Sicherheit*, 4/2001, p. 26; Reiner K. Huber and Schmidt, *The Challenge for Defense Reform in Europe*; Meiers, 'A German Defence Review?', p. 24.

44 Defence expenditures of NATO member countries are available at www.nato.int. General Klaus Naumann, cited in *Welt am Sonntag*, 6 October 1991; General Klaus Naumann, 'Sicherheit in Europa – Konsequenzen für die Bundeswehr', *Europäische Sicherheit* 1/1995, p. 14; Inspector of the Army, Helmut Willmann, cited in 'Heeresinspekteur warnt vor Kürzungen', *Die Welt*, 19 June 1997.

45 *IAP-DIENST Sicherheitspolitik*, Nr. 7/Juli 2001, p. 8.

46 Inspector General Harald Kujat, cited in 'Letzter Ausweg Berufsarmee', *Süddeutsche Zeitung*, 6 August 2001, p. 2. For critical evaluations of the budgetary assumptions of

Cornerstones, see Klaus Becher, 'Reforming German Defence', *Survival*, 42:3 (Autumn 2000), p. 167; Matthias Geis, 'Der Verteidigungsminister muss jetzt beweisen, dass er die Armee wirklich erneuern will', *Die Zeit*, 22/2000; Wolfgang Hoffmann, 'Bundeswehr: Das wird teuer!', *Die Zeit*, 43/2000; Constanze Stelzenmüller, 'Druck von allen Seiten', *Die Zeit*, 37/1999; 'Das ist insofern tough', *Die Zeit*, 12/2001.

47 François Heisbourg, *Emerging European Power Projection Capabilities*, GCSP-RAND Workshop Paper, Geneva, 15–16 July 1999, p. 3, available on Columbia International Affairs Online, www.ciaonet.org/conf/hef01/.

48 In order to compare the modernisation level of armed forces in a systematic way one can apply either a 'bottom-up' or a 'top-down' approach. 'Bottom-up' approaches estimate the quality of armed forces by assigning scores to different weapon systems and individual combat units. They are based on the combined judgement of military experts and draw on field experience and computer simulations. The more crude 'top-down' approaches look at the sum invested relative to the number of active soldiers that must be equipped. Most defence analyses today rely on the 'top-down' approach since there are no good 'bottom-up' measurements applicable to post-Cold War armed forces – existing models were developed during Cold War times and apply mainly to armies equipped for classical armoured warfare. Huber and Schmidt, *The Challenge for Defense Reform in Europe*, p. 3; Reiner K. Huber and Bernhard Schmidt, 'Wo steht die Bundeswehr in der NATO?', *Europäische Sicherheit*, 5/1999, p. 48.

49 Hanns W. Maull, 'Germany and the Use of Force: Still a "Civilian Power"?', *Survival*, 42:2 (2000), p. 75; Meiers, 'A German Defence Review?', p. 24; Michael Stürmer, 'Ein Diplomat spricht aus, was die Politik nicht zu sagen wagt', *Die Welt*, 4 August 2001; Johannes Varwick, 'Die Bundeswehr reformieren', *Internationale Politik*, 7/2000.

50 The French army constitutes 56 per cent, the British 53 per cent, and the American 34 per cent of total armed forces, while the German army, according to *Cornerstones*, will amount to 67 per cent of total forces upon completion of the current reforms. *The Military Balance 1999–2000* (London: IISS).

51 *Material- und Ausrüstungskonzept für die Streitkräfte der Zukunft*, Ministerium der Verteidigung, Berlin, March 2001, p. 29.

52 The British and French navies, respectively, dispose of twenty-one and twenty-nine countermeasure units, while Germany has thirty-four. *The Military Balance 1999–2000*.

53 Author's interview, Embassy of Germany, Washington, DC, 26 November 2001. See also Lt Gen. Helmut Willmann, Inspector of the Army, cited in *Die Welt*, 4 February 2000.

54 Huber and Schmidt, 'Wo steht die Bundeswehr in der NATO?', pp. 49–50.

55 Duffield, *World Power Forsaken*, p. 162; Geoffrey van Orden, 'The Bundeswehr in Transition', *Survival*, 33:4 (1991), p. 357.

56 Van Orden, 'The Bundeswehr in Transition', p. 356; *Weißbuch 1994*, German Ministry of Defence, Bonn, April 1994, p. 112.

57 General Harald Kujat, Inspector General of the Bundeswehr, interview with *Der Tagesspiegel*, 26 November 2000; Hans-Jürgen Leersch, 'Gerhardt fordert Generalstab', *Die Welt*, 6 August 1999 and 'Kehrtwende der CDU in der Sicherheitspolitik', *Die Welt*, 8 October 1999; Rupert Scholz, 'Bundeswehr auch zur Grenzsicherung einsetzen', *Die Welt*, 8 October 1999. The FDP embraced the proposal to establish a General Staff as official policy in March 1999. FDP, *Bundeswehr 2000*, Berlin, 23 March 1999.

58 Egon Bahr, 'Ein Generalstab ist kein Taboo mehr', *Europäische Sicherheit*, 3/1992; 'CDU und Grüne wollen keinen Generalstab', *Die Welt*, 7 August 1999; Lothar Gutjahr, *German Foreign and Defence Policy after Unification* (London: Pinter, 1994), p. 57; Charima Reinhardt, 'Kontroverse um Militärstrategie', *Frankfurter Rundschau*, 20 February 1992; Wolfram Wette, 'Der Wünsch nach Weltmacht', *Die Zeit*, 30 July 1993, p. 4.

59 Johannes Bohnen, 'Germany', in Jolyon Howorth and Anand Menon (eds), *The European Union and National Defence Policy* (London: Routledge, 1997), p. 59; *Militärpolitische und*

Militärstrategische Grundlagen und konzeptionelle Grundrichtung der Neugestaltung der Bundeswehr, reprinted in *Blätter für deutsche und internationale Politik*, No. 4, 1992, pp. 506–510; *Weißbuch 1994*, Bundesministerium der Verteidigung, Bonn, p. 114.

60 Author's interview, Embassy of Germany, Washington, DC, November 2001 and Chancellery, Berlin, March 2002.

Conclusion

Germany, pacifism, and pre-emptive strikes

The Germany that declined involvement in the 2003 Iraq War was, in a number of respects, different from the Germany that had abstained in 1991. The geostrategic context of the 1990s permitted competing schools of thought within Germany's strategic culture to converge on a new consensus. International calls for an active German engagement in out-of-area crisis management, together with the nature of the era's crises, paved the way for a novel German international military activism.

With the terror attacks of 11 September 2001 and the new US doctrine of military pre-emption the context for German security policy changed. Yet, as argued above, there will be no German backtracking on the development that took place over the 1990s. Despite the 'no' to Iraq, Germany through 2003 maintained thousands of peace keepers abroad, expanded its engagement in Afghanistan, and committed troops to an EU intervention in Congo. Pacifism remained a factor to be reckoned with, but by the mid-1990s it had ceased to define Germany's position on the out-of-area question. In sum, German policy makers have given up a piece of the country's post-Second World War exceptionalism in military affairs – the principled renunciation of using military means for other purposes than self-defence. Thus, Germany changed, that much is certain.

Other questions, however, remain open:

- Why did Germany change?
- What are the limits and possibilities of Germany's new willingness to use military force?
- Do Germany's neighbours have any reason to be concerned over the German transformation?

- What does the German change entail for the organisation of Western security and where will Germany look for partners in a world of terrorist violence and pre-emptive military strikes?

The culturalist analysis of the previous chapters offers some answers.

Realism, culturalism, and the German transformation

Why did Germany change? An observer informed by the notions of realist international relations theory might see his expectations confirmed by the change that occurred in Germany's out-of-area policy over the 1990s: post-unification Germany's augmented power base and improved security position opened up new possibilities for German policy makers. The bigger and more secure Germany responded to its amplified room for manoeuvre by gradually abandoning the military exceptionalism of the Cold War years and started participating in international military crisis management in line with other major European powers.

As argued in the book's introduction, an analysis based on a culturalist perspective is not at odds with the realist notion about the importance of systemic pressure in influencing state behaviour. The culturalist framework, however, suggests that both structures – the domestic security culture and the international distribution of power – and actors are important in accounting for the security policy of states. Thus, whereas realist theory would predict a relatively linear and progressive movement in which the foreign and security policy role of a country is readjusted to its new relative power position, culturalism would not expect the foreign policy behaviour of a state to respond directly to the apparent logic of external circumstances.

These notions were confirmed by the analysis. Chapters 3–5 showed how the response of German politicians to the external pressure of the 1990s was mediated and channelled through the domestic German security culture and its two competing schools of thought. It also showed how political entrepreneurs were both limited and aided by these schools of thought.

Arguably, the strategic rationale for extending Germany's international role had existed since superpower relations started 'warming' in the late 1980s, making a major conflict on the central European front appear less and less likely. Already at this time a small group of Conservative security experts had started advocating German participation in the management of global security. Yet, only once they managed to link their cause to 'never again alone' by exploiting, in the wake of the Gulf War, the widespread international criticism of Germany's 'security free-riding' and 'risk avoidance', when a majority within the Conservative party was willing to go along.

The Liberals maintained their resistance to a German military engagement throughout the Gulf conflict. The break-up of Yugoslavia, however, challenged central and operational Liberal beliefs about the nature of the international system to such an extent that it forced an intellectual revision. In the spring of 1993, the Conservative coalition partner was able to pull the Liberals along in support of a German military contribution to manage the crisis.

The massacre at Srebrenica was the key event that challenged the German left's central beliefs about Germany and Germany's role in the world – pacifism – as well as its operational beliefs about the effectiveness of diplomatic versus more forceful means of foreign policy. Translating the lessons of Srebrenica into terms that spoke to Germany's historical experience, the proponents of German participation in international crisis management catalysed a turnaround among numerous former pacifists as 'never again war' was supplanted by 'never again Auschwitz'.

In sum, though realism can indicate the general direction of change, the analysis of Chapters 3–5 demonstrates that neither the reasons, nor the timing of Germany's transformation can be adequately understood without taking into account the different domestic German schools of thought about security, as well as political entrepreneurs who translated external pressures and events into a language that resonated with Germany's strategic culture. Germany's transformation did not occur as a smooth progressive movement. Instead, Germany moved at those points in time when external events resonated with the domestic culture or seriously challenged ingrained cultural beliefs.

Realism, culturalism, and Germany's military transformation

Looking at the military side of Germany's transformation, a quick glance at the overall change in Germany's security posture and capability profile during the 1990s might again seem to confirm the realist's expectations. During the 1990s Germany certainly expanded her military options and realised more of her potential military power by modernising her armed forces and participating in managing the more diversified threat environment of the post-Cold War world. Again, culturalism would not object to this general description.

However, whereas realist theory would predict the eventual realisation of a country's full military–political power potential, culturalism would not. Instead, the endpoint of change would be a foreign and security policy that brings external pressure into balance with the stable and fundamental beliefs that make up the core of a country's security policy culture – beliefs about the nature of the international system, about the self, and about the other. A culturalist would thus expect Germany to aim for a projection capability just big enough to silence international accusations of security free-riding and to shoulder new humanitarian interventions – but a projection capability which might well remain far below the country's potential.

As illustrated in Chapter 7, the projected endpoint of Germany's military transformation would leave Germany with a power projection capability in line with that of France and the UK. Considering that Germany's population exceeds that of these two countries by about one-third, a realist might have expected Germany to aim higher. Moreover, the political will to allocate sufficient funds to actually realise the force projection goal of 50,000 troops by 2010 has so far not materialised. As a culturalist might expect, defence spending retained a low priority in the context of Germany's strategic culture. Germany remains far from dedicating the same percentage of GDP as France and the UK to its armed forces. Apparently, Germany is not in a process of fully realising her potential power.

Moreover, as Chapters 6 and 7 have shown, a closer look also reveals that Germany even as it aligned its force structures with those of other major European powers simultaneously preserved elements of her post-Second World War military exceptionalism. German policy makers, for example, remained committed to conscription. In addition, they increased their efforts to embed the German military potential in bi-national or multinational structures, making her armed forces the most integrated among the major Western European powers. Finally, German military exceptionalism appeared to find a new kind of expression in the way German armed forces approached international crisis management. German soldiers apparently took a distinctly 'civilised' approach, engaging comprehensively in humanitarian and civilian tasks and cultivating a non-offensive style towards local parties and populations.

Thus, to account for the finer picture it is helpful to draw on culturalism. As pointed out in Chapter 6, for instance, the approach of German peace keepers might be explained in part as a result of the peculiar post-war ethos of German armed forces. Similarly, the German choice to stick with conscription could be explained by pointing to fading, but still existing historical and cultural anti-militarism. Finally, the continued efforts to integrate German armed forces with those of allied countries also appear natural considering the strong cultural inclination towards cooperation within Germany's security culture – 'never again alone'.

A slightly more challenging case is Germany's unresponsiveness to repeated calls from European and NATO partners to align the German defence budget with the budgets of France and Great Britain. Germany's 'special path', as played out in military spending, risked undermining her influence and standing within organisations of vital importance to her security. Yet considering that the cooperative inclination epitomised in 'never again alone' had to compete and coexist with residual anti-militarism within Germany's security culture, the unwillingness to increase the defence budget makes more sense.

In sum, a realist perspective may account for the general direction of change in Germany's military posture, force structures, and equipment profile during the 1990s. But culturalism provides a better tool to understand the choices and actions of German policy makers on a more detailed level.

Conditions of engagement: what for, where, with whom?

Between 1991 and 2003 Germany went from having no soldiers deployed in international peacekeeping missions to having between 6,000 and 10,000 soldiers permanently deployed abroad. Today more than $1 bn a year are earmarked to cover the direct costs of these missions.

With such an engagement of resources, an external observer might have expected at least some debate of how this served German national interest, where in the world Germany should focus its efforts, and within which institutional framework it should prefer to operate. Yet, Germany's transformation was not preceded or accompanied by a grand strategy debate about Germany's place in the world, its interests, and its goals. Terms such as 'national security' and 'national interest' were hardly ever used. Instead, the debate centred on abstract notions such as 'Germany's historical responsibility', 'moral responsibility', 'international solidarity', and 'requirements of partnership'.

The geographical limits of the policy, if any, were not debated and though the Constitutional Court in 1994 established that Germany could engage only within a multinational framework, the question of which framework would better serve German interests was not raised. In other words, the questions what for, where, and with whom Germany would engage the Bundeswehr remained unanswered. The evidence of previous chapters, however, helps shed light on what German policy makers did not address explicitly in the out-of-area battle.

What for? The past, the partners, and the national interest

From a culturalist perspective the absence of a discussion over Germany's national interest was not surprising. Considering Germany's past it would appear natural that the reformulation of Germany's out-of-area policy was driven by aversions – Auschwitz and a national separate path – more than by positive notions of what Germany could hope to achieve by expanding its military role. The 'never again!' that had resounded after the end of the Second World War still, in the 1990s, pervaded the German way of thinking and talking about security policy. The culturalist would thus suggest that the language of German politicians mirrored their real concerns and that Germany actually extended its international military role in an attempt to heed the lessons of the past and for the sake of partnership.

As pointed out in Chapter 1, there are ways to reduce the reliability problem of culturalist analysis, but no foolproof method for testing the sincerity of political language. Indeed, an observer informed by realist assumptions might remain sceptical as to the sincerity of the internationalist, anti-militarist, and self-effacing language of German politicians. He might consider the topics of the out-of-area debate to be smokescreens for the real issue at stake – the reemergence of Germany as a major power, disposing of the full vocabulary of such a power, including the military part. Yet, as shown in Chapters 3 and 4 culturalism does a better job in accounting for what actually happened to German policy over the 1990s, and Chapter 5 shows how German reactions to East Timor, Macedonia, Afghanistan, Iraq, and Congo did not appear to be guided by realist notions about the national interest.

Of course, a realist might still maintain that it is premature too conclude on the basis of thirteen years' evidence that Germany is maintaining a security policy based on cooperation and civility. It is impossible to falsify such an assertion. Yet, as argued above, the projected endpoint of Germany's military transformation does not support this realist assumption. However, even if accepting for a moment realist notions about rational, self-seeking state behaviour and the existence of a time lag between changes in the distribution of international power and changes in policy behaviour, it remains difficult to see how Germany would gain by amplifying and exploiting a new space for independent military action.

The increasing density of international contacts and transactions, the new prevalence of border-crossing security threats, and the increasing political, economic, financial, and monetary integration within Europe creates a situation in which the factors impacting Germany's well-being extend far beyond the factors Germany can possibly deal with independently. With an export economy, dependence on energy imports, a geography giving it more neighbours than any other European country, and a position on the border between the former East and West, Germany is more dependent than most other countries on international cooperation to deal with border-crossing security, political, social, economic, and environmental issues. This arguably makes the preservation of trust and cooperative structures more important in the pursuit of German national interests than what Germany could hope to achieve individually by acquiring a full-blown independent projection force commensurate with its demographic and economic influence in Europe.

Thus, even if accepting realist premises about self-seeking state actors, it is difficult to see what nationalist designs German politicians could hide beneath their internationalist language. Arguably, if indeed, as indicated in this study, German politicians changed German policy on the out-of-area question for the sake of the past and the partners, it was not based on idealistic self-deception. It *was* German 'Real-Politik'.

The members of Germany's relatively small strategic community might be right in lamenting that German politicians at large did not respond to the international crises of the 1990s based on a comprehensive idea about German interests in connection with international crisis management. Yet, the debate's focus on the partners and the past was, arguably, informed by a good deal of cultural wisdom about Germany's position in Europe, the constraints on its room for independent action, the nature of its national interest, and the importance of working within multilateral structures and organisations to realise it.

Where? The geographical limits

German politicians did not directly address the question of what Germany would deploy the Bundeswehr internationally for. The question of where Germany should concentrate its efforts was also left open.

A realist would expect the transformed Germany to intervene in conflicts where substantial direct German political, economic, or security interests were at stake. Germany's geographic position at the border between the former East and West should make it one of the countries with the strongest interests in maintaining stability and dousing potential conflicts in Europe's Eastern and South-Eastern neighbourhood. A realist would thus assume that a re-unified Germany would be more inclined to intervene in conflicts in Europe's immediate neighbourhood and possibly in the Middle East due to Germany's energy import dependence than in the conflicts of more far-flung regions.

The culturalist would not necessarily assume a direct connection between Germany's 'objective' national interests and the German willingness to intervene with military means in an international conflict. Instead, culturalism would expect German policy makers to be most inclined to engage when an intervention appeals simultaneously to both schools of thought within Germany's security culture – that is, if it takes place in such a way as to confirm and strengthen international cooperation and Germany's standing as a partner, and if the intervention serves to limit or prevent violence and human rights violations.

Table 8.1 provides an overview of the geography, size, mandate, and composition of the actual crisis management efforts to which Germany contributed to between 1991 and 2003. Looking at this overall picture, it becomes clear that Germany committed the largest number of troops in Europe's neighbourhood – in Croatia, Bosnia, Kosovo, and Macedonia – to help manage the Yugoslavian succession wars and the instability following in their wake. Of the eleven analysed cases of German military engagement, seven missions were in Europe. This geographical focus confirms the expectations of a realist observer. The abstention in both Gulf Wars, however, presents a puzzle to the realist. Based on Germany's dependence on energy imports the country should have a strong interest in participating in shaping the security situation of that region – something, which is arguably better done through aligning to some extent with the US and engaging instead of abstaining.

Moreover, the new German policy was not limited to Europe. The first deployment ever of ground troops beyond NATO area was in Somalia in 1993; in 1999, Germany dispatched a medical contingent as far as East Timor; and in 2001 it committed the second biggest number of troops ever – 3,900 military personnel – to the American campaign *Enduring Freedom* in Afghanistan. Finally, 350 troops were committed to the French-led EU mission, *Operation Artemis* in Congo in June 2003. The latter three commitments – commitments to areas in which Germany had no or limited direct interests at stake – came at a time when the Bundeswehr was already overstretched due to existing obligations in the

Conclusion

Table 8.1 Location, size, mandate, and national composition of the crisis management missions to which Germany contributed, 1990–2003

Military operation	Total size of operation/German contribution	Mandate and auspices	Other participating nations
Adriatic Sea 1992–96 *Operation Sharp Guard* Monitoring embargo against FRY in the Adriatic Sea	22 ships/2 destroyers	UN mandate, UNSCR 820 Joint NATO and WEU operation	12 nations, including US, Great Britain, Greece, Turkey, the Netherlands
Somalia 1993–94 *UNOSOM II*	28.000 troops/1,700 troops	UN mandate, UNSCR 814 UN operation	28 nations, including US, France, Italy, Greece
Bosnia-Herzegovina 1993–95 *Operation Deny Fly* Monitoring and enforcing no-fly zone over Bosnia	4,500 airmen/500 airmen	UN mandate, UNSCR 816 NATO-led operation	US, France, Great Britain, Turkey, Italy, the Netherlands
Bosnia-Herzegovina 1995–96 IFOR	60,000 troops/3,000 troops	UN mandate, UNSCR 1031 NATO-led operation	All NATO members, 22 non-NATO members
Bosnia-Herzegovina, since 1996 SFOR	3,000 troops/3,000 troops	UN mandate, UNSCR 1088 NATO-led operation.	All NATO members, 22 non-NATO members
Kosovo, since 1999 KFOR	50,000 troops/8,000 troops	UN mandate, UNSCR 1244 UN auspices but substantial NATO presence	All NATO members, 22 non-NATO members
East Timor 1999–2000 INTERFET	9,800 troops/100 military personnel	UN mandate, UNSCR 1264 Australian-led multinational operation	29 nations, including Australia, UK, US
Macedonia, since 2001 *Operation Essential Harvest*	1,000 troops/500 troops	No UN mandate NATO operation requested by the parties to the conflict	Belgium, Canada, Czech Rep., France, Greece, Italy, the Netherlands, Spain, Turkey, UK

Table 8.1 (*continued*)

Military operation	Total size of operation/German contribution	Mandate and auspices	Other participating nations
Macedonia, since 2001 *Operation Amber Fox*	1,000 troops/600 troops	UN mandate, UNSCR 1371 NATO operation	Denmark, France, Greece, Italy, Portugal, Poland, Spain
Afghanistan, since 2001 *Operation Enduring Freedom*	3 US carrier battle groups, at least 18,000 allied forces excl. American army and air force personnel[a]/3,900 troops	No UN mandate but support in UNSCR 1368 and 1373 US-led multinational operation	Australia, Canada, France, Italy, Japan, UK
Iraq, since 2003 *Operation Iraqi Freedom*	Between 200,000 and 150,000 troops/ No German contribution	No UN mandate US-led coalition of the willing	Denmark, Italy, Poland, (Spain), UK, US
Congo June–September 2003 *Operation Artemis*	1,400 troops/350 troops French-led EU operation	UN mandate, UNSCR 1484	Belgium, Brazil, Canada, France, Hungary, the Netherlands, South Africa, Sweden, UK

Note: [a] These numbers are estimates as some deployments were, as of September 2002, undisclosed or unspecified. *Operation Enduring Freedom Deployments,* Global Security.org, www.globalsecurity.org/military/ops/enduring-freedom_orbat-03.htm. Spain withdrew its troops during the summer of 2004.

Balkans. Though Germany committed the greatest number of soldiers in absolute terms to Europe, there appeared to be no fixed geographical limits to the new German policy. It further became clear, with the vote on *Operation Essential Harvest* in Macedonia, that the fact alone that a crisis was erupting in Europe and had the potential to impact Germany directly by no means guaranteed broad political support for dispatching the Bundeswehr.

In sum, there were no fixed geographical limits to Germany's new willingness to engage the Bundeswehr. Instead, the peculiar nature of Germany's security culture seemed to determine when and where Germany would engage, and when not.

With whom: a European alternative?

Both in words and action the re-unified Germany's political elite expressed a strong preference for multilateralism. Germany never during the analysed period deployed troops outside of multinational frameworks. Yet, the question whether German interests were better served by contributing within one or another of the possible multinational frameworks was not debated. The actual deployments seem to reveal a preference for NATO. As illustrated in Table 8.1, five of the eleven analysed cases of German out-of-area deployment were NATO operations. Yet, judging from German reactions to the 2003 Iraq War, one might assume that German policy makers in future will throw their new military weight decisively behind the fledgling European Security and Defence Policy (ESDP) and thus promote an alternative voice to that of the US.

Indeed, both a realist and a culturalist observer might have expected German policy makers to favour a European framework for crisis management. A realist might have anticipated that German policy makers would prefer a security organisation focusing mainly on providing stability in and around Europe instead of a US-led NATO, clearly in the process of refocusing on extra-European conflict areas. Though combating terrorism by deterring potential state sponsors and stabilising far-flung crisis areas to prevent terrorists from gaining a territorial basis is arguably a common Western interest, a hard-nosed realist might judge that the direct threat to Germany from such phenomena was far lower than the direct threat from instability in Germany's immediate neighbourhood. The war in Yugoslavia, for example, caused an influx of 350,000 refugees into Germany.

Moreover, a too close alignment with the US might invite the wrath of international terrorist groups, as appeared to be the case when Spain – a member of the anti-Saddam Hussein coalition in Iraq – was struck by terrorists in March 2003. In sum, a realist might have expected Germany to place more eggs in the EU basket during the 1990s instead of relying on a US-dominated NATO whose leading member – the US – had no real interest at stake in the crisis areas of most immediate concern to Germany.

A culturalist, in turn, would point to how the new US emphasis on military pre-emption carried out by coalitions of the willing jarred with Germany's security culture. Indeed, the debate surrounding the crises in Iraq, Macedonia, and Afghanistan revealed how politicians from across the political spectrum perceived substantial differences in the German and American approaches to international crisis management. Most of the aspects of US foreign policy singled out for criticism by German policy makers were regarded with equal scepticism among the national elites of other continental European countries as well as in Brussels.[1] Thus, arguably, German notions about crisis management would find more accommodation within a European framework than within a NATO dominated by US concepts and methods.

The EU's 2003 Security Strategy indeed enjoyed a favourable reception in Germany. The emphasis on preventive political and economic engagement in conflict areas, the need for dialogue to defuse tensions, and the emphasis on military force as an important option, but one of last resort, was embraced by commentators from across Germany's political spectrum. There is little doubt that the EU document was more in tune with Germany's security culture than the new US security strategy.[2]

To be sure, there had been indications of a move towards Europe. As illustrated in this book, proponents of an extended German military role frequently invoked 'Europe', arguing that only if Germany were willing to contribute to crisis management on an equal basis with other major European countries could Europe develop into a real political union with a real common foreign and security policy. 'Europe' proved an effective device in the domestic battle due to the positive connotations it carried across the political spectrum. Europeanism has remained a constant feature of German political life, whereas Atlanticism has had its ups and downs.

Moreover, during the 1990s Germany promoted a variety of initiatives aimed at strengthening European security and defence cooperation. Together with France, the German Government pushed for the inclusion of defence issues in the 1992 Maastricht Treaty, which established the development of a European Common Foreign and Security Policy (CFSP) as an objective of the Union.[3] German elites also declared their support for the French–British St Malo initiative aimed at strengthening Europe's military capabilities. Yet, they took a backseat role in the process and while the German defence budget kept shrinking, few German voices were heard in the debate over the fledgling ESDP. German elites, if pressed, insisted that the ESDP should remain firmly within NATO.[4] The April 2003 initiative of Germany, France, Belgium, and Luxembourg to create the 'nucleus of a European planning capability' might have sent a strong political signal due to its timing – the reiterated commitment to a number of the goals for enhanced EU military cooperation already established in the wake of St Malo coincided with the war in Iraq and came at a time of unprecedented US–European disagreement over key strategic issues. Yet, the initiative again eschewed concrete budgetary commitments and the German chancellor later went out of his way to underline that the initiative did not entail that Europe should develop as a counterweight to NATO and the US. Eventually, the EU planning unit was nested inside NATO headquarters in Brussels.[5]

The reason for this German ambiguity goes back to the composite nature of Germany's security culture. The establishment of a European alternative to NATO would require substantial investments to upgrade Europe's military capabilities. Europe has no common military planning and command capabilities or strategic intelligence gathering capabilities, insufficient military transportation capabilities, and too little precision ammunition to undertake a mission such as, for example, *Operation Allied Force* in Kosovo without relying on NATO assets.[6] A European alternative to what is seen as an excessively trigger-happy US appeals to some German politicians, especially on the centre left. However, just as there are deeply ingrained historical limits to the German faith in military solutions, there are limits to the willingness to spend on the armed forces as would be necessary if Europe was to develop an independent ESDP. In effect, Germany voted against ESDP by maintaining military spending at a relatively low level.

Furthermore, if there was one clear lesson from the debacle over Iraq it arguably was that attempts to unify Europe against the US were doomed to fail. When forced into making a choice between the US and a French–German alternative, numerous European states eventually rallied to the US. This illustrated that a policy aiming at an autonomous ESDP would quickly come into conflict with 'never again alone'.

In sum, in spite of a new US security strategy that jars with core notions of Germany's security culture, German policy makers will not throw their increasing military weight behind an ESDP independent from NATO and the US. Such a move would split Germany, not just from the US and UK, but also from numerous smaller European countries. That would be equally jarring within Germany's strategic culture and would at the same time require budgetary commitments that few are willing to make in a country characterised by limited belief in military solutions. Thus, Germany's transformation will not entail a revolution in the Western security architecture and Germany will keep looking both to Europe and across the Atlantic for security policy partners.

What kind of power? Continuity and change

Less than a decade after re-unification, Germany had dispatched Bundeswehr units to regions as distant as East Timor and participated in missions as difficult as *Operation Enduring Freedom* in Afghanistan. In the summer of 2002, moreover, Germany was the first European country to stand up to the American ally and issue a plain 'no' to a potential war in Iraq. Such behaviour differed fundamentally from the path Germany had followed throughout the post-war era and might be a cause for concern among Germany's partners and neighbours. However, a close look at the competing logics within Germany's security culture and the way they developed during the 1990s indicated that, beneath the outward change, a number of the core notions about Germany's interest and role in international security remained constant.

The most central cultural belief of the German centre right – the conviction that multilateralism and international integration were in Germany's national interest – remained constant throughout the 1990s. The very reason why the German centre right came to accept an extended role in international crisis management was the need to preserve Germany's influence and standing in organisations such as NATO and the EU. What changed was the assessment of the concrete requirements of partnership in the post-Cold War world, an operational belief challenged by the international criticism directed at Germany's original policy of out-of-area abstinence.

On the German left, one central belief – the pacifist notion that the use of force is always and under all circumstances wrong – changed. But another central belief – the notion of a special German responsibility to work for international civility, peace, and human rights – was unaltered. The left came around on the out-of-area question due to a perceived German historical responsibility and moral obligation to resist genocide and massive human rights abuses – in its starkest form 'never again Auschwitz'. What the post-Cold War era did challenge and change was the centre left's operational beliefs about the efficiency of respectively political and more forceful means of international diplomacy. The events in ex-Yugoslavia, particularly the mass killing of Bosnian Muslims in Srebrenica, prompted this revision. Most of the change that drove Germany's transformation thus took place at the level of operational beliefs.

The continuity in the central beliefs of German policy makers found expression in the conditions attached to Germany's new policy of engagement as well as in the way it approached the task of international crisis management. Germany participated only in missions that involved its major Western partners, the military intervention needed to be a measure of last resort, and it needed to serve a plausible humanitarian goal besides the political and military objectives. While coming around to accept the occasional indispensability of the use of force, German policy makers simultaneously reiterated their commitment to political and preventive non-military strategies of crisis management, and consistently embedded military contributions to crisis management in broadly conceived political, economic, and cultural stabilisation and development programmes. As illustrated with the resistance to the 2003 war against Iraq, the German centre left's belief in military means remained circumscribed.

The political logics that went into forming German out-of-area policy found parallels within the German armed forces. The Bundeswehr was permeated by internationalist attitudes, placed a high price on political education of the peace keepers, rejected the cult of the warrior, and accepted the civilian and humanitarian aspects of crisis management as an integral part of the tasks of the armed forces. As a result, deployed German units took a non-offensive approach towards local parties and populations and engaged extensively in civil and humanitarian aspects of crisis management.

In sum, Germany abandoned one of the traits of a civilian power during the 1990s – the renunciation of the use of military force for other purposes than self-defence. Yet, while stepping up its military engagement in international crisis management and developing force structures and military capabilities akin to those of other major European powers, Germany maintained a good deal of its post-Second World War 'civility'. It developed a policy towards international crises that from conception to implementation had a distinctly civilised cast. Germany became willing and able to use military means, however, only in cooperation with other Western democracies, taking a broad and non-forceful approach including political, social, economic, and humanitarian measures, and pursuing goals that went beyond purely national interests, including international cooperation and the protection of human rights.

In the world of theory this pattern of continuity and change confirms the assumptions of cognitive and culture theory – that culture can change, but that individuals as well as collective entities tend towards minimal attitude change in as few peripheral regions of their belief systems as possible.

In the world of politics it should assuage potential fears among Germany's neighbours regarding the change in Germany's military posture of the 1990s. There is little reason to believe that the new out-of-area policy heralds a German reversion to the power politics of the past or that Germany will use its enhanced military capabilities for purposes of domineering or asserting national interests at the cost of its neighbours and partners. The international role conception of post-war Germany remained largely constant, as did many fundamentals of German security thinking. The 'no' to participate in the Iraq War did not indicate a dramatic new turn in Germany's security posture. It did not reflect that 'never again alone' had been jettisoned. Instead, the circumstances of the Iraq crisis simply illustrated that, like most other civilised nations, Germany has conditions for lining up.

Notes

1 Gilles Andréani, 'The Disarray of US Non-Proliferation Policy', *Survival* 41/4, Winter 1999–2000, pp. 42–61; Jacques Andréani, Speech given at Johns Hopkins SAIS, Washington, DC, 22 February 2000; Egon Bahr, 'Ein Protektorat wird selbstständlich', *Die Zeit*, 23/2000, pp. 6–7; Jacques Beltran, 'US "Rogue" Policy Isn't the French Way', *Los Angeles Times*, 16 October 2000; Chris Patten, 'Europe Must Solve its Own Conflicts', *Die Zeit*, 6 February 2000; Chris Patten, Speech before joint meeting of European Parliament Foreign Affairs Committee and Members of the NATO Parliamentary Assembly, Brussels, 22 February 2000; Chris Patten, Speech before the Institut Français des Relations Internationales (ifri), Paris, 15 June 2000; Chris Patten, 'The EU Counterweight to American Influence', *International Herald Tribune*, 16 June 2000; Ignacio Ramonet, 'New World Order', *Le Monde diplomatique*, June 1999; 'Hubert Védrine, 'France's Voice in the World', *The Economist*, 11 November 2000.
2 *A Secure Europe in a Better World: European Security Strategy*, Brussels, December 2003; 'Regierungserklärung von Bundesaussenminister Fischer vor dem Deutschen Bundestag zu den Ergebnissen des Europäischen Rats von Thessaloniki', 26 June 2003, available at www.auswaertiges-amt.de/www/de/ausgabe_archiv?archiv_id=4667#5 (accessed on 17 January 2005); Katja Ridderbusch, 'Kontinentaldrift aufgehalten', *Die Welt*, 25 June 2003; Jacques Schuster, 'Sicherheit schaffen auch mit Waffen', *Die Welt*, 21 June 2003.
3 Charles Grant, *Intimate Relations: Can Britain Play a Leading Role in European Defense – and Keep its Special Links to US intelligence?*, Centre for European Reform, Working Paper, April 2000; Jolyon Howorth, 'Britain, France and the European Defence Initiative', *Survival*, 42/2 (Summer 2000), pp. 33–55 and *European Integration and Defence: The Ultimate Challenge?*, Chaillot Paper, 43, Institute for Security Studies of the WEU, Paris, xx; Anand Menon, 'Security Relations: Mehr Schein als Sein', in Patrick McCarthy (ed.), *France–Germany in the Twenty-First Century* (New York: Palgrave, 2001), p. 116; 'Paris and Berlin Hold Course for EU Enlargement', *Financial Times*, 13 June 2001; Peter Schmidt, *The Special Franco-German Security Relationship in the 1990s*, Chaillot Paper, 8, Institute for Security Studies of the WEU, Paris, June 1993; Bryan Wells, 'European Force Structures after St-Malo – The British Approach', in Gordon Wilson (ed.), *European Force Structures*, WEU Occasional Paper, 6, May 1999, p. 11.
4 Joschka Fischer 'Wer redet von Neuanfang', *Die Zeit*, 25/1999 and speech to the Council

of Foreign Relations, New York, 5 November 1999; Ralf Fücks, 'Was ist neu an der Berliner Republik?', Lecture at the Goethe Institute, Washington, DC, 12 December 1999; Wolfgang Ischinger, 'Die Gemeinsame Aussen- und Sicherheitspolitik der Europäischen Union', *Europäische Sicherheit*, 7/1998; Josef Joffe, 'Weltmacht USA', *Die Zeit*, 09/2001; General Klaus Naumann, 'Warum wir und die USA auf einander angewiesen bleiben', *Die Welt*, Oktober 22, 2000; Rudolf Scharping, 'Europas Stimme in der Allianz', *Die Zeit*, 8/1999; Rudolf Scharping, Speech at Berliner Dialog – Internationale Sicherheit, Berlin, 3 July 2001; Rudolf Scharping, Speech at Berliner Dialog – Internationale Sicherheit, Berlin, 3 July 2001; Klaus Wiesmann, 'Die Entwicklung der Europäische Sicherheits- und Verteidigungspolitik: Ambitionen und Realitäten', *Europäische Sicherheit*, 5/2001, p. 17.
5 'Stärkung des europäischen Pfeilers der Nato', Pressemitteilung, 29 April 2003.
6 François Heisbourg, *Emerging European Power Projection Capabilities*, GCSP-RAND Workshop Paper, Geneva, 15–16 July 1999, available at Columbia International Affairs Online, www.ciaonet.org/conf/hef01/.

Appendix A

German contributions to out-of-area military operations. The table lists the analysed cases and the parliamentary debates relating to each case.

Conflict/Military operation	Total size of of operation	German contribution	Bundestag debates
Gulf War 1990–91		Financial and logistical support Dispatch of 200 soldiers and 18 fighter jets to Turkey as part of NATO's ACE Mobile Force	23 August 1990 31 January 1991
Adriatic Sea 1992–96 *Operation Sharp Guard* Monitoring embargo against FRY	22 NATO and WEU ships	2 destroyers (no combat operation)	6 June 1991 15 November 1991 22 July 1992
Somalia 1993–94 UNOSOM II	28,000 troops	Supply and transport units, 1,700 troops	17 June 1993 22 July 1993 22 July 1994
Bosnia-Herzegovina 1993–95 *Operation Deny Fly* Monitoring no-fly zone	4,500 airmen	Air force personnel as part of AWACS unit, 500 airmen	15 January 1993 24 June 1993 2 July 1993
Bosnia-Herzegovina 1995–96 IFOR	60,000 troops	3.000 ground troops, logistical and supply tasks, no security tasks	30 November 1995 6 December 1995
Bosnia-Herzegovina, since 1996 SFOR	32,000 troops	3.000 ground troops, incl. combat troops	13 December 1996 19 June 1998

Conflict/Military operation	Total size of of operation	German contribution	Bundestag debates
Kosovo, since 1998 *Operation Allied Force* KFOR	50,000 KFOR troops	Participation in NATO air strikes in *Allied Force* 8,000 KFOR ground troops	16 October 1998 16 February 2001
East Timor 1999–2000 INTERFET	9,800 troops	100 medical personnel	7 October 1999 16 September 1999
Macedonia, since 2001 *Operation Essential Harvest* *Operation Amber Fox*	Each operation comprising 1,000 troops	500 ground troops to *Essential Harvest* 600 ground troops to *Amber Fox*, Germany lead nation	29 August 2001 27 September 2001
Afghanistan, since 2001 *Operation Enduring Freedom*	3 carrier battle groups with strike aircrafts, 300 fighter jets and support aircraft, 18,000 troops excluding American army and airforce personnel[a]	3,900 troops incl. 100 troops from the elite unit KSK	16 September 2001 16 November 2001
Congo June–September 2003 *Operation Artemis*	1,400 troops	Up to 350 troops, transportaion capabilities, medical support, staff officers	18 June 2003

Note: [a] These numbers are estimates as some deployments as by September 2002 were undisclosed or unspecified. *Operation Enduring Freedom Deployments*, Global Security.org, www.globalsecurity.org/military/ops/enduring-freedom_orbat-03.htm.

Appendix B

The table lists cases that were not analysed for reasons explained in Chapter 1, p. 18.

Cambodia 1991–92, UNAMIC	140 medical personnel in support of UN transitional administration
Bosnia-Herzegovina 1993–95, UNPROFOR	Logistical support for airlift to Sarajevo
Georgia, since 1994, UNOMIG	10 medical officers and military observers as part of UN peacekeeping force

Appendix C

Interviews conducted during research in the period between May 1999 and April 2002.

Government officials	
Chancellery	1
Foreign Ministry	3
Defence Ministry	3
Political party officials/Political advisors	
CDU/CSU	2
SPD	3
FDP	1
The Greens	2
PDS	0
Bundeswehr leaders	
Officers of the rank General and Major General	5
Educational leaders	3
Others	
Security policy experts/Think tank employees	8
Mass media leaders	3

Appendix D

The table lists the analysed cases of German military participation in out-of-area crisis management, the mandate on which intervention was based, the organisation under whose auspices the intervention took place, and other participating nations, with focus on Germany's NATO and European allies, and finally the distribution of votes in the German Bundestag as an indication of the base of support for each individual mission.

Conflict/Military operation	Mandate/Auspices	Other participating nations	Distribution of votes in the Bundestag
Adriatic Sea 1992–96 Operation Sharp Guard Monitoring embargo against FRY in the Adriatic Sea	UN mandate, UNSCR 820 Joint NATO and WEU operation	12 nations, including US, Great Britain, Greece, Turkey, and the Netherlands	No Bundestag vote SPD, Greens, and PDS against German participation
Somalia 1993–94 UNOSOM II	UN mandate, UNSCR 814 UN operation	28 nations, including US, France, Italy, Greece	No Bundestag vote SPD, Greens, and PDS against German participation
Bosnia-Herzegovina 1993–95 Operation Deny Fly Monitoring and enforcing no-fly zone over Bosnia	UN mandate, UNSCR 816 NATO-led operation	US, France, Great Britain, Turkey, Italy, the Netherlands	No Bundestag vote SPD, Greens, and PDS against German participation
Bosnia-Herzegovina 1995–96 IFOR	UN mandate, UNSCR 1031 NATO-led operation	All NATO members, 22 non-NATO members	Yes: 543 No: 107 Abstentions: 6

Conflict/Military operation	Mandate/Auspices	Other participating nations	Distribution of votes in the Bundestag
Bosnia-Herzegovina, since 1996 SFOR	UN mandate, UNSCR 1088 NATO-led operation	All NATO members, 22 non-NATO members	Yes: 499 No: 93 Abstentions: 0
Air-strikes against Serbia March–June 1999 Operation Allied Force	No UN mandate NATO operation	All NATO members contributed 650 US aircraft and 554 from other NATO members involved	Yes: 500 No: 62 Abstentions: 18
Kosovo since 1999 KFOR	UN mandate, UNSCR 1244 UN auspices but substantial NATO presence	All NATO members, 22 non-NATO members	Yes: 540 No: 24 Abstentions: 11
East Timor 1999–2000 INTERFET	UN mandate, UNSCR 1264 Australian-led multinational operation	29 nations, including Australia, UK, US	Approved[a]
Macedonia, since 2001 Operation Essential Harvest	No UN mandate NATO operation requested by parties to the conflict	Belgium, Canada, Czech Rep., France, Greece, Italy, the Netherlands, Spain, Turkey, UK	Yes: 497 No: 130 Abstentions: 8
Macedonia, since 2001 Operation Amber Fox	UN mandate, UNSCR 1371 NATO operation	Denmark, France, Greece, Italy, Portugal, Poland, Spain	Yes: 528 No: 40 Abstentions: 10
Afghanistan, since 2001 Operation Enduring Freedom	No UN mandate but support in UNSCR 1368 and 1373 US-led multinational operation	Australia, Canada, France, Italy, Japan, UK	Yes: 336 No: 326 Abstentions: 0
Congo, June–September 2003 Operation Artemis	UN mandate, UNSCR 1484 EU operation.	Belgium, Brazil, Canada, France, Hungary, the Netherlands, South Africa, Sweden, UK	Yes: 441 No: 30 Abstentions: 7

Note: [a] In uncontroversial votes the Bundestag does not hold roll calls and the *Plenarprotokoll* simply records whether a proposal was passed or rejected.

Bibliography

Books and articles

Abenheim, Donald, 'The Citizen in Uniform: Reform and its Critics in the Bundeswehr', in Stephen F. Szabo (ed.), *The Bundeswehr and Western Security* (New York: St Martin's Press, 1990).
Abenheim, Donald, *Reforging the Iron Cross* (Princeton: Princeton University Press, 1988).
Almond, Gabriel and Sydney Verba, *The Civic Culture* (Boston: Little, Brown, 1965).
Anderson, Jeffrey J. and John B. Goodman, 'Mars or Minerva? A United Germany in a Post-Cold War Europe', in Robert O. Keohane, Joseph S. Nye, and Stanley Hoffmann (eds), *After the Cold War: International Institutions and State Strategies in Europe, 1989–1991* (Cambridge, MA: Harvard University Press, 1993).
Andréani, Gilles, 'The Disarray of US Non-Proliferation Policy', *Survival* 41:4 (Winter 1999–2000).
Bagger, Hartmut, 'Wir haben genug Wehrpflichtige', *Stuttgarter Nachrichten*, 23 January 1997.
Bahr, Egon, 'Ein Generalstab ist kein Taboo mehr', *Europäische Sicherheit*, 3/1992.
Bahr, Egon, 'Ein Protektorat wird selbstständlich', *Die Zeit*, 23/2000.
Bald, Detlef, *Militär und Gesellschaft 1945–1990* (Baden-Baden: Nomos Verlagsgesellschaft, 1994).
Bartels, Henning, 'Modernisierung und Ausrüstung unserer Streitkräfte', *Europäische Sicherheit*, 5/2001.
Baudissin, Count Wolf von, 'The New German Army', *Foreign Affairs*, 34:1 (October 1955).
Baumann, Rainer and Gunther Hellmann, 'Germany and the Use of Military Force: "Total War", the "Culture of Restraint", and the Quest for Normality', *German Politics*, 10:1 (April 2001).
Becher, Klaus, 'Reforming German Defence', *Survival*, 42:3 (Autumn 2000).
Beck, Major General Hans-Christian, *Anforderungen an die Erziehung in den Streitkräften vor dem Hintergrund ihrer aktuellen und künftigen Aufgaben*, Zentrum Innere Führung, Koblenz, April 1999.

Beck, Major General Hans-Christian, *Identität und Professionalität des deutschen Soldaten*, Zentrum Innere Führung, Koblenz, 1999.
Beer, Angelika, 'Antimilitärische Verständnis der Grünen', *Europäische Sicherheit*, 4/1996.
Beltran, Jacques, 'US "Rogue" Policy Isn't the French Way', *Los Angeles Times*, 16 October 2000.
Berger, Thomas U., *Cultures of Antimilitarism: National Security in Germany and Japan* (Baltimore: Johns Hopkins University Press, 1998).
Berger, Thomas U., 'Norms, Identity, and National Security in Germany and Japan', in Peter J. Katzenstein (ed.), *The Culture of National Security: Norms and Identity in World Politics* (New York: Columbia University Press, 1996).
Berndt, Michael, *Deutsche Militärpolitik in der neuen Weltunordnung* (Münster: Agenda, 1997).
Bohnen, Johannes, 'Germany', in Jolyon Howorth and Anand Menon (eds), *The European Union and National Defence Policy* (London: Routledge, 1997).
Borkenhagen, Franz H.U., *Außenpolitische Interessen Deutschlands: Rolle und Aufgabe der Bundeswehr* (Bonn: Bouvier Verlag, 1997).
Boynton, G. R., 'The Expertise of the Senate Foreign Relations Committee', in Valerie M. Hudson (ed.), *Artificial Intelligence and International Politics* (Boulder: Westview Press, 1991).
Brandt, Gerhard, 'Diverging Functions of Military Armament', in Jacques van Doorn (ed.), *Armed Forces and Society: Sociological Essays* (The Hague: Mouton, 1968).
Brauch, Hans Günter, 'SDI – The Political Debate in the Federal Republic of Germany', in Hans Günter Brauch (ed.), *Star Wars and European Defense* (London: Macmillan, 1987).
Bredow, Wilfried von and Gerhard Kümmel, *Das Militär und die Herausforderung globaler Sicherheit*, SOWI-Arbeitspapier, No. 119, Strausberg, September 1999.
Brüderle, Rainer, 'Die Wehrpflicht ist von Gestern', *Der Tagesspiegel*, 14 August 1997.
Buchholz, Frank, 'Ernstfall Frieden – Ernstfall Krieg', in Paul Klein and Andreas Prüfert, *Militärische Ausbildung Heute und in der Zukunft* (Baden-Baden: Nomos Verlagsgesellschaft, 1994).
Buchsteiner, Jochen, 'Three Green Parliamentarians in George Bush's Court', *Frankfurter Allgemeine Zeitung*, 9 October 2001.
Budde, Hans-Otto, 'Gleiche Rechte und Pflichten – Die deutsche Beteiligung an SFOR', in General Peter Goebel (ed.), *Von Kambodscha bis Kosovo: Auslandseinsätze der Bundeswehr* (Frankfurt am Main: Report Verlag, 2000).
Buras, Piotr and Kerry Longhurst, 'The Berlin Republic, Iraq, and the Use of Force', *European Security*, 13:3 (2004).
Calleo, David, 'Germany and the Balance of Power', in Wolfram F. Hanrieder (ed.), *West German Foreign Policy 1949–1979* (Boulder: Westview Press, 1980).
Cavanagh Hodge, Carl, 'Konrad Adenauer, Arms, and the Redemption of Germany', in Cathal J. Nolan (ed.), *Ethics and Statecraft: The Moral Dimension of International Affairs* (London: Praeger, 1995).
Clay, Lucius D., *Decision in Germany* (New York: Doubleday and Co, 1950).
Cohn-Bendit, Daniel, 'Wir werden die Welt verbessern', *Die Zeit*, 50/2000.
Collmer, Sabine, 'Neuer Auftrag – neue Soldaten?', in Paul Klein and Dieter Walz (eds), *Die Bundeswehr an der Schwelle zum 21. Jahrhundert* (Baden-Baden: Nomos Verlagsgesellschaft, 2000).

Cox, Robert W., 'Social Forces, States, and World Orders: Beyond International Relations Theory', in Robert O. Keohane (ed.), *Neorealism and its Critics* (New York: Columbia University Press, 1986).
Craig, Gordon A., *Europe, 1815–1914* (New York: Harcourt Brace Jovanovich College Publishers, 1971).
Craig, Gordon A., *The Politics of the Prussian Army 1640–1945* (London: Oxford University Press, 1979).
Crawford, Beverly, 'Explaining Defection from International Cooperation', Germany's Unilateral Recognition of Croatia', *World Politics*, No. 48 (July 1996).
Crawford, Beverly and Jost Halfmann, 'Domestic Politics and International Change: Germany's Role in Europe's Security Future', in Beverly Crawford (ed.), *The Future of European Security*, Center for German and European Studies, University of California at Berkeley, Research Series, No. 4, 1992.
Czempiel, Ernest-Otto, 'Seltsame Stille', *Die Zeit*, 14/1999.
Daalder, Ivo H. and Michael E. O'Hanlon, *Winning Ugly: NATO's War to Save Kosovo* (Washington, DC: Brookings Institution Press, 2000).
Dalgaard-Nielsen, Anja, 'Homeland Security and the Role of the Armed Forces: A Scandinavian Perspective', in Heiko Borchert (ed.), *Mehr Sicherheit – Weniger Souveränität* (Hamburg: Verlag E. S. Mittler & Sohn, 2004).
Dalvi, Sameera, 'The Post-Cold War Role of the Bundeswehr: A Product of Normative Influences', *European Security*, 7:1 (1998).
Davis, Lynn E., 'Defining the Army's Homeland Security Needs', in Lynn E. Davis and Jeremy Shapiro (eds), *The US Army and the New National Security Strategy*, Santa Monica: RAND, 2003.
Dettke, Dieter, 'Civil Foreign Policy: German Domestic Constraints and New Security Arrangements in Europe', in Beverly Crawford (ed.), *The Future of European Security*, Berkeley, University of California Center for German and European Studies, University of California at Berkeley, Research Series, No. 84, 1992.
Dettke, Dieter, 'Multilateralism and Re-Nationalization: European Security in Transition', in Paul Michael Lützeler, *Europe After Maastricht* (Providence: Berghahn Books, 1994).
Deutsch, Karl W., Lewis J. Edinger, Roy C. Macridis, and Richard L. Merritt, *France, Germany and the Western Alliance* (New York: Charles Scribner's Sons, 1967).
Dinke, Albert, 'Nicht die Bundeswehr ist in der Sinnkrise – die ganze Gesellschaft ist es', *Europäische Sicherheit*, 7/1993.
Drozdiak, William, 'Germany Vows Balkan Recognition', *Washington Post*, 11 January 1992.
Duffield, John S., *World Power Forsaken: Political Culture, International Institutions, and German Security Policy after Unification* (Stanford, CA: Stanford University Press, 1998).
Durch, William J., 'Introduction to Anarchy: Humanitarian Intervention and "State-Building" in Somalia', in William J. Durch (ed.), *UN Peacekeeping, American Politics, and the Uncivil Wars of the 1990s* (New York: St Martin's Press, 1996).
Dyson, Kenneth, *The State Tradition of Western Europe* (New York: Oxford University Press, 1980).
Enzenberger, Hans-Magnus, 'Hitlers Wiedergänger', *Der Spiegel*, 1 February 1991.
Feld, W., 'Franco-German Military Cooperation and European Unification', *Journal of European Integration*, 12:2 (1989).

Feldmeyer, Karl, 'Mehr Geld gibt es nicht', *Frankfurter Allgemeine Zeitung*, 18 November 1997.
Fischer, Joschka, 'Wer redet von Neuanfang', *Die Zeit*, 25/1999.
Fraps, Peter K., 'Unter dem Blauen Barett', in General Peter Goebel (ed.), *Von Kambodscha bis Kosovo': Auslandseinsätze der Bundeswehr* (Frankfurt am Main: Report Verlag, 2000).
Friedeburg, Ludwig von 'Rearmament and Social Change', in Jacques van Doorn (ed.), *Armed Forces and Society: Sociological Essays* (The Hague: Mouton, 1968).
Fuchs, Katrin, *Die Architektur einer neuen europäischen Sicherheitsordnung*, press release, 25 September 1991
Fuchs, Katrin, 'Keine deutschen Soldaten an den Golf', *Vorwärts*, January 1991.
Gantzel-Kress, Gisela and Klaus Jürgen Gantzel, 'The Development of IR Studies in West Germany', in Ekkehart Krippendorf and Volker Rittberger (eds), *The Foreign Policy of West Germany: Formation and Contents* (Beverly Hills, CA: Sage, 1988).
Garten, Jeffrey, *Cold Peace: America, Japan, Germany, and the Struggle for Supremacy* (New York: Times Books, 1992).
Garton Ash, Timothy, *In Europe's Name: Germany and the Divided Continent* (London: Jonathan Cape, 1993).
Geertz, Clifford, 'Ideology as a Cultural System', in David E. Apter (ed.), *Ideology and Discontent* (London: Macmillan, 1964).
Geis, Matthias, 'Der Verteidigungsminister muss jetzt beweisen, dass er die Armee wirklich erneuern will', *Die Zeit*, 22/2000.
Genscher, Hans-Dietrich, 'Die Bundeswehr ist eine Armee mitten im Volk', *General Anzeiger*, 12 (August 1997).
Genscher, Hans-Dietrich, 'Die neue europäische Friedensordnung', *Europa-Archiv*, No. 15, 1990.
Genscher, Hans-Dietrich, 'Kontinuität und Wandel: Moderne Außenpolitik in der Perspektive 2000', in Hans-Dietrich Genscher (ed.), *Nach vorn gedacht: Perspektiven deutscher Außenpolitik* (Bonn: Bonn aktuell, 1987).
Giddens, Anthony, *The Constitution of Society* (Cambridge: Polity Press, 1984).
Giesen, Bernhard, *Die Intellektuellen und die Nation* (Frankfurt am Main: Suhrkamp, 1993).
Goebel, General Peter, 'Beteiligung der Bundeswehr am Wiederaufbau in Bosnien-Herzegowina', in General Peter Goebel (ed.), *Von Kambodscha bis Kosovo: Auslandseinsätze der Bundeswehr* (Frankfurt am Main: Report Verlag, 2000).
Goldstein, Judith and Robert O. Keohane, *Ideas and Foreign Policy* (Ithaca: Cornell University Press, 1993).
Gompert, David C., Richard L. Kugler, and Martin C. Libicki, *Mind the Gap: Promoting a Transatlantic Revolution in Military Affairs* (Washington, DC: National Defense University Press, 1999).
Gow, James, *Triumph of the Lack of Will: International Diplomacy and the Yugoslav War* (New York: Colombia University Press, 1997).
Grant, Charles, *Intimate Relations: Can Britain Play a Leading Role in European Defense – And Keep its Special Links to US Intelligence?*, Centre for European Reform, Working Paper, April 2000.
Gray, Colin, 'National Styles in Strategy: The American Example', *International Security*, 6:2 (Fall 1981).
Gress, David, *Peace and Survival: West Germany, the Peace Movement, and European*

Security (Stanford, CA: Hoover Institution Press, 1985).
Gutjahr, Lothar, *German Foreign and Defence Policy after Unification* (London: Pinter, 1994).
Haas, Peter M., 'Epistemic Communities', *International Organization*, 46 (1992).
Habermas, Jürgen, 'Bestialität und Humanität', *Die Zeit*, 18/1999.
Hacke, Christian, *Weltmach wider Willen* (Stuttgart: Ernst Klett Verlag, 1988).
Hamann, Rudolf, 'Abscheid vom Staatsbürger in Uniform', in Paul Klein and Dieter Walz (eds), *Die Bundeswehr an der Schwelle zum 21. Jahrhundert* (Baden-Baden: Nomos Verlagsgesellschaft, 2000).
Hanrieder, Wolfram F., 'West German Foreign Policy, 1949-1979: Necessities and Choices', in Wolfram F. Hanrieder (ed.), *West German Foreign Policy 1949–1979* (Boulder: Westview Press, 1980).
Hauser, Otto, 'Ende der Wehrpflicht – Beginn der Dienstpflicht?', *Europäische Sicherheit*, 4/1994.
Hedetoft, Ulf, *Signs of Nations: Studies in the Political Semiotics of Self and Other in Contemporary European Nationalism* (Aldershot: Dartmouth, 1995).
Heisbourg, François, *Emerging European Power Projection Capabilities*, GCSP-RAND Workshop Paper, Geneva, 15–16 July 1999, available at Columbia International Affairs Online, www.ciaonet.org/conf/hef01/.
Heisbourg, François, *European Defense: Making it Work*, Chaillot Paper, 42, Institute for Security Studies of the WEU, Paris, September 2000.
Herf, Jeffrey, *Divided Memory: The Nazi Past in the Two Germanies* (Cambridge, MA: Harvard University Press, 1997).
Herf, Jeffrey, *War by Other Means: Soviet Power, West German Resistance, and the Battle of the Euromissiles* (New York: Free Press, 1991).
Hintze, Peter, 'Zur Diskussion eine Abschaffung der allgemeinen Wehrpflicht', *Mittagsmagazin*, 8 August 1997.
Hobsbawn, Eric J., 'Die neuen Nationalismen', *Die Zeit*, 19/1999.
Hoffmann, Arthur and Kerry Longhurst, 'German Strategic Culture in Action', *Contemporary Security Policy*, 20:2, 1999.
Hoffmann, Wolfgang, 'Bundeswehr: Das wird teuer!', *Die Zeit*, 43/2000.
Hofmann, Gunter, 'Wie Deutschland in den Krieg geriet', *Die Zeit*, 12 May 1999.
Holbrooke, Richard, *To Stop a War* (New York: Random House, 1998).
Holsti, K. J., 'National Role Conceptions in the Study of Foreign Policy', in Stephen G. Walker (ed.), *Role Theory and Foreign Policy Analysis* (Durham: Duke University Press, 1987).
Holsti, Ole R., 'Foreign Policy Formation Viewed Cognitively', in Robert Axelrod (ed.), *Structure of Decision: The Cognitive Maps of Political Elites* (Princeton: Princeton University Press, 1976).
Howorth, Jolyon, 'Britain, France and the European Defence Initiative', *Survival*, 42:2 (Summer 2000).
Howorth, Jolyon, *European Integration and Defence: The Ultimate Challenge?*, Chaillot Paper, 43, Institute for Security Studies of the WEU, Paris, November 2000.
Hrbek, Rudolf and Wolfgang Wessels (eds), *EG-Mitgliedschaft: Ein vitales Interesse der Bundesrepublik Deutschland?* (Bonn: Europa Union Verlag, 1984).
Huber, Reiner K., 'Die Erneuerung der Bundeswehr', *Europäische Sicherheit*, 4/2001.
Huber, Rainer K. and Bernhard Schmidt, *The Challenge for Defense: Reform in Europe*, The Potomac Papers, May 2000.

Huber, Reiner K. and Bernhard Schmidt, 'Wo steht die Bundeswehr in der NATO?', *Europäische Sicherheit*, 5/1999.

Human Rights Watch, *Failure to Protect: Anti-Minority Violence in Kosovo, March 2004*, Human Rights Watch Report, 16:6 (D), July 2004 at http://hrw.org/reports/2004/kosovo0704/.

Inacker, Michael J., 'Die mentale Ausrichtung von Streitkräften', *Europäische Sicherheit*, 10/1995.

Ischinger, Wolfgang, 'Die Gemeinsame Aussen- und Sicherheitspolitik der Europäischen Union', *Europäische Sicherheit*, 7/1998.

Jakobsen, Peter Viggo, *PRTs in Afghanistan: Successful but not Sufficient*, DIIS Report, 6 (Copenhagen: Danish Institute for International Studies, 2005).

Jepperson, Ronald L., Alexander Wendt, and Peter J. Katzenstein, 'Norms, Identity, and Culture in National Security Policy', in Peter J. Katzenstein (ed.), *The Culture of National Security: Norms and Identity in World Politics* (New York: Columbia University Press, 1996).

Jermer, Helmut, 'Innere Führung – auf den Punkt gebracht', in Oskar Hoffmann and Andreas Prüfert, *Innere Führung 2000* (Baden-Baden: Nomos Verlagsgesellschaft, 2001).

Jertz, Walter, 'Einsatz der Luftwaffe über Bosnien', in General Peter Goebel (ed.), *Von Kambodscha bis Kosovo: Auslandseinsätze der Bundeswehr* (Frankfurt am Main: Report Verlag, 2000).

Jervis, Robert, *Perception and Misperception in International Politics* (Princeton: Princeton University Press, 1976).

Joffe, Josef, 'Feldzug gegen Unbekannt', *Die Zeit*, 66/2001.

Joffe, Josef, 'Peace and Populism: Why the European Anti-Nuclear Movement Failed', *International Security*, 11:4 (Spring 1987).

Joffe, Josef, 'Weltmacht USA', *Die Zeit*, 09/2001.

Johnston, Alastair Iain, 'Thinking about Strategic Culture', *International Security*, 19:4 (Spring 1995).

Jones, David R., 'Soviet Strategic Culture', in Carl G. Jacobsen (ed.), *Strategic Power: USA/USSR* (London: St Martin's Press, 1990).

Judt, Tony, *The Burden of Responsibility* (Chicago: University of Chicago Press, 1998).

Kaiser, Karl and Klaus Becher, 'Germany and the Iraq Conflict', in Nicole Gnesotto and John Roper (eds), *Western Europe and the Gulf* (Paris: Institute for Security Studies of the WEU, 1992).

Kammerhoff, Holger, 'Unter Blauhelm am Horn von Afrika', in General Peter Goebel (ed.), *Von Kambodscha bis Kosovo: Auslandseinsätze der Bundeswehr* (Frankfurt am Main: Report Verlag, 2000).

Kelleher, Catherine M., 'Fundamentals of German Security: The Creation of the Bundeswehr – Continuity and Change', in Stephen F. Szabo, *The Bundeswehr and Western Security* (New York: St Martin's Press, 1990).

Kielmansegg, Major General Johann Adolf Graf von, 'Der Krieg ist der Ernstfall', *Truppenpraxis*, 3/1991.

Kinkel, Klaus, 'Die Außenpolitik der Bundesrepublik Deutschland nach der Wiedervereinigung', *Europäische Sicherheit*, 1/1993.

Kinkel, Klaus, 'Deutsche Außen- und Sicherheitspolitik bei der internationalen Krisenbewältigung seit 1990', *Bulletin*, 98, 9 December 1997.

Kinkel, Klaus, 'Germany's Role in Peacemissions', *NATO Brief*, 10/1994.

Kirchbach, General Inspector Hans Peter von, 'Neue Herausforderungen an die Ausbildung des Heeres in der Zukunft', in Paul Klein and Andreas Prüfert, *Militärische Ausbildung Heute und in der Zukunft* (Baden-Baden: Nomos Verlagsgesellschaft, 1994).

Kirchbach, General Inspector Hans Peter von, 'Soldaten können nicht Frieden herbeibringen und nicht die Köpfe ändern', *Berliner Zeitung*, 29 December 1999.

Kissinger, Henry, *Diplomacy* (New York: Simon & Schuster, 1994).

Kitchen, Martin, *A Military History of Germany: From the Eighteenth Century to the Present Day* (London: Weidenfeld & Nicolson, 1975).

Klein, Paul, 'Multinationale Streitkräfte: Modell für die Zukunft oder bereits wieder Vergangenheit?', in Paul Klein and Dieter Walz (eds), *Die Bundeswehr an der Schwelle zum 21. Jahrhundert* (Baden-Baden: Nomos Verlagsgesellschaft, 2000).

Klose, Hans-Ulrich, 'Die Deutschen und der Krieg am Golf – eine schwierige Debatte', *Frankfurter Allgemeine Zeitung*, 25 January 1991.

Kohl, Helmut, 'Aufbruch in die Zukunft: Deutschland gemeinsam erneuern', *Bulletin*, No. 108, 24 November 1994.

Kohler, Berthold, 'In Reserve', *Frankfurter Allgemeine Zeitung*, 9 October 2001.

Köppelin, Jürgen, 'Rühe kann der FDP Debatte um Wehrpflicht nicht verbieten', *Thüringer Allgemeine Zeitung*, 9 August 1997.

Krause, Joachim, 'The Role of the Bundestag in German Foreign Policy', in Wolf-Dieter Eberwein and Karl Kaiser (eds), *Germany's New Foreign Policy: Decision-Making in an Interdependent World* (New York: Palgrave, 1998).

Kreile, Michael, 'Verantwortung und Interesse in der deutschen Außen- und Sicherheitspolitik', *Aus Politik und Zeitgeschichte*, 5 (1996), pp. 3–11.

Kremp, Herbert, 'Erste NATO-Soldaten in Mazedonien erwartet', *Die Welt*, 17 August 2001.

Kremp, Herbert, 'Wir brauchen belebenden deutschen Eigenwillen', *Die Welt*, 29 May 2000.

Kuhn, Friedrich, 'Im freien Fall ins Krisengebiet', *Die Welt*, 29 March 1997.

Kutz, Martin, *Berufsbilder und politische Orientierung: Zur soziologischen Typologisierung und politischen Entwicklungen des Offizierskorps der Bundeswehr*, Führungsakademie der Bundeswehr, Hamburg, October 1998.

Lafontaine, Oskar, 'Verzweifelte Aussichten', *Die Tageszeitung*, 9 February 1991.

Lambeck, Martin S., 'Erster Einsatz der Bundeswehr-Elitetruppe', *Die Welt*, 16 June 1998.

Lamers, Karl, 'Schwarze Löcher in der Weltpolitik müssen verschwinden', *Financial Times Deutschland*, 8 October 2001.

Lange, Manfred, 'Die Bundeswehr auf dem Weg ins 21. Jahrhundert', *Europäische Sicherheit*, 10/2000.

Lankowski, Carl, 'Modell Deutschland and the International Regionalization of the West German State in the 1970s', in Andrei Markowits (ed.), *The Political Economy of West Germany: Modell Deutschland* (New York: Praeger, 1982).

Lantis, Jeffrey S., 'Rising to the Challenge: German Security Policy in the Post-Cold War Era', *German Politics and Society*, 14:2 (1996).

Layne, Christopher, 'The Unipolar Illusion: Why New Great Powers Will Rise', *International Security*, 17:4 (1993).

Leder, Dieter, 'Internationale Minenräumoperationen im Arabischen Golf', in General Peter Goebel (ed.), *Vom Kambodscha bis Kosovo: Auslandseinsätze der Bundeswehr* (Frankfurt am Main: Report Verlag).

Leersch, Hans-Jürgen, 'Gerhardt fordert Generalstab', *Die Welt*, 6 August 1999.
Leersch, Hans-Jürgen, 'Kämpfen statt zahlen ist diesmal die deutsche Devise', *Die Welt*, 2 October 2001.
Leersch, Hans-Jürgen, 'Kehrtwende der CDU in der Sicherheitspolitik', *Die Welt*, 8 October 1999.
Leersch, Hans-Jürgen, 'Leere Kassen machen den Soldaten das Leben schwer', *Die Welt*, 14 September 1999.
LeGloannec, Anne-Marie, 'West German Security: Less of a Consensus?', in Catherine McArdle Kelleher and Gale A. Mattox (eds), *Evolving European Defense Policies* (Lexington, MA: Lexington Books, 1987).
Lennartz, Klaus, 'Wehpflicht ganz abschaffen', *Express*, 7 January 1997.
Libal, Michael, *Limits of Persuasion: Germany and the Yugoslav Crisis, 1991–1992* (Westport: Praeger, 1997).
Longhurst, Kerry, *Germany and the Use of Force: The Evolution of German Security Policy 1990–2003* (Manchester and New York: Manchester University Press, 2004).
Marienfeld, Claire, 'Allgemeine Wehrpflicht – die Verantwortung des Bürgers in der Demokratie', *Europäische Sicherheit*, 9/1997.
Mass, Heiko, 'Relikt des Kalten Krieges', *Süddeutsche Zeitung*, 8 August 2001.
Maull, Hanns W., 'Germany and Japan: The New Civilian Powers', *Foreign Affairs*, 69:5 (1990).
Maull, Hanns W., 'Germany and the Use of Force: Still a "Civilian Power"?' *Survival*, 42:2, 2000.
Maull, Hanns W.. 'Germany in the Yugoslav Crisis', *Survival*, 37:4 (Winter 1995–96).
Maull, Hanns W., 'Germany's Foreign Policy, post-Kosovo: Still a "Civilian Power"?', in Sebastian Harnisch and Hanns W. Maull (eds), *Germany as a Civilian Power? The Foreign Policy of the Berlin Republic* (Manchester: Manchester University Press, 2001).
Mearsheimer, John J., 'Back to the Future: Instability in Europe after the Cold War', *International Security*, 15:1 (1990).
Meiers, Franz-Josef, 'A German Defence Review?', in Gordon Wilson (ed.), *European Force Structures*, Paris: Institute for Security Studies of the WEU, Occasional Paper, 8, May 1999.
Menkhaus, Ken, 'The Security Paradox of Failed States', *National Strategy Forum Review*, 12:3 (Spring 2003).
Menon, Anand, 'Security Relations: Mehr Schein als Sein', in Patrick McCarthy (ed.), *France–Germany in the Twenty-First Century* (New York: Palgrave, 2001).
Meyer, Berthold and Roberto Zadra, *Die Grünen und List Verdi – Sicherheitspolitische Alternativen für Europa?*, Münster/Hamburg, 1992.
Meyers, Reinhard, 'Weltmarkt oder Weltpolitik?', *Neue Politische Literatur*, 31:2 (1986).
Molitor, Andreas, Sabine Rückert, Stefan Willeke, Stefan Merx, and Michael Schwellen, 'Aus Dienst wird Ernst', *Die Zeit* 15/1999.
Moniac, Rüdiger, 'Der Kampfeinsatz gehört zum neuen Berufsalltag', *Die Welt*, 22 September 1998.
Moniac, Rüdiger, 'Grünen streiten über Verhältnis zum Militär', *Die Welt*, 20 June 1998.
Moniac, Rüdiger, 'Vorgelebte Versöhnung', *Die Welt*, 2 July 1997.
Müller, Harald, 'Military Intervention for European Security: The German Debate', in Lawrence Freedman (ed.), *Military Intervention in European Conflicts* (Oxford: Blackwell, 1994).

Mutz, Reinhard, 'Schiessen wie die anderen?', in Dieter S. Lutz (ed.), *Deutsche Soldaten weltweit? Blauhelme, Eingreiftruppen, 'out-of-area' – Der Streit um unsere sicherheitspolitische Zukunft* (Reinbek: Rowohlt, 1993).
Naumann, General Klaus, *Die Bundeswehr in einer Welt im Umbruch* (Berlin, 1994).
Naumann, General Klaus, 'Die Bundeswehr steht für Frieden und Freiheit', *Europäische Sicherheit*, 1/1996.
Naumann, General Klaus, *Erfahrungen aus dem Kosovo-Einsatz*, Führungsakademie der Bundeswehr, Hamburg, Akademie-Information, Sonderheft, August 1999.
Naumann, General Klaus, 'Sicherheit in Europa – Konsequenzen für die Bundeswehr', *Europäische Sicherheit*, 1/1995.
Naumann, General Klaus, 'Warum wir und die USA auf einander angewiesen bleiben', *Die Welt*, 22 Oktober 2000.
Naumann, General Klaus, 'Zuverlässiger Instrument in den Händen der Politik', *Frankfurter Rundschau*, 27 October 1995.
Nolting, Günther, 'Noch eine Reform ist jetzt nicht sinnvoll', *Bonner Rundschau*, 9 August 1997.
Nolting, Günther F., 'So muss die Bundeswehr aussehen!', *Die Welt*, 19 May 2000.
Opel, Manfred, 'Plädoyer für eine moderne und flexible Freiwilligenarmee', *Frankfurter Rundschau*, 20 August 1997.
Opel, Manfred, 'Wehrpflicht hilft nicht gegen moderne Waffen', *Sonntagsblatt*, 29 August 1997.
Orden, Geoffrey van, 'The Bundeswehr in Transition', *Survival*, 33:4 (1991).
Patten, Chris, 'Europe must solve its own conflicts', *Die Zeit*, 6 February 2000.
Patten, Chris, 'The EU Counterweight to American Influence', *International Herald Tribune*, 16 June 2000.
Philippi, Nina, 'Civilian Power and War: The German Debate about Out-of-Area Operations 1990–99', in Sebastian Harnisch and Hanns W. Maull (eds), *Germany as a Civilian Power: The Foreign Policy of the Berlin Republic* (Manchester: Manchester University Press, 2001).
Pond, Elizabeth, 'Federal Republic of Germany: Westpolitik, Ostpolitik, and Security', in Catherine McArdle Kelleher and Gale A. Mattox (eds), *Evolving European Defense Policies* (Lexington, MA: Lexington Books, 1987).
Prüfert, Andreas, 'Politische Bildung mit und für Soldaten – Ein tragfähiges Handlungskonzept für die Zukunft', in Oskar Hoffmann and Andreas Prüfert (eds), *Innere Führung 2000* (Baden-Baden: Nomos Verlagsgesellschaft, 2001).
Putnam, Robert D., *The Beliefs of Politicians: Ideology, Conflict, and Democracy in Britain and Italy* (New Haven: Yale University Press, 1973).
Ramonet, Ignacio, 'New World Order', *Le Monde diplomatique*, June 1999.
Randow, Gero von and Constanze Stelzenmüller, 'Zivis fürs Grobe', *Die Zeit*, 12/2000.
Rattinger, Hans, 'The Bundeswehr and Public Opinion', in Stephen F. Szabo (ed.), *The Bundeswehr and Western Security* (New York: St Martin's Press, 1990).
Rattinger, Hans, 'The Federal Republic of Germany: Much Ado About (Almost) Nothing', in Gregory Flynn and Hans Rattinger (eds), *The Public and Atlantic Defense* (London: Rowman & Allanheld, 1985).
Rau, Johannes, 'Wir müssen den Terrorismus bekämpfen', *Die Welt*, 15 October 2001.
Reinhardt, Charima, 'Kontroverse um Militärstrategie', *Frankfurter Rundschau*, 20 February 1992.
Riechmann, Friedrich W., 'Von Kroatien in die "Box"', in General Peter Goebel (ed.), *Von*

Kambodscha bis Kosovo: Auslandseinsätze der Bundeswehr (Frankfurt am Main: Report Verlag, 2000).
Rokeach, Milton, *The Open and the Closed Mind* (New York: Basic Books, 1960).
Ropers, Frank, 'Embargo-Überwachung in der Adria', in General Peter Goebel (ed.), *Von Kambodscha bis Kosovo: Auslandseinsätze der Bundeswehr* (Frankfurt am Main: Report Verlag, 2000).
Ropers, Norbert, 'Security Policy in the Federal Republic of Germany', in Colin McInnes (ed.), *Security and Strategy in the New Europe* (London: Routledge, 1992).
Rosen, F. V., *Soldatenbeteiligung in integrierten Stäben*, SOWI, Beiträge zu Lehre und Forschung, 2/1999.
Rühe, Volker, 'Abschluss der humanitären Hilfsaktion für Somalia', *Bulletin*, 25 March 1993.
Rühe, Volker, 'Berufsarmee lockt die Söldner-Typen', *Neue Ruhr Zeitung*, 7 May 1997.
Rühe, Volker, 'Bundeswehr und europäische Sicherheit', *Europäische Sicherheit*, 1/1996.
Rühe, Volker, 'Die Bundeswehr hat alle die Probleme der Gesellschaft auch', *Süddeutsche Zeitung*, 28 August 1997.
Rühe, Volker, 'Mogelpackung Schröder', *Focus*, 18 August 1997.
Rühe, Volker, 'Über den Kopf gewachsen', *Der Spiegel*, No. 16, 15 April 1996.
Rühe, Volker, 'Rolle Deutschlands im zusammenwachsenden Europa und der Beitrag der Bundeswehr', *Bulletin*, No. 91, 14 November 1996.
Rühe, Volker, 'Vierzig Jahre Bundeswehr – fünf Jahre Armee der Einheit', *Bulletin*, 12 October 1995.
Rühl, Lothar, 'Security Policy: National Structures and Multilateral Integration', in Wolf-Dieter Eberwein and Karl Kaiser (eds), *Germany's New Foreign Policy: Decision-Making in an Interdependent World* (New York: Palgrave, 1998).
Saalfeld, Thomas, 'The West German Bundestag after 40 Years: The Role of the Parliament in a Party Democracy', in Philip Norton (ed.), *Parliaments in Western Europe*, Special Issue, *West European Politics*, 13:3 (1990).
Sampson, M., 'Cultural Influences on Foreign Policy', in C. F. Hermann, C. W. Kegley, and J. N. Rosenau (eds), *New Directions in the Study of Foreign Policy* (Boston: Allen & Unwin, 1987).
Scharping, Rudolf, 'Europas Stimme in der Allianz', *Die Zeit*, 8/1999.
Scharping, Rudolf, 'Frieden und Stabilität in Europa', *Bulletin*,No. 6, 9 February 1999.
Schauer, Hans, *Europäische Identität und demokratische Tradition: Zum Staatsverständnis in Deutschland, Frankreich und Großbritannien* (Munich: Günter Olzog Verlag, 1996).
Schmidt, Helmut, 'Die NATO gehört nicht Amerika', *Die Zeit*, 17/1999.
Schmidt, Helmut, 'Zum AWACS-Beschluss des Bundeskabinetts', *Stichworte zur Sicherheitspolitik*, 4/1993.
Schmidt, Peter, *The Special Franco-German Security Relationship in the 1990s*, Chaillot Paper, 8, Institute for Security Studies of the WEU, Paris, June 1993.
Schmitz, Peter, 'The Out-of-Area Issue: Is NATO an Island?', in Catherine McArdle Kelleher and Gale A. Mattox (eds), *Evolving European Defense Policies* (Lexington, MA: Lexington Books, 1987).
Schneckener, Ulrich, *Transnationale Terroristen als Profiteure fragiler Staatlichkeit*, Berlin: SWP-Studie, Stiftung Wissenschaft und Politik, Deutsches Institut für Internationale Politik und Sicherheit, May 2004.
Schneider, Peter, 'Krieg und Frieden: Die Lehren von Sarajevo', *Die Zeit*, 18 June 1998.

Scholz, Rupert, 'Auch Deutschland muss UNO-Friedensaktionen mittragen', *Truppenpraxis*, No. 2, 1993.
Scholz, Rupert, 'Bundeswehr auch zur Grenzsicherung einsetzen', *Die Welt*, 8 October 1999.
Schröder, Gerhard, 'Deutsche Russlandpolitik – europäische Ostpolitik', *Die Zeit*, 15/2001.
Schröder, Gerhard, 'Die Grundkoordinaten deutscher Außenpolitik sind unverändert', *Bulletin*, No. 83, 6 December 1999.
Schröder, Gerhard, 'Weil wir Deutschlands Kraft vertrauen', Government Declaration to the Bundestag, 10 November 1998, reprinted in *Bulletin*, 11 November 1998.
Schwarz, Hans-Peter, *Die gezähmten deutschen* (Stuttgart: Deutsche Verlagsanstalt, 1985).
Schwarz, Hans-Peter, *Die Zentralmacht Europas: Deutschlands Rückkehr auf die Weltbühne* (Berlin: Siedler Verlag, 1994).
Schwarz, Hans-Peter, *Konrad Adenauer*, I (Providence: Berghahn Books, 1986).
Schwellen, Michael, 'Hilfe, die Helfer sind gekommen', *Die Zeit* 19/1999.
Smyser, W. R., *From Yalta to Berlin: The Cold War Struggle over Germany* (New York: St Martin's Griffin, 1999).
Snyder, Jack L., *The Soviet Strategic Culture: Implications for Nuclear Options* (Santa Monica: Rand Corporation, 1977).
Sommer, Theo, 'Allein ist der Starke hilflos', *Die Zeit*, 66/2001.
Sommer, Theo, 'New World Order?', *The Guardian*, 13 April 1991.
Sommer, Theo, 'Wehrpflicht oder Berufsheer?', *Die Zeit*, 10/1996.
Sommer, Theo, 'Wir trauern mit', *Die Zeit*, 38/2001.
Stadlmeyer, Tina, 'Grüne stimmen für Militäreinsätze', *Financial Times Deutschland*, 8 October 2001.
Stehr, Uwe, 'Damit deutsche Soldaten in der Krieg ziehen können?', *Frankfurter Rundschau*, 30 November 1990.
Steinhoff, Günter, 'Nicht nur Wissen – GE-wissen ist gefragt', in Oskar Hoffmann and Andreas Prüfert, *Innere Führung 2000* (Baden-Baden: Nomos Verlagsgesellschaft, 2001).
Stelzenmüller, Constanze, 'Deutschland braucht eine von Grund auf erneuerte Bundeswehr', *Die Zeit*, 20/2000.
Stelzenmüller, Constanze, 'Die Reform-Armee', *Die Zeit*, 20/2000.
Stelzenmüller, Constanze, 'Druck von allen Seiten', *Die Zeit*, 37/1999.
Stelzenmüller, Constanze, 'Hebammen in Uniform', *Die Zeit*, 39/2004.
Stürmer, Michael, 'Abschied von der Wehrpflicht', *Die Welt*, 8 August 2001.
Stürmer, Michael, 'Aussenpolitik im Stande der Unschuld', *Die Welt*, 29 May 2000.
Stürmer, Michael, *Die Grenzen der Macht: Begegnung der Deutschen mit der Geschichte* (Berlin: Siedler Verlag, 1990).
Stürmer, Michael, 'Ein Diplomat spricht aus, was die Politik nicht zu sagen wagt', *Die Welt*, 4 August 2001.
Szabo, Stephen F. *Parting Ways: The Crisis in German–American Relations* (Washington, DC: Brookings Institution Press, 2004).
Szabo, Stephen F., *The Changing Politics of German Security* (New York: St Martin's Press, 1990).
Thadden, Rudolf von, *Nicht Vaterland, nicht Fremde: Essays zu Geschichte und Gegenwart* (Munich: C. H. Beck Verlag, 1989).
The Military Balance 1999–2000 (London: IISS, 2000).

Tiersky, Ronald, 'French Military Reform and NATO Restructuring', *Joint Force Quarterly*, No. 15 (Spring 1997).
Varwick, Johannes, 'Die Bundeswehr reformieren', *Internationale Politik*, 7/2000.
Vernet, Daniel, 'Le retour de la question allemande', *Le Monde*, 22–23 December 1991.
Voigt, Karsten D., *The Discussion of a European Security and Defense Policy: Labor Pains of a New Atlanticism*, www.auswaertiges-amt.de.
Vogt, Hannah, *The Burden of Guilt: A Short History of Germany, 1914–1945* (New York: Oxford University Press, 1964).
Waltz, Kenneth N., *Theory of International Politics* (Reading, MA: Addison-Wesley, 1979).
Weise, Hans-Heinrich, 'Erfahrungen aus dem Einsatz der Bundeswehr auf dem Balkan', *Europäische Sicherheit*, 11/2000.
Wells, Bryan, 'European Force Structures after St-Malo – The British Approach', in Gordon Wilson (ed.), *European Force Structures*, WEU Occasional Paper, 6, May 1999.
Wette, Wolfram, 'Der Wünsch nach Weltmacht', *Die Zeit*, 30 July 1993.
Whitney, Craig, 'Gulf Fighting Shatters Europeans' Fragile Unity', *New York Times*, 25 January 1991.
Wiedemann, Günther M., 'Das Frühwarnsystem AWACS', *Kölner Stadtanzeiger*, 26 March 1993.
Wiesmann, Klaus, 'Die Entwicklung der Europäische Sicherheits- und Verteidigungspolitik: Ambitionen und Realitäten', *Europäische Sicherheit*, 5/2001.
Wolffsohn, Michael, 'Wie wichtig ist für uns die Wehrpflicht?', *Bild*, 10 June 1997.
Wörner, Manfred, 'West Germany and New Dimensions of Security', in Wolfram F. Hanrieder (ed.), *West German Foreign Policy 1949–1979* (Boulder: Westview Press, 1980).
Zürn, Michael, 'We Can Do Much Better! Aber muss es auf amerikanisch sein?', *Politische Vierteljahreschrift*, 1990/21.

Official documents

Auswärtiges Amt, 'Kooperation in der Golfkrise', Informationserlass des Auswärtigen Amts, 19 February 1991, reprinted in *Außenpolitik der Bundesrepublik Deutschland: Dokumente von 1949 bis 1994* (Bonn: Auswärtiges Amt, 1995).
Auswärtiges Amt, Regierungserklärung von Bundesaussenminister Fischer vor dem Deutschen Bundestag zu den Ergebnissen des Europäischen Rats von Thessaloniki', 26 June 2003, available at www.auswaertiges-amt.de/www/de/ausgabe_archiv?archiv_id=4667#5.
Bundesministerium der Verteidigung, *Auftrag Kommando Spezialkräfte (KSK)*, available at www.deutschesheer.de/C1256B6C002D670C/vwContentFrame/N2582A8G725PTILDE.
Bundesministerium der Verteidigung, *Bestandsaufnahme: Die Bundeswehr an der Schwelle zum 21. Jahrhundert*, Bundesministerium der Verteidigung, Bonn, May 1999.
Bundesministerium der Verteidigung, *Corps Concept 1 (German/Netherlands) Corps*, Münster, Section Press and Information 1(GE/NL) Corps, 2001.
Bundesministerium der Verteidigung, *Defence Policy Guidelines*, Berlin, 21 May 2004.
Bundesministerium der Verteidigung, 'Der Generalinspekteur der Bundeswehr zur

Allgemeine Wehrpflicht am 15.5.1996 Paris', press release, 5 May 1996, reprinted in *Stichworte zur Sicherheitspolitik*, 6/1996.
Bundesministerium der Verteidigung, *Die Bundeswehr der Zukunft: Sachstand der Reform 1. Juni 2001*, Bundesministerium der Verteidigung, www.bundeswehr.de.
Bundesministerium der Verteidigung, *Eckwerte für die konzeptionelle und planerische Weiterentwicklung der Streitkräfte*, Generalinspekteur der Bundeswehr, Bonn, 23 May 2000.
Bundesministerium der Verteidigung, *Konzeptionelle Leitlinie*, Bonn, 1994, reprinted in *Stichworte zur Sicherheitspolitik*, 9/1994.
Bundesministerium der Verteidigung, Lt Gen. Helmut Willmann, *Leadership: Der militärische Führer im Einsatz – Forderung für Erziehung und Ausbildung*, Bonn, 25 June 1998.
Bundesministerium der Verteidigung, *Material- und Ausrüstungskonzept für die Streitkräfte der Zukunft*, Berlin, March 2001.
Bundesministerium der Verteidigung, *Militärpolitische und Militärstrategische Grundlagen und konzeptionelle Grundrichtung der Neugestaltung der Bundeswehr*, reprinted in *Blätter für deutsche und internationale Politik*, No. 4, 1992.
Bundesministerium der Verteidigung, Tagesbefehl an die Bundeswehr, *Bulletin*, No. 1, 2 January 1997.
Bundesministerium der Verteidigung, *The Bundeswehr Advancing Steadily into the 21st Century: Cornerstones of a Fundamental Renewal*, Bundesministerium der Verteidigung, Bonn, 14 June 2000.
Bundesministerium der Verteidigung, *Verteidigungspolitische Richtlinien für den Geschäftsbereich des Bundesministers der Verteidigung*, Bonn, 26 November 1992.
Bundesministerium der Verteidigung, *Wegmarken für den neuen Kurs*, reprinted in *Stichworte zur Sicherheitspolitik*, 1/2004.
Bundesministerium der Verteidigung, *Weißbuch 1970*, Bundesministerium der Verteidigung Bonn.
Bundesministerium der Verteidigung, *Weißbuch 1994*, Ministerium der Verteidigung, Bonn, April 1994.
Bundesregierung, 'Bemühungen der Bundesregierung zur friedlichen Lösung der Golf-Krise', *Bulletin*, No. 2, 11 January 1991.
Bundesregierung, 'Bericht der Bundesregierung', 23 August 1990, reprinted in *Bulletin*, No. 102, 25 August 1990.
Bundesregierung, 'Beschluss der Bundesregierung zur Unterstützung von UNOSOM II in Somalia', *Bulletin*, No. 208, 23 April 1993.
Bundesregierung, 'Beschlussempfehlung der Bundesregierung', Drucksachen 14/7296, Presse und Informationsamt der Bundesregierung.
Bundesregierung, 'Bundesregierung bedauert Ergebnislosigkeit der Genfer Gespräche zur Lösung der Golfkrise', reprinted in *Stichworte zur Sicherheitspolitik*, 1/1991.
Bundesregierung, 'Erklärung von Bundeskanzler Gerhard Schröder zur Lage in Kosovo', 24 March 1999, reprinted in *Bulletin*, No. 13, 30 March 1999.
Bundesregierung, Helmut Kohl, 'Erklärung der Bundesregierung zum Krieg am Golf', reprinted in *Bulletin*, No. 6, 19 January 1991.
Bundesregierung, Helmut Kohl, 'Erklärung der Bundesregierung zur Lage in der Golfregion', 14 January 1991, reprinted in *Außenpolitik der Bundesrepublik Deutschland. Dokumente von 1949 bis 1994* (Bonn: Auswärtiges Amt, 1995).
Bundesregierung, Helmut Kohl, 'Regierungserklärung', 6 December 1995, *Bulletin*, 11 December 1995.

Bundesregierung, 'Neuer Bundeswehreinsatz in Mazedonien beschlossen', www.bundesregierung.de/dokumente/Artikel/ix.55736.1499.htm.
Bundesregierung, Regierungsbeschluss, 'Überwachung des Flugverbots über Bosnien-Herzegowina unter deutscher Beteiligung', *Bulletin*, No. 29, 7 April 1993.
Bundesregierung, 'Regierungserklärung', 7 July 1992, *Bulletin*, No. 83, 23 July 1992.
Bundesregierung, 'Regierungserklärung', 21 April 1993, *Bulletin*, 23 April 1993.
Bundesregierung, 'Regierungserklärung', reprinted in *Bulletin*, No. 22, 30 March 1998.
Bundestag, debate in the Bundestag, 31 January 1991, reprinted in *Das Parlament*, No. 7–8, 15 February 1991.
Bundestag, debate in the Bundestag, 6 June 1991, reprinted in *Bulletin*, No. 64, 7 June 1991.
Bundestag, debate in the Bundestag, 15 January 1993, reprinted in *Stichworte zur Sicherheitspolitik*, 2/1993.
Bundestag, debate in the Bundestag, 16 February 2001, full transcript reprinted in *Die Zeit*, 20 February 2001.
Bundestag, *Plenarprotokoll Deutscher Bundestag*, 12/101.
Bundestag, *Plenarprotokoll Deutscher Bundestag*, 12/132.
Bundestag, *Plenarprotokoll Deutscher Bundestag*, 12/166.
Bundestag, *Plenarprotokoll Deutscher Bundestag*, 12/169.
Bundestag, *Plenarprotokoll Deutscher Bundestag*, 12/240.
Bundestag, *Plenarprotokoll Deutscher Bundestag*, 12/243.
Bundestag, *Plenarprotokoll Deutscher Bundestag*, 12/41.
Bundestag, *Plenarprotokoll Deutscher Bundestag*, 12/58.
Bundestag, *Plenarprotokoll Deutscher Bundestag*, 13/242.
Bundestag, *Plenarprotokoll Deutscher Bundestag*, 13/244.
Bundestag, *Plenarprotokoll Deutscher Bundestag*, 13/248.
Bundestag, *Plenarprotokoll Deutscher Bundestag*, 13/74.
Bundestag, *Plenarprotokoll Deutscher Bundestag*, 13/76.
Bundestag, *Plenarprotokoll Deutscher Bundestag*, 14/184.
Bundestag, *Plenarprotokoll Deutscher Bundestag*, 14/190.
Bundestag, *Plenarprotokoll Deutscher Bundestag*, 14/202.
Bundestag, *Plenarprotokoll Deutscher Bundestag*, 14/43.
Bundestag, *Plenarprotokoll Deutscher Bundestag*, 14/55.
Bundestag, *Plenarprotokoll Deutscher Bundestag*, 14/58.
Bundestag, *Plenarprotokoll Deutscher Bundestag*, 14/61.
Bundestag, *Plenarprotokoll Deutscher Bundestag. Stenographischer Bericht*, 51. Sitzung, Berlin, 18 June 2003.
Bundesverfassungsgericht, 2 BvQ 17/93, reprinted in *Stichworte zur Sicherheitspolitik*, 7/1993.
Bundesverfassungsgericht, Urteil des Bundesverfassungsgericht vom 12 July 1994 zu Auslandseinsätzen der Bundeswehr, reprinted in *Stichworte zur Sicherheitspolitik*, 7/1994.
CDU, 'Allgemeine Wehrpflicht', available at www.cdu.de/politik-a-z/sicherheit/kap21.htm.
CDU, *Die Zukunft gemeinsam gestalten: Die neuen Aufgaben deutscher Politik*. Resolution passed at the CDU party convention, 14–17 December 1991. CDU-Dokumentation 39/40, 1991.

Embassy of France in the US, *Reform of French National Defense*, 12 June 2001, www.info-france-usa.org.
European Union, *A Secure Europe in a Better World: European Security Strategy*. Document proposed by Javier Solana and adopted by the Heads of State and Government at the European Council in Brussels on 12 December 2003.
FDP, 'Beschluss des Bundeshauptausschusses der FDP', 25 May 1991, reprinted in Bundes Presse Amt, Referat III B 5, Dokumentation, *Freiheit und Verantwortung gehören zusammen*, June 1991.
FDP, *Bundeswehr Einsatz II: FDP für uneingeschränkte Solidarität/Aussetzung der Wehrpflicht gefördert*, 12 November 2001, www.fdp.de.
FDP, *Gemeinsame europäische Golf-Initiative nötig*, FDP Fachinfo, Irak, 11 January 1991.
FDP, *Zukunftsfähigkeit der Bundeswehr sichern – Wehrpflicht aussetzen*, Bill introduced by the FDP parliamentary group in the Bundestag on 10 October 2000, www.fdp.de.
Gemeinsame Sicherheit und Zukunft der Bundeswehr, Bericht der Kommission and die Bundesregierung, Berlin, 23 May 2000.
German Embassy, Washington, DC, 'German Role in Afghanistan Gains US Praise', *Germany Info*, 11 August 2003, at www.germany-info.org/relaunch/politics/new/pol_isaf_nato.html.
NATO Handbook, Chapter 5, p. 114, available at www.nato.int.
NATO, 'Task Force Fox', available at NATO's website, www.afsouth.nato.int.
NATO, 'Task Force Harvest Mission', available at NATO's website, www.afsouth.nato.int.
NATO, *Strategic Concept 1991*, NATO On-line library, www.nato.int/docu/basictxt/b911108a.htm.
Operation Enduring Freedom – Deployments, available at www.globalsecurity.org.
PDS, *BRD im Golfkriege: Von der Wiedervereinigung an die Nah-Ostfront*, PDS-Pressedienst, Bonn, 30 January 1991.
PDS, decision of the 2nd PDS party convention, PDS Pressedienst, 12 July 1991.
Petersberg Declaration, WEU Document, www.weu.int.
Schröder, Gerhard, Rede von Bundeskanzler Gerhard Schröder zum Wahlkampfauftakt, 5 August 2002, Hannover (Opernplatz), p. 8, www.spd.de/servlet/PB/show/1019520/Schr%F6der%20Rede%20WahlkampfauftaktHannover.doc (accessed on 8 February 2005).
SPD, *Außen-, Friedens-, und Sicherheitspolitik*, Beschlüsse des Parteitages in Bremen, 28–31 May 1991.
SPD, *Perspektiven*, Wiesbaden, November 1993.
SPD, *SPD-Sofortprogramm*, Bonn, November 1992.
SPD, *Stellungnahme der Kommission Sicherheitspolitik beim SPD-Parteivorstand zur sicherheitspolitischen Verantwortung der Bundesrepublik Deutschland*, press release, 17 May 1991.
UK Ministry of Defence, *The Strategic Defence Review White Paper*, July 1998
UK Ministry of Defence, *UK Regular Forces and Civilian Personnel Strengths at 1 April 2002*, SCPS1 Monthly Publication, Ministry of Defence, London, available at www.dasa.mod.uk.
United Nations, *A More Secure World: Our Shared Responsibility*. Report of the Secretary-General's High-Level Panel on Threats, Challenges and Change, New York: United Nations, 2004.
United Nations Security Council Resolution 1199, available at www.un.int.
United Nations Security Council Resolution 1203, available at www.un.int.

United Nations Security Council Resolution 1368, available at www.un.org.
Wehrbeauftragte des Deutschen Bundestages, *Jahresbericht 1996*.
Wehrbeauftragte des Deutschen Bundestages, *Jahresbericht 1997*.
Wehrbeauftragte des Deutschen Bundestages, *Jahresbericht 1998*.
Wehrbeauftragte des Deutschen Bundestages, *Jahresbericht 1999*.
Wehrbeauftragte des Deutschen Bundestages, *Jahresbericht 2000*.
Wehrbeauftragte des Deutschen Bundestages, *Jahresbericht 2001*.
The White House, *National Strategy for Combating Terrorism*, Washington, DC, February 2003.
The White House, *The National Security Strategy of the United States*, Washington, DC, September 2002.
Zentrum Innere Führung, *Legitimitätsfragen bei Auslandseinsätze der Bundeswehr*, Strausberg, Arbeitspapier, 3/1996.

Newspaper articles

'Beschluss-Begründung des Bundesverfassungsgerichts im AWACS-Streit', *Süddeutsche Zeitung*, 10 April 1993.
Blome, Nikolaus and Torsten Krauel, 'Gerhard und George', *Die Welt*, 26 February 2004.
'Breite Mehrheit im Bundestag für Beteiligung der Bundeswehr an einem Nato-Einsatz', *Frankfurter Allgemeine Zeitung*, 17 October 1998.
'CDU und Grüne wollen keinen Generalstab', *Die Welt*, 7 August 1999.
'CDU will Bundeswehreinsatz außerhalb Europas', *Stichworte zur Sicherheitspolitik*, 6/1991.
'CDU will eine Atlantische Charta', *Frankfurter Allgemeine Zeitung*, 29 September 2001.
'CSU und Grüne gegen Interventionsarmee', *Die Welt*, 10 May 2000.
'Das ist insofern tough', *Die Zeit*, 12/2001.
'Deutsche Elitesoldaten bereiten sich in Oman auf den Einsatz vor', *Die Welt*, 27 November 2001.
'Die Bundeswehr steigt in die Bezirksklasse ab', *Die Welt*, 28 July 1999.
'Die Deutschen als Opfer', *Der Spiegel*, 25 March 2002.
'Die heile Welt der Kleinen an der Führungsakademie', *Die Welt*, 22 November 2000.
'Die Wehrpflicht steht nicht zur Disposition', *Die Welt*, 13 January 2000.
'Ein sanfter Mann fürs Militär', *Die Zeit*, 13/1999.
'FDP fühlt sich bei Wehrpflicht bestätigt', *Süddeutsche Zeitung*, 8 August 2001.
'FDP stellt Wehrpflicht in Frage – Truppe hält dagegen', *Berliner Morgenpost*, 28 July 2001.
'Fischer warnt vor Krieg der Zivilisationen', *Die Welt*, 16 October 2001.
'Generalinspekteur Naumann zur Lage der Bundeswehr nach dem Karlsruher Urteil', *Frankfurter Rundschau*, 2 August 1994.
'Grosse Mehrheit für Verlängerung des Sfor-Einsatzes', *Frankfurter Allgemeine Zeitung*, 20 June 1998.
'Grünes Konzept zur Sicherheits- und Außenpolitik führt Deutschland ins Abseits', IAP, November 1997, reprinted in *Stichworte zur Sicherheitspolitik*, 11/1997.
'Grüne-Spitze unterstützt US-Angriff auf Afghanistan', *Die Welt*, 9 October 2001.
'Heeresinspekteur warnt vor Kürzungen', *Die Welt*, 19 June 1997.

'Hier kommt die Berufsarmee!', *Die Welt*, 7 August 2001.
'Huber: Bundeswehr trägt auch zur Strukturpolitik bei', *Die Welt*, 19 June 2000.
'Hubert Védrine, France's Voice in the World', *The Economist*, 11 November 2000.
'Irak: Union wirft Regierung Täuschungsmanöver vor', *Die Welt*, 23 December 2002.
Ja zum Kriegseinsatz spaltet grüne Basis', *Frankfurter Allgemeine Sonntagszeitung*, 18 November 2001.
'Keine halben Nato-Sachen', *Die Welt*, 21 August 2001.
'Kleinere Bundeswehr ohne Wehrpflicht: Gutachten der Friedensinstitute', *Frankfurter Allgemeine Zeitung*, 11 June 1997.
'Konflikt in ehemaligen Jugoslawien', *Stichworte zur Sicherheitspolitik*, 11/1996.
'Krieg der Köpfe', *Der Spiegel*, 15/1999.
'Krieg und Wahlkampf', *Die Welt*, 21 December 2002.
'Letzter Ausweg Berufsarmee', *Süddeutsche Zeitung*, 6 August 2001.
'Make Arms, Not War?', *The Economist*, 16 February 1991.
'Nach 2002 brauchen wir den Euro-Fighter', *Frankfurter Allgemeine Sonntagszeitung*, 3 March 1997.
'NATO-Chef: Bundeswehr hat großartige Arbeit geleistet', *Bild am Sonntag*, 23 March 1997.
'Paris and Berlin Hold Course for EU enlargement', *Financial Times*, 13 June 2001.
'Paris übt Kritik an deutschem Verteidigungsetat', *Financial Times Deutschland*, 1 August 2001.
'Reserven kann man nicht wieder herbeizaubern', *Die Welt*, 24 July 1999.
Ridderbusch, Katja, 'Kontinentaldrift aufgehalten', *Die Welt*, 25 June 2003.
'Rühe: Ich halte an der Wehrpflicht fest', *Westdeutsche Allgemeine Zeitung*, 20 May 1997.
'Scharping fordert weltweite Solidarität gegen den Terror', *Die Welt*, 4 October 2001.
'Schäuble fordert zu Irak-politik klaren Positionen im Sicherheitsrat', *Die Welt*, 3 January 2003.
Schuster, Jacques, 'Sicherheit schaffen auch mit Waffen', *Die Welt*, 21 June 2003.
'Skeptische Blicke der Partner auf den Reformer Scharping', *Die Welt*, 9 June 2000.
'Union fürchtet um Wehrpflicht und warnt vor Eingrifftruppe', *Die Welt*, 24 May 2000.
'Unklarheiten in der deutsch-französischen Sicherheitspolitik', *Frankfurter Allgemeine Zeitung*, 2 March 1996.
'US Condemns "Poisoned Relations" with Berlin', *Financial Times*, 21 September 2003.
'USA warnen Deutschland', *Berliner Zeitung*, 2 August 2001.
Vincour, John, 'Berlin Says Europeans Need Close Bond to US', *International Herald Tribune*, 17 July 2004.
Wetzel, Hubert, 'Bush und Schröder wägen Interessen ab', *Financial Times Deutschland*, 25 February 2004.
'Wo stehen die Bundestagsparteien?', *Die Welt*, 9 October 2001.
'Zu den geplanten Veränderungen in den französischen Streitkräften', *Stichworte zur Sicherheitspolitik*, 5/1996.

Speeches and interviews

Andréani, Jacques, speech given at Johns Hopkins SAIS, Washington, DC, 22 February 2000.
Bagger, Hartmut, interview with *Außenpolitik*, 19 December 1995, reprinted in *Stichworte zur Sicherheitspolitik*, 12/1995.
Breuer, Paul, interview with Deutschlandfunk, 8 June 1993, reprinted in *Stichworte zur Sicherheitspolitik*, 7/1993.
Erler, Gernot, interview with *Die Zeit*, 8 May 2001.
Essen, Jörg van, interview with *Die Zeit*, 2 July 2001.
Fischer, Joschka, speech to the Council of Foreign Relations, New York, 5 November 1999.
Genscher, Hans-Dietrich, interview with SAT 1, 5 January 1991, reprinted in *Stichworte zur Sicherheitspolitik*, 1/1991.
Klaus Kinkel, 'BM des Auswärtiges Dr. Kinkel zu den Luftangriffen auf serbische Stellungen', interview reprinted in *Stichworte zur Sicherheitspolitik*, 11/1995.
Kinkel, Klaus, interview with *Fuldauer Zeitung*, 28 July 1998.
Kinkel, Klaus, speech at 'Forum Bundeswehr and Gesellschaft', Berlin, reprinted in *Bulletin*, No. 47, 9 June 1997.
Kinkel, Klaus, 'Vor weitere Militäraktionen warne ich', interview with *Bild Zeitung*, 25 August 1995.
Klose, Hans-Ulrich, interview with ZDF, 30 August 1993, reprinted in *Stichworte zur Sicherheitspolitik*, 9/1993.
Kohl, Helmut, interview with SAT 1, 2 April 1993, reprinted in *Stichworte zur Sicherheitspolitik*, 5/1993.
Kuhn, Fritz, interview with *Die Welt*, 18 November 2001.
Kujat, General Harald, interview in *Der Tagesspiegel*, 26 November 2000.
Chris Patten, speech before the Institut Français des Relations Internationales (ifri), Paris, 15 June 2000.
Rau, Johannes, speech at the 38th Kommandeurtagung der Bundeswehr, Leipzig, 14 November 2000, reprinted in *Bulletin*, No. 76–1, 14 November 2000.
Richard, Alain, speech at 'Berliner Dialog – Internationale Sicherheit', Berlin, 3 July 2001
Richard, Alain, speech at 'Forum Bundeswehr und Gesellschaft', Berlin, 2 October reprinted in 'Bundeswehr & Gesellschaft', a special section of *Welt am Sonntag*, 7 October 2001.
Robertson, Lord and Alain Richard, speech at 'Forum Bundeswehr und Gesellschaft', reprinted in 'Bundeswehr & Gesellschaft', a special section of *Welt am Sonntag*, 7 October 2001.
Rühe, Volker, 'BM der Verteidigung Rühe zur Fragen der Bundeswehr und deutscher Sicherheitspolitik', interview with *Die Welt*, 24 November 1996.
Rühe, Volker, interview with ADR, 30 November 1995, reprinted in *Stichworte zur Sicherheitspolitik*, 12/1995.
Rühe, Volker, interview with *Bild am Sonntag*, 2 July 1995.
Rühe, Volker, interview with *Der Spiegel*, 16 November 1995.
Rühe, Volker, interview with *Die Zeit*, 1 December 1995.
Rühe, Volker, interview with *Rheinischer Merkur*, 29 December 1996.
Rühe, Volker, interview with *Welt am Sonntag*, 27 November 1994.

Rühe, Volker, speech to the Rheinisch-Westfälischen Handwerkerbundes, 12 January 1993, reprinted in *Bulletin*, No. 6, 18 January 1993.

Rühe, Volker, *Zur Rolle der Bundeswehr in einer sich wandelnden Welt*, speech at 'Forum Bundeswehr und Gesellschaft', Berlin, 22 March 1994.

Rüttgers, Jürgen, interview with ZDF, 22 July 1993, reprinted in *Stichworte zur Sicherheitspolitik*, 8/1993.

Scharping, Rudolf, 'Der Vorsitzende der SPD-Bundestagsfraktion Scharping zur deutschen Beteiligung an der Friedenstruppe für Bosnien', interview reprinted in *Stichworte zur Sicherheitspolitik*, 12/1995.

Scharping, Rudolf, interview with *Die Zeit*, 15 September 2001.

Schröder, Gerhard, 'Die Krise, die Europa eint', interview with *Die Zeit*, 14/2003.

Schröder, Gerhard, speech at reception of the report 'Gemeinsame Sicherheit und Zukunft der Bundeswehr', reprinted in *Bulletin* No. 30–1, 26 May 2000.

Schröder, Gerhard, speech in Berlin, 23 May 2000, reprinted in *Bulletin*, No. 30–1, 26 May 2000.

Stoiber, Edmund, interview with *Die Zeit*, 14/2003.

Stoltenberg, Gerhard, interview with *Bonn Direkt ZDF*, 6 January 1991, reprinted in *Stichworte zur Sicherheitspolitik*, 2/1991.

Stoltenberg, Gerhard, interview with SDR 1, 3 March 1991, reprinted in *Stichworte zur Sicherheitspolitik*, 3/1991.

Stoltenberg, Gerhard, interview with ZDF, 6 January 1991, reprinted in *Stichworte zur Sicherheitspolitik*, 1/1991.

Stoltenberg, Gerhard, speech, CDU Congress, Bonn, 15 May 1991, reprinted in *Stichworte zur Sicherheitspolitik*, 6/1991.

Verheugen, Günter, interview with ZDF, 7 June 1993, reprinted in *Stichworte zur Sicherheitspolitik*, 9/1993.

Vollmer, Antje, 'Hundertgähriges Chaos', interview with *Die Zeit*, 05/2003.

Weizsäcker, Richard von, interview with *Die Zeit*, 8 February 1991.

Index

Adenauer, Konrad, 25–34
Afghanistan, 1, 14–15, 18, 47, 81, 86–89, 92, 94, 108–110, 119, 130, 132, 142, 147–148, 150–151, 153, 158, 162
Al-Qaeda, 14
'Auftragstaktik', 107
Auschwitz, 36, 47, 70–71, 75, 77, 81, 83, 86, 88, 90, 92, 144, 146, 154

Bahr, Egon, 31–33, 35, 133
Belgium, 83, 89, 107, 149–150, 152, 162
Bosnia and Herzegovina, 18, 46, 53–56, 69–71, 73, 75, 84–85, 108, 110, 148–149, 154, 157, 159, 161–162
Brandt, Willy, 26, 31–35, 38
Bundestag, 2, 4, 6, 15–20, 26, 29, 36, 47, 52, 55, 62, 71, 73–77, 81–82, 85, 87–88, 91, 121, 128, 157–158, 161–162
Bundeswehr, 1–5, 16, 20, 29–31, 38–40, 46–47, 50, 55–56, 61–62, 71–72, 74–76, 81–84, 86, 91–92, 99, 101–112, 119–135, 146, 148, 150, 153–154, 160

Christian Democratic Union of Germany (CDU), 16, 25, 34, 49–50, 55–56, 59, 71, 75, 84, 91–92, 133–134, 160
Christian-Social Union of Bavaria (CSU), 16, 25, 34, 56, 59, 71, 91–92, 160
'citizen in uniform', 30, 107, 111
Cold War, 2–6, 10, 15–16, 32, 49, 54, 57, 93, 101, 103–105, 107, 111, 120, 125, 129, 134, 143–144, 153–154

conscription, 30, 119–120, 125–129, 135, 145
Croatia, 53, 59, 71, 73, 75, 125, 148
cultural change, 20, 76
culturalism, 3, 143–145, 147–148

Dayton Peace Agreement, 54, 71
Defence policy guidelines, 40, 123–124, 126
Democratic Republic of Congo (DRC), 4, 18, 45, 48, 81, 91–92, 94, 103, 121, 133, 142, 147–148, 150, 158, 162
Denmark, 89, 107, 150, 162

East Timor, 1, 18, 47, 81–83, 86, 108, 147, 148–149, 153, 158, 162
elite discourse, 14
European Security and Defence Policy, 5, 151–153
European Union, 40, 45, 48, 53, 55, 62, 73, 77, 81, 83–84, 91, 93–94, 124, 133, 142, 149–153
Ex-Yugoslavia, 54, 57–58, 73, 83–85, 105–106, 154

Fischer, Joschka, 47, 72, 75, 82
France, 4, 27, 51, 53, 56, 58–60, 71, 73, 82–84, 86, 89–91, 107, 109–110, 119–121, 123–125, 128–133, 135, 144–145, 148–150, 152–153, 161–162
Free Democratic Party (FDP), 16, 25, 34, 36, 49–51, 55–56, 59, 61, 71, 73, 75, 84, 133–134, 160

Genscher, Hans Dietrich, 28, 46, 49–50, 53
German Constitutional Court, 16, 45–46, 56, 60–63, 85, 102, 106, 146
Germany
   historical responsibility, 5, 7, 38, 40, 46–47, 58, 62, 71–72, 74–75, 82, 84, 246, 254
   partnership, 5, 7, 26, 34, 38, 45, 47, 59, 62, 73, 87, 130, 146, 153
   trust, 25–27, 30–32, 34, 37, 125, 134–135, 147
Great Britain, 4, 50–51, 53, 55–56, 58–59, 71, 81, 83–84, 86, 109–110, 120–124, 129–132, 145, 149, 152, 161
Green Party, 16, 26, 47, 51, 56, 60, 62, 70, 72, 74–77, 84–91, 104, 106, 110, 123, 126, 160–161
Gulf War, 1–2, 4, 15, 18, 45–46, 49–55, 58, 64, 77, 81, 86, 91, 101, 143, 148, 157
Holocaust, 28, 36

Implementation Force (IFOR), 18, 47, 71–78, 105, 108, 121–122, 135, 149, 157, 161
intermediate-range nuclear forces (INF), 14, 34–36
International Force East Timor (INTERFET), 18, 82–83, 149, 158, 162
International Security and Assistance Force (ISAF), 81, 92, 132
Italy, 55–56, 58, 60, 82–83, 86, 89, 117, 128–131, 149–150, 161–162

Kinkel, Klaus, 54, 63
Kohl, Helmut, 16, 36, 55, 57, 63, 73, 102, 105
Kosovo, 1, 18, 45, 47–48, 74–77, 81, 83, 93, 108, 110, 119, 130, 148–149, 152, 158, 162
Kosovo Force (KFOR), 18, 76, 83, 105, 121–122, 135, 149, 158, 162

liberal IR theory/liberalism, 51, 54–55, 143

Macedonia, 18, 47, 81–88, 147–151, 158, 162

Netherlands, 55–56, 70, 83, 107, 149, 161–162
'never again alone', 6, 25–26, 34–39, 45, 49–50, 57, 59, 61–62, 72, 77, 81, 83–86, 88, 90, 92, 143, 145, 153, 155

'never again Auschwitz', 47, 70–71, 75, 77, 81, 83, 86, 88, 90, 92, 144, 154
'never again war', 6, 25–26, 28, 35, 37–39, 46–47, 49, 51–52, 57, 63, 70–71, 74, 76, 81, 88, 90, 92–93, 144
North Atlantic Treaty Organisation, 1, 5, 11, 16, 26–31, 34–36, 39–40, 46–47, 50, 54–56, 60–63, 71–75, 77, 83–87, 102, 105, 107, 121–122, 124, 128, 130, 133, 145, 148–153, 157–158, 161–162
Nuremberg Trials, 24

Operation Allied Force, 1, 18, 47, 70, 74–77, 84, 119, 130, 152, 158, 162
Operation Amber Fox 18, 83–84, 150, 158, 162
Operation Artemis, 18, 45, 48, 81, 91, 103, 121, 133, 148, 150, 158, 162
Operation Deny Fly, 18, 55–58, 61, 149, 157, 161
Operation Desert Storm, 50–51
Operation Enduring Freedom, 1, 15, 18, 86–91, 121, 130, 132, 150, 153, 158, 162
Operation Essential Harvest, 18, 83–85, 149, 158, 162
Operation Iraqi Freedom, 1, 18, 89, 91, 150
Operation Sharp Guard, 18, 55–58, 61, 149, 157, 161
Organisation for Security and Co-operation in Europe, 63, 83
'out-of-area missions', 1–6, 15–20, 30, 38–39, 45–47, 50–52, 55, 58–63, 72–77, 83, 85, 92–94, 99–108, 112, 119–126, 130–135, 142–143, 146–147, 151–155, 157, 161

Party of Democratic Socialism (PDS), 20, 52, 60, 72, 75, 82, 85–87, 89, 91, 110, 160–161
peace enforcement, 47, 59, 72, 103, 131–132
peacekeeping, 39–40, 46–47, 50, 52, 55, 58–59, 66–68, 71–73, 76–77, 81, 84, 90–91, 94, 102–109, 120, 122, 131–132, 146, 159
Potsdam Agreement, 24
pre-emptive strike, 88, 142
projection capability, 4, 95, 119, 123, 135–136, 144

realist IR theory/realism, 3, 11, 33, 38, 40, 76, 81–82, 85–86, 143–148, 151
Russia, 90

Schröder, Gerhard, 14, 16, 86–89
Second World War, 1, 10–11, 24, 30, 36, 46, 49, 55, 71, 73, 142, 145–146, 154
security culture, 3–6, 10–16, 18, 24, 26, 36–37, 39–40, 86, 88–89, 143, 145, 148, 150–153
Serbia and Montenegro, 46–47, 55–56, 74–75, 83, 162
Slovenia, 53, 59, 125
Social Democratic Party (SPD), 16, 25, 28–29, 31, 34–36, 51–52, 55–63, 72–77, 85, 89–91, 160–161
Somalia, 18, 45–46, 49, 60–62, 68, 103, 105, 122, 148, 149, 157, 161
Soviet Union, 24–27, 31–39
Srebrenica, 45–46, 70–74, 77, 87, 105, 144, 154
Stabilisation Force in Bosnia and Herzegovinia (SFOR), 47, 73–74, 105–108, 121–122, 135, 149, 157, 162

Taleban, 1, 81, 86
territorial defence, 31, 99, 103, 119–126, 129, 135
terrorism, 2, 15, 86–89, 93–94, 126–128, 135, 142–143, 151
two-plus-four Treaty, 3, 133

United Nations, 5, 14, 18, 39–40, 46, 50–63, 71–74, 77, 79, 81–89, 93–94, 103, 108
United States, 1, 3, 9, 14, 24, 26, 28, 31, 33, 35–36, 39, 47, 49–56, 59–60, 64, 71, 84–93, 96, 107, 109, 119, 128–132, 135, 140, 148, 150–153

White Book, 19, 121
Weapons of Mass Destruction (WMDs) (ABCs), 29, 86–87, 93–95
'Wehrbeauftragte', 29, 104, 110–111